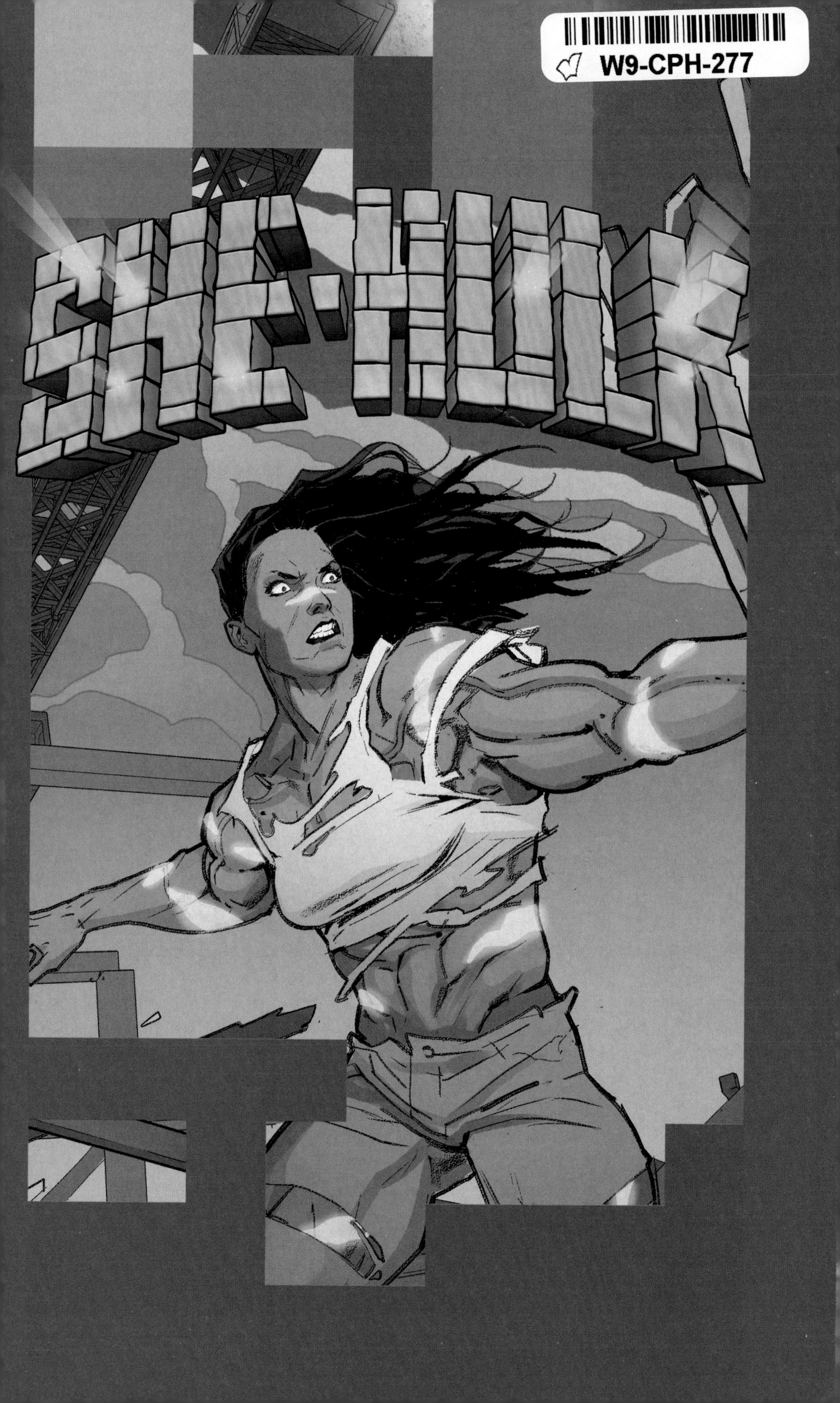
SHE-HULK

SHE-HULK VOL. 2: LET THEM EAT CAKE. Contains material originally published in magazine form as HULK #7-11. First printing 2017. ISBN 978-1-302-90568-2. Published by MARVEL WORLDWIDE, INC., a subsidiary of MARVEL ENTERTAINMENT, LLC. OFFICE OF PUBLICATION: 135 West 50th Street, New York, NY 10020. Copyright © 2017 MARVEL No similarity between any of the names, characters, persons, and/or institutions in this magazine with those of any living or dead person or institution is intended, and any such similarity which may exist is purely coincidental. **Printed in Canada.** DAN BUCKLEY, President, Marvel Entertainment; JOE QUESADA, Chief Creative Officer; TOM BREVOORT, SVP of Publishing; DAVID BOGART, SVP of Business Affairs & Operations, Publishing & Partnership; DAVID GABRIEL, SVP of Sales & Marketing, Publishing; JEFF YOUNGQUIST, VP of Production & Special Projects; DAN CARR, Executive Director of Publishing Technology; ALEX MORALES, Director of Publishing Operations; SUSAN CRESPI, Production Manager; STAN LEE, Chairman Emeritus. For information regarding advertising in Marvel Comics or on Marvel.com, please contact Jonathan Parkhideh, VP of Digital Media & Marketing Solutions, at jparkhideh@marvel.com. For Marvel subscription inquiries, please call 888-511-5480. **Manufactured between 11/17/2017 and 12/19/2017 by SOLISCO PRINTERS, SCOTT, QC, CANADA.**

10 9 8 7 6 5 4 3 2 1

SHE-HULK

LET THEM EAT CAKE

WRITER **MARIKO TAMAKI**

ISSUES #7-8
ARTIST **GEORGES DUARTE**
COLOR ARTIST **MATT MILLA**
LETTERER **VC's CORY PETIT**

ISSUES #9-10
ARTISTS **JULIAN LOPEZ** & **FRANCESCO GASTÓN**
COLOR ARTIST **MATT MILLA**
LETTERER **VC's CORY PETIT**

ISSUE #11
ARTIST **BACHAN**
COLOR ARTIST **FEDERICO BLEE**
LETTERER **VC's TRAVIS LANHAM**

COVER ART **JOHN TYLER CHRISTOPHER**

EDITOR **CHRISTINA HARRINGTON**
SENIOR EDITOR **MARK PANICCIA**

COLLECTION EDITOR **JENNIFER GRÜNWALD** | ASSISTANT EDITOR **CAITLIN O'CONNELL**
ASSOCIATE MANAGING EDITOR **KATERI WOODY** | EDITOR, SPECIAL PROJECTS **MARK D. BEAZLEY**
VP PRODUCTION & SPECIAL PROJECTS **JEFF YOUNGQUIST** | SVP PRINT, SALES & MARKETING **DAVID GABRIEL**
BOOK DESIGNER **JAY BOWEN**

EDITOR IN CHIEF **C.B. CEBULSKI** | CHIEF CREATIVE OFFICER **JOE QUESADA**
PRESIDENT **DAN BUCKLEY** | EXECUTIVE PRODUCER **ALAN FINE**

#7 MARY JANE
VARIANT BY
RAHZZAH

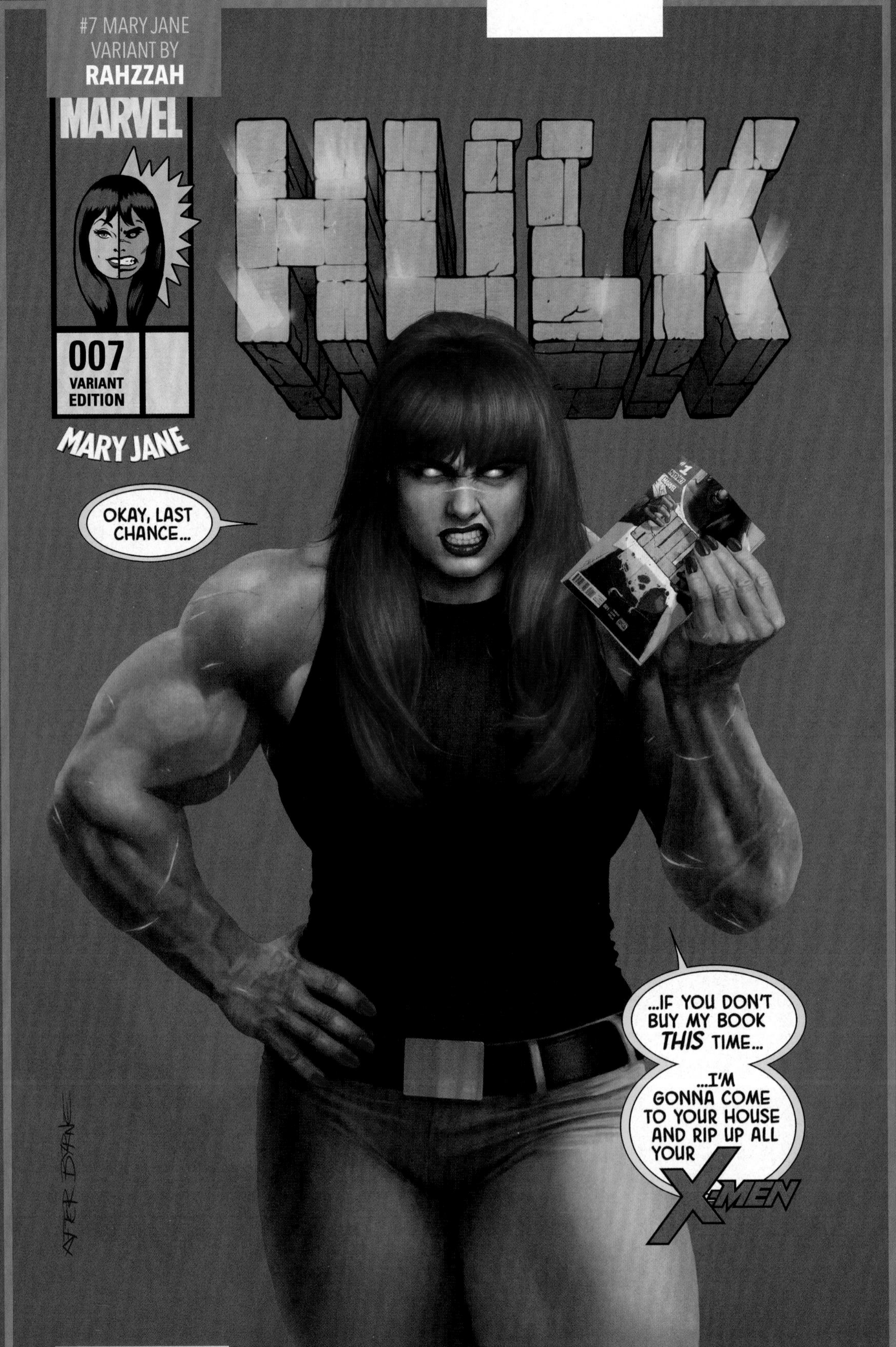
MARVEL
HULK
007
VARIANT EDITION
MARY JANE
OKAY, LAST CHANCE...
...IF YOU DON'T BUY MY BOOK THIS TIME...
...I'M GONNA COME TO YOUR HOUSE AND RIP UP ALL YOUR
X-MEN
AFTER BYRNE

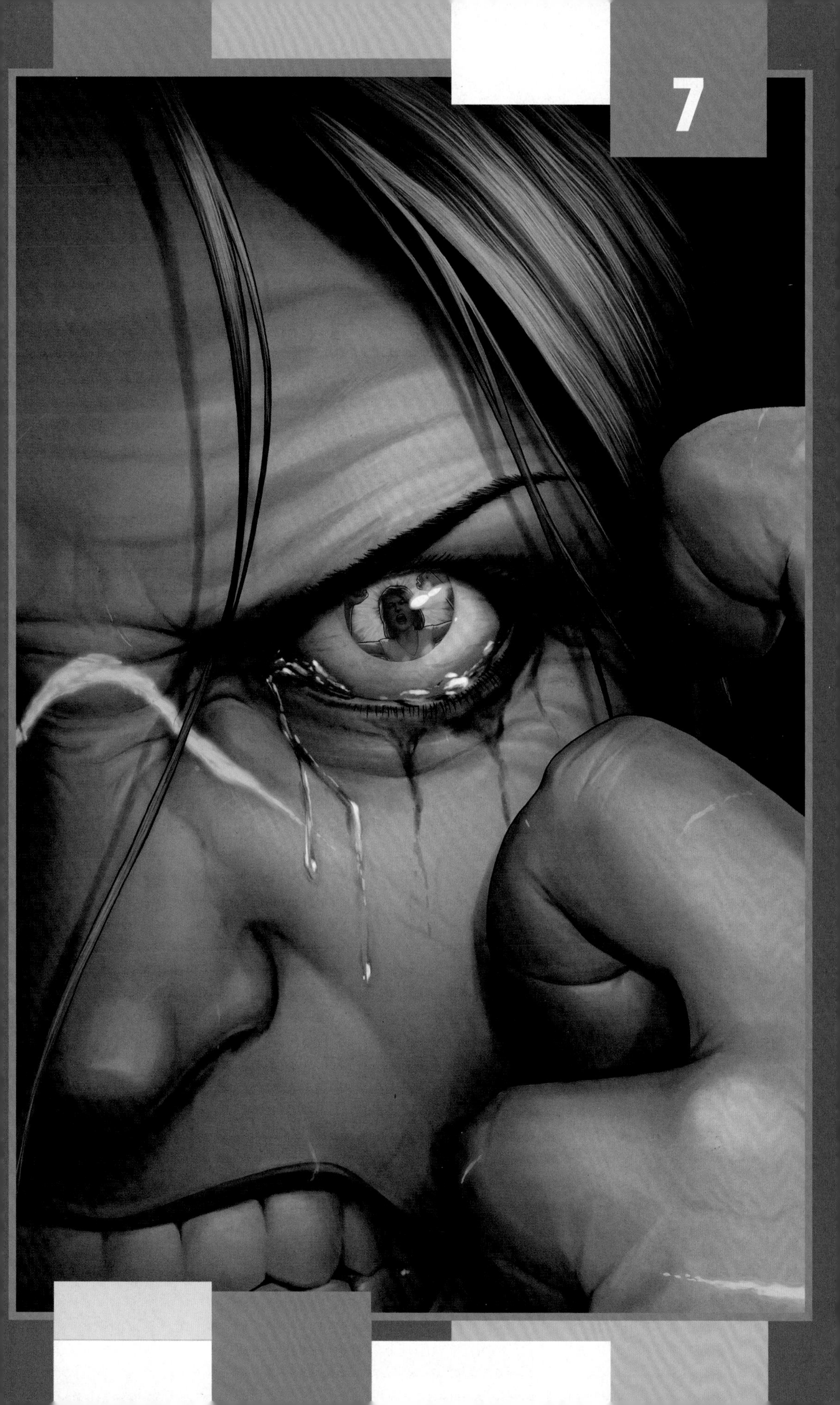
7

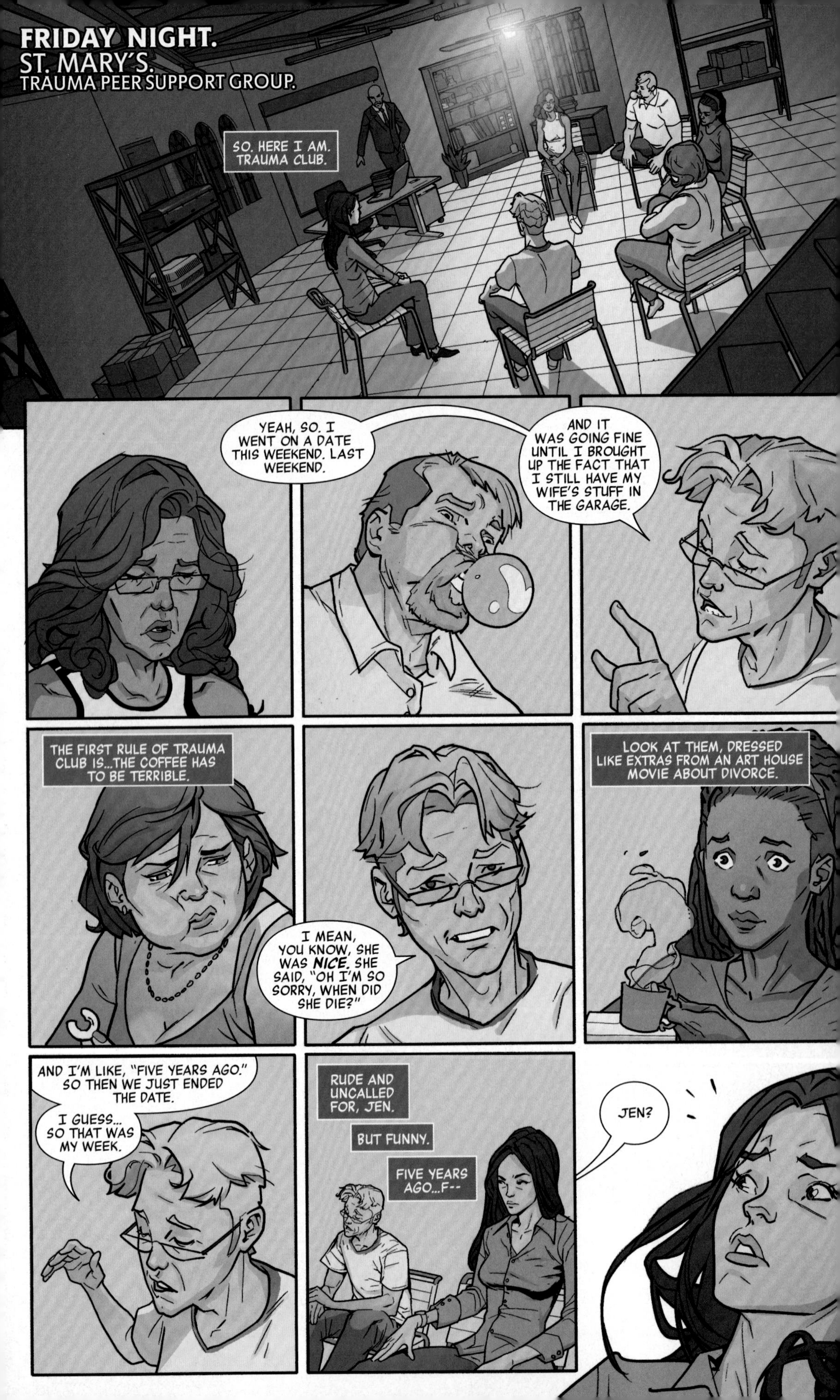
FRIDAY NIGHT.
ST. MARY'S.
TRAUMA PEER SUPPORT GROUP.
SO. HERE I AM. TRAUMA CLUB.
YEAH, SO. I WENT ON A DATE THIS WEEKEND. LAST WEEKEND.
AND IT WAS GOING FINE UNTIL I BROUGHT UP THE FACT THAT I STILL HAVE MY WIFE'S STUFF IN THE GARAGE.
THE FIRST RULE OF TRAUMA CLUB IS...THE COFFEE HAS TO BE TERRIBLE.
I MEAN, YOU KNOW, SHE WAS NICE. SHE SAID, "OH I'M SO SORRY, WHEN DID SHE DIE?"
LOOK AT THEM, DRESSED LIKE EXTRAS FROM AN ART HOUSE MOVIE ABOUT DIVORCE.
AND I'M LIKE, "FIVE YEARS AGO." SO THEN WE JUST ENDED THE DATE.
I GUESS... SO THAT WAS MY WEEK.
RUDE AND UNCALLED FOR, JEN.
BUT FUNNY.
FIVE YEARS AGO...F--
JEN?

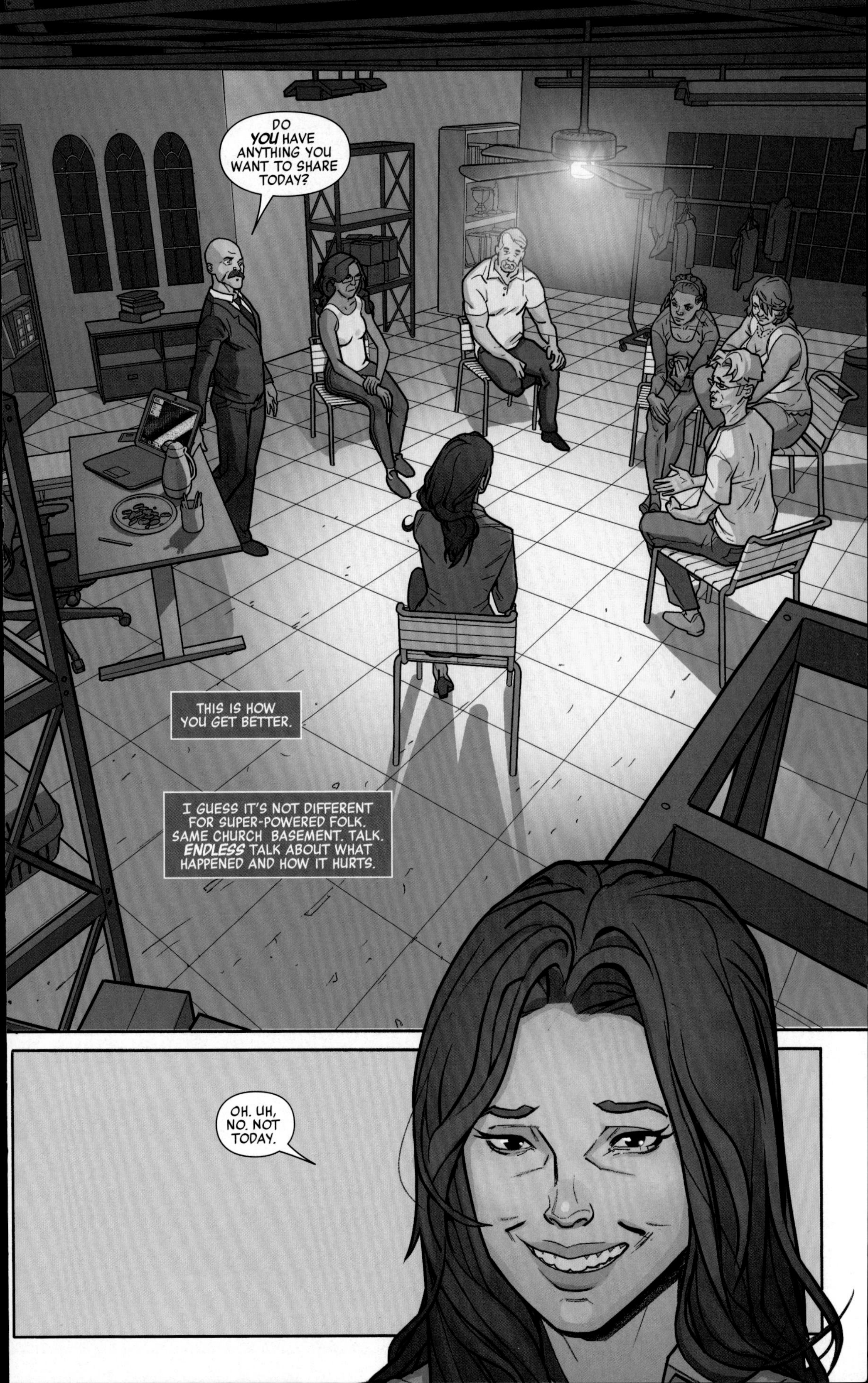
DO *YOU* HAVE ANYTHING YOU WANT TO SHARE TODAY?
THIS IS HOW YOU GET BETTER.
I GUESS IT'S NOT DIFFERENT FOR SUPER-POWERED FOLK. SAME CHURCH BASEMENT. TALK. *ENDLESS* TALK ABOUT WHAT HAPPENED AND HOW IT HURTS.
OH. UH, NO. NOT TODAY.

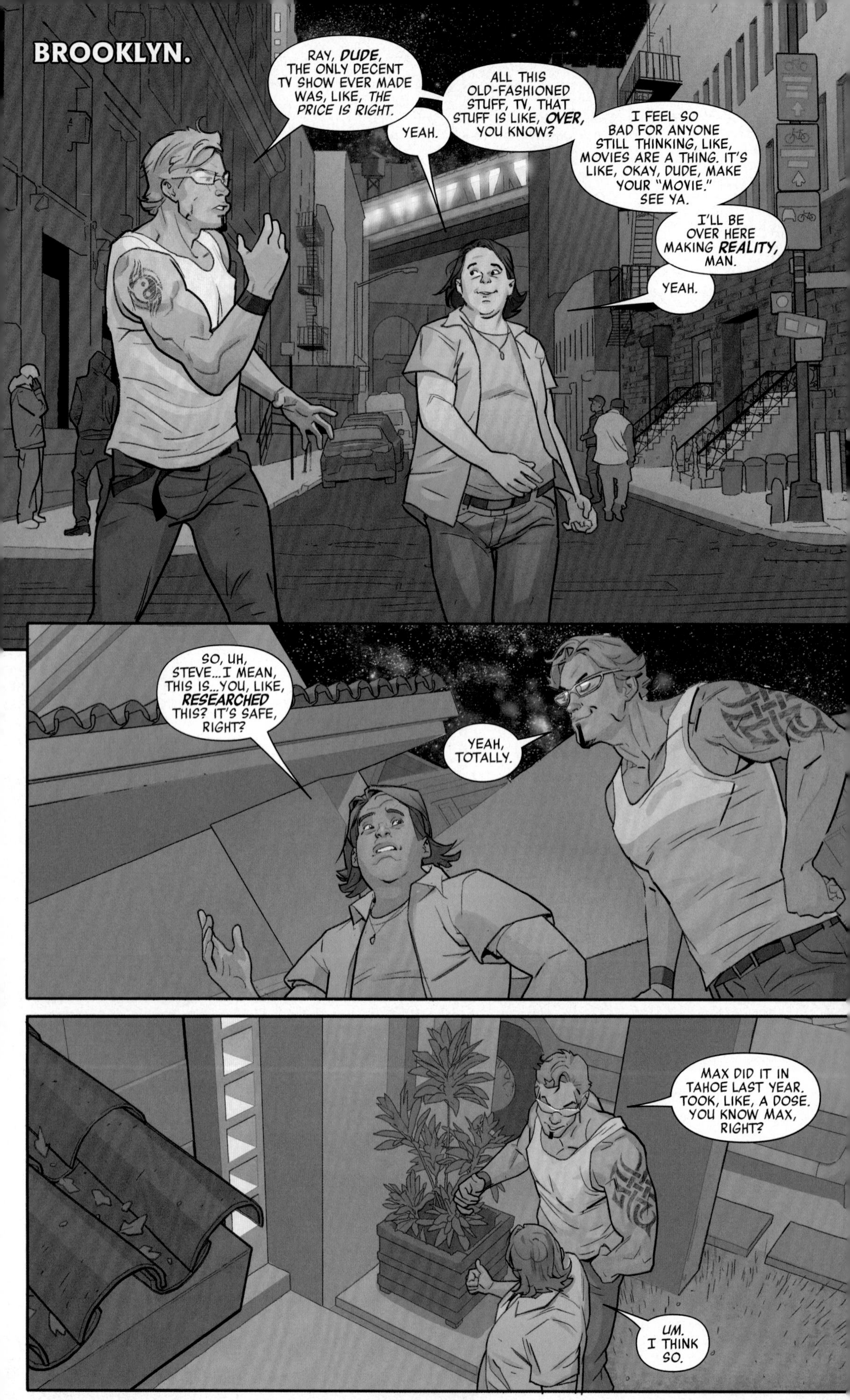
BROOKLYN.
RAY, DUDE, THE ONLY DECENT TV SHOW EVER MADE WAS, LIKE, THE PRICE IS RIGHT.
YEAH.
ALL THIS OLD-FASHIONED STUFF, TV, THAT STUFF IS LIKE, OVER, YOU KNOW?
I FEEL SO BAD FOR ANYONE STILL THINKING, LIKE, MOVIES ARE A THING. IT'S LIKE, OKAY, DUDE, MAKE YOUR "MOVIE." SEE YA.
I'LL BE OVER HERE MAKING REALITY, MAN.
YEAH.
SO, UH, STEVE...I MEAN, THIS IS...YOU, LIKE, RESEARCHED THIS? IT'S SAFE, RIGHT?
YEAH, TOTALLY.
MAX DID IT IN TAHOE LAST YEAR. TOOK, LIKE, A DOSE. YOU KNOW MAX, RIGHT?
UM. I THINK SO.

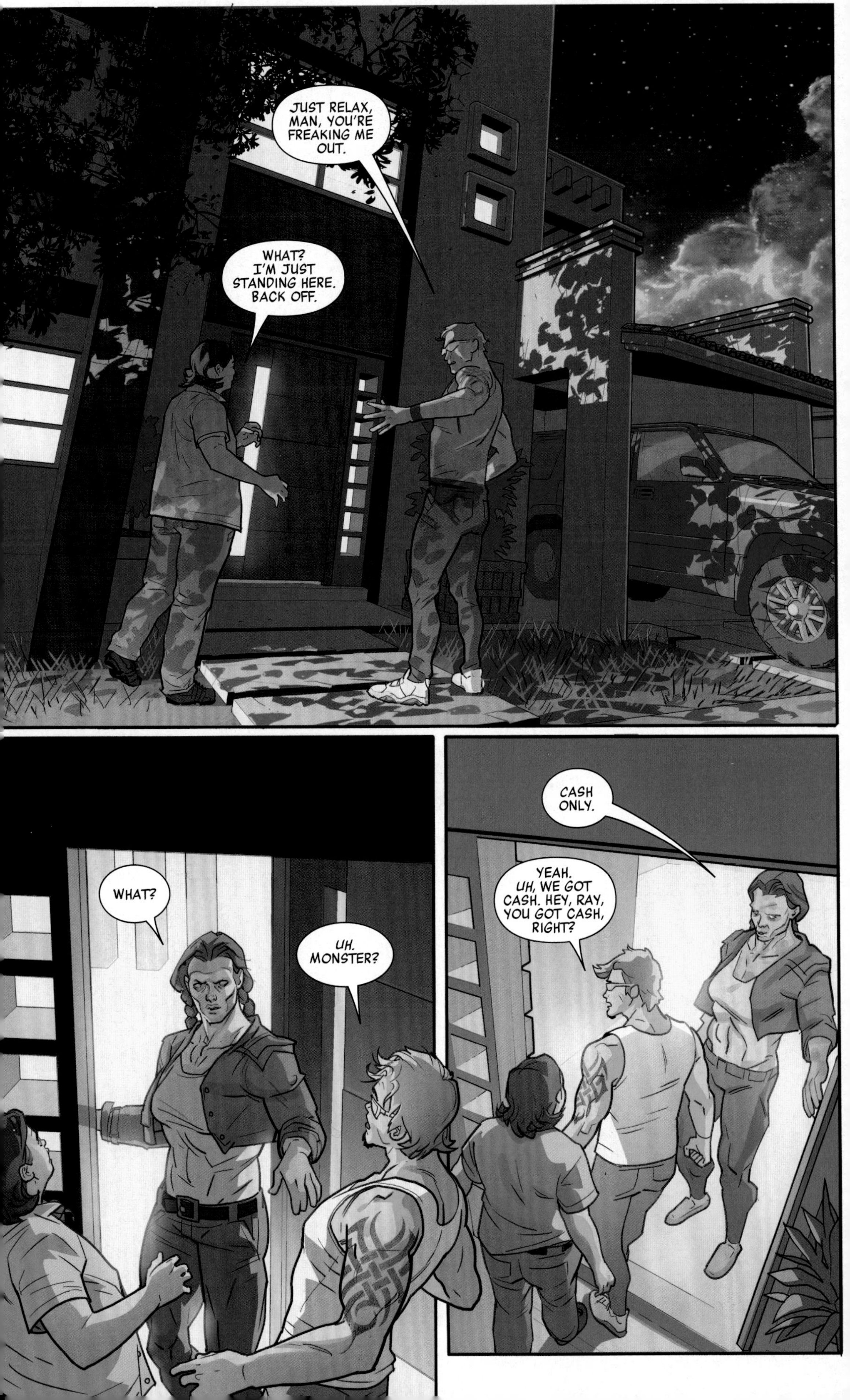
JUST RELAX, MAN, YOU'RE FREAKING ME OUT.
WHAT? I'M JUST STANDING HERE. BACK OFF.
WHAT?
UH. MONSTER?
CASH ONLY.
YEAH. UH, WE GOT CASH. HEY, RAY, YOU GOT CASH, RIGHT?

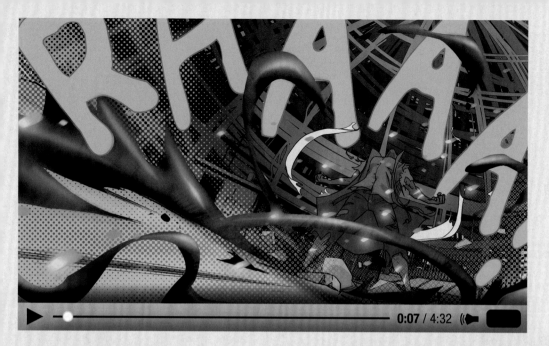

0:07 / 4:32

Uploaded by CHxMP_HLK17 on 06/14/2017.

Jennifer Walters has always battled for justice, both as a lawyer and as the super hero She-Hulk. But during the last super hero civil war, Jen was critically injured. At the same time, Jen's cousin, Bruce Banner A.K.A. the original Hulk, was murdered.

Since her accident, Jen's Hulk persona has changed. No longer articulate, no longer green, this new Hulk is gray and scarred, an enormous creature whose thoughts are often muddied by rage.

She-Hulk is no more. Now, there is only HULK

What does the future hold for this new hero?

Related:

2:56

1:09

0:56

6:35

Load more...

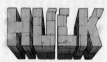

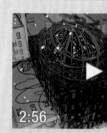

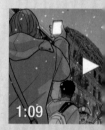

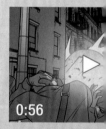

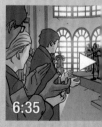

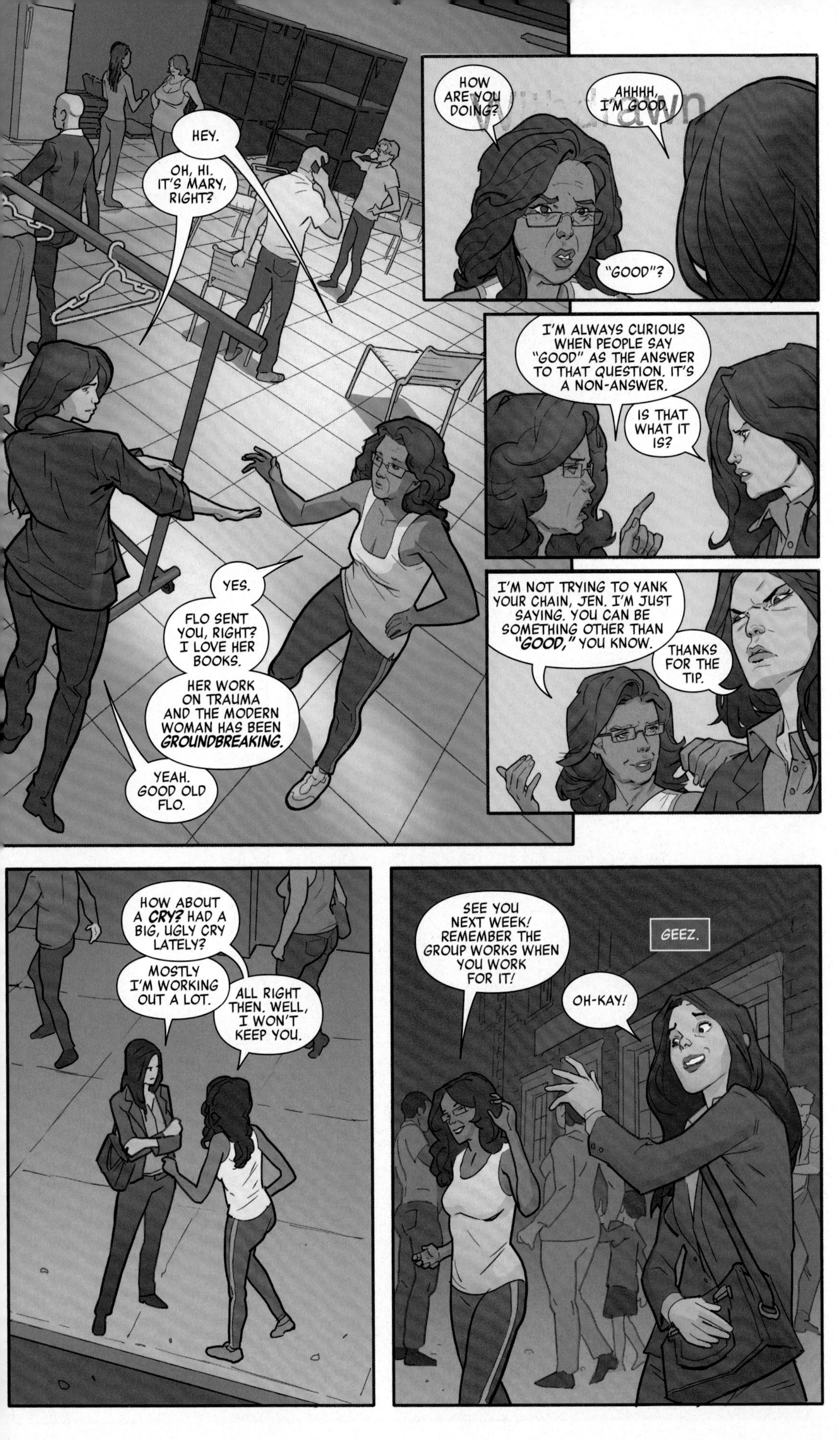
HEY.
OH, HI. IT'S MARY, RIGHT?
YES.
FLO SENT YOU, RIGHT? I LOVE HER BOOKS.
HER WORK ON TRAUMA AND THE MODERN WOMAN HAS BEEN **GROUNDBREAKING.**
YEAH. GOOD OLD FLO.
HOW ARE YOU DOING?
AHHHH, I'M GOOD.
"GOOD"?
I'M ALWAYS CURIOUS WHEN PEOPLE SAY "GOOD" AS THE ANSWER TO THAT QUESTION. IT'S A NON-ANSWER.
IS THAT WHAT IT IS?
I'M NOT TRYING TO YANK YOUR CHAIN, JEN. I'M JUST SAYING. YOU CAN BE SOMETHING OTHER THAN ***"GOOD,"*** YOU KNOW.
THANKS FOR THE TIP.
HOW ABOUT A ***CRY?*** HAD A BIG, UGLY CRY LATELY?
MOSTLY I'M WORKING OUT A LOT.
ALL RIGHT THEN. WELL, I WON'T KEEP YOU.
SEE YOU NEXT WEEK! REMEMBER THE GROUP WORKS WHEN YOU WORK FOR IT!
GEEZ.
OH-KAY!

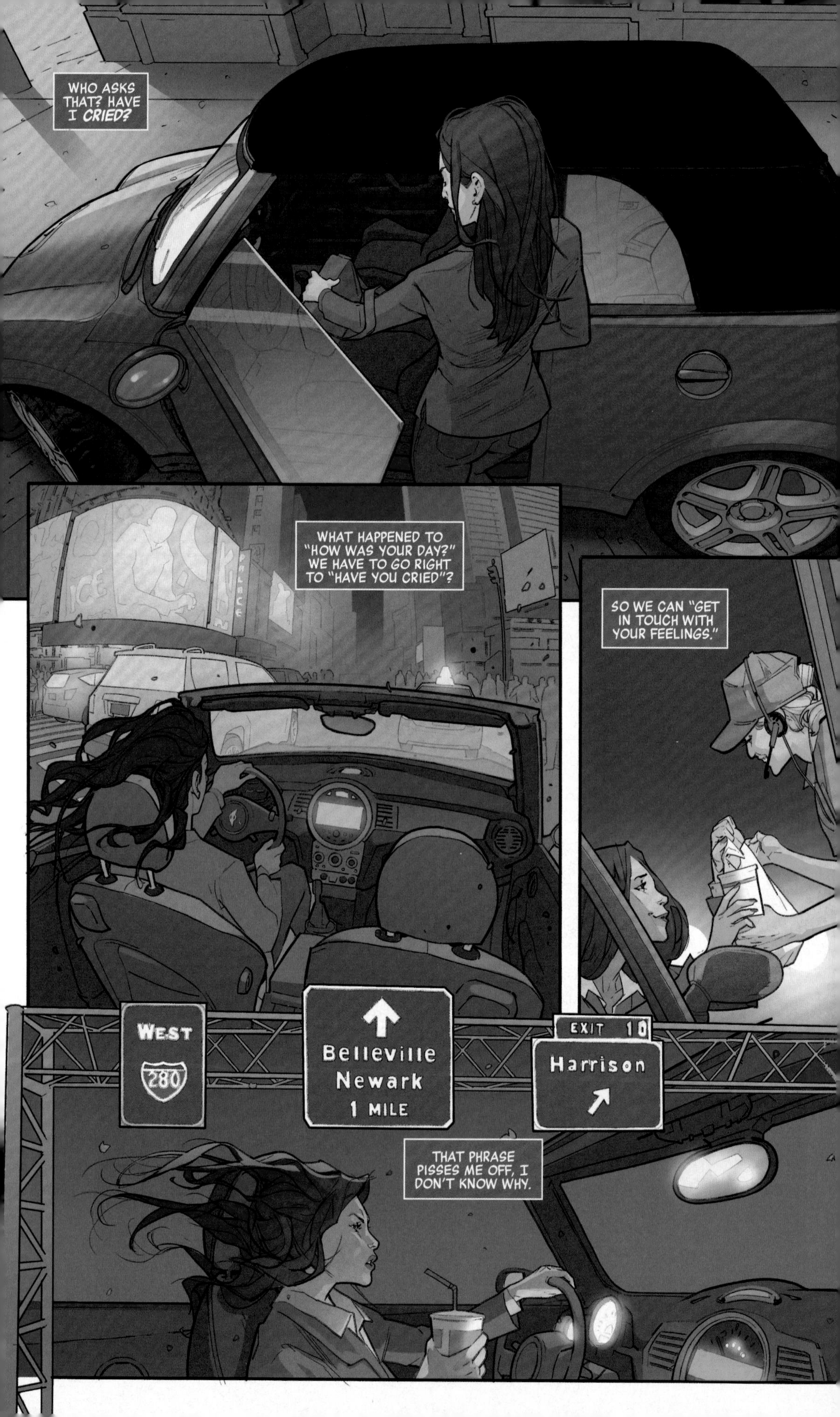
WHO ASKS THAT? HAVE I *CRIED*?
WHAT HAPPENED TO "HOW WAS YOUR DAY?" WE HAVE TO GO RIGHT TO "HAVE YOU CRIED"?
SO WE CAN "GET IN TOUCH WITH YOUR FEELINGS."
WEST
280
Belleville
Newark
1 MILE
EXIT 10
Harrison
THAT PHRASE PISSES ME OFF, I DON'T KNOW WHY.

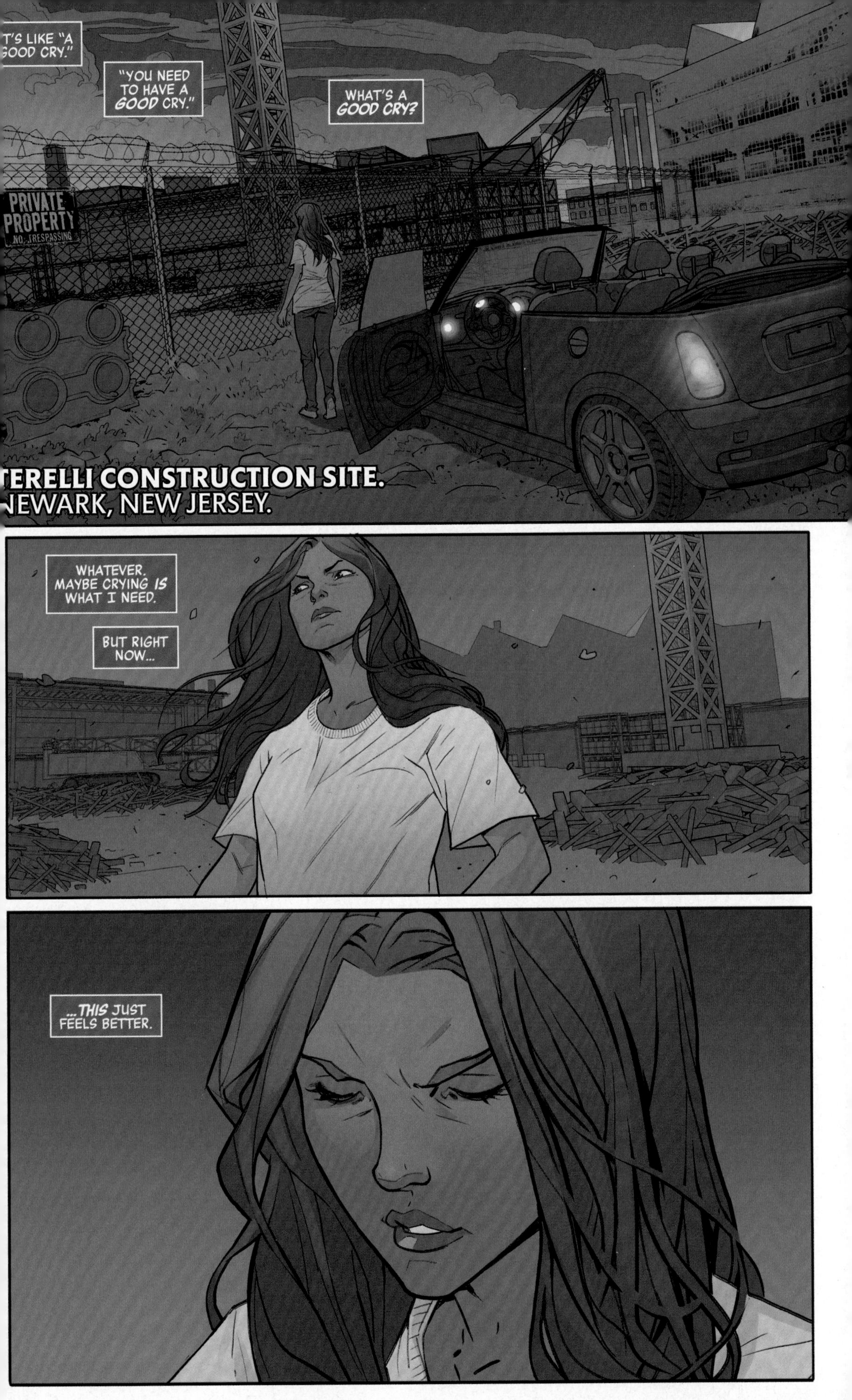

T'S LIKE "A GOOD CRY."
"YOU NEED TO HAVE A GOOD CRY."
WHAT'S A GOOD CRY?
PRIVATE PROPERTY
NO TRESPASSING
TERELLI CONSTRUCTION SITE.
NEWARK, NEW JERSEY.
WHATEVER. MAYBE CRYING IS WHAT I NEED.
BUT RIGHT NOW...
...THIS JUST FEELS BETTER.

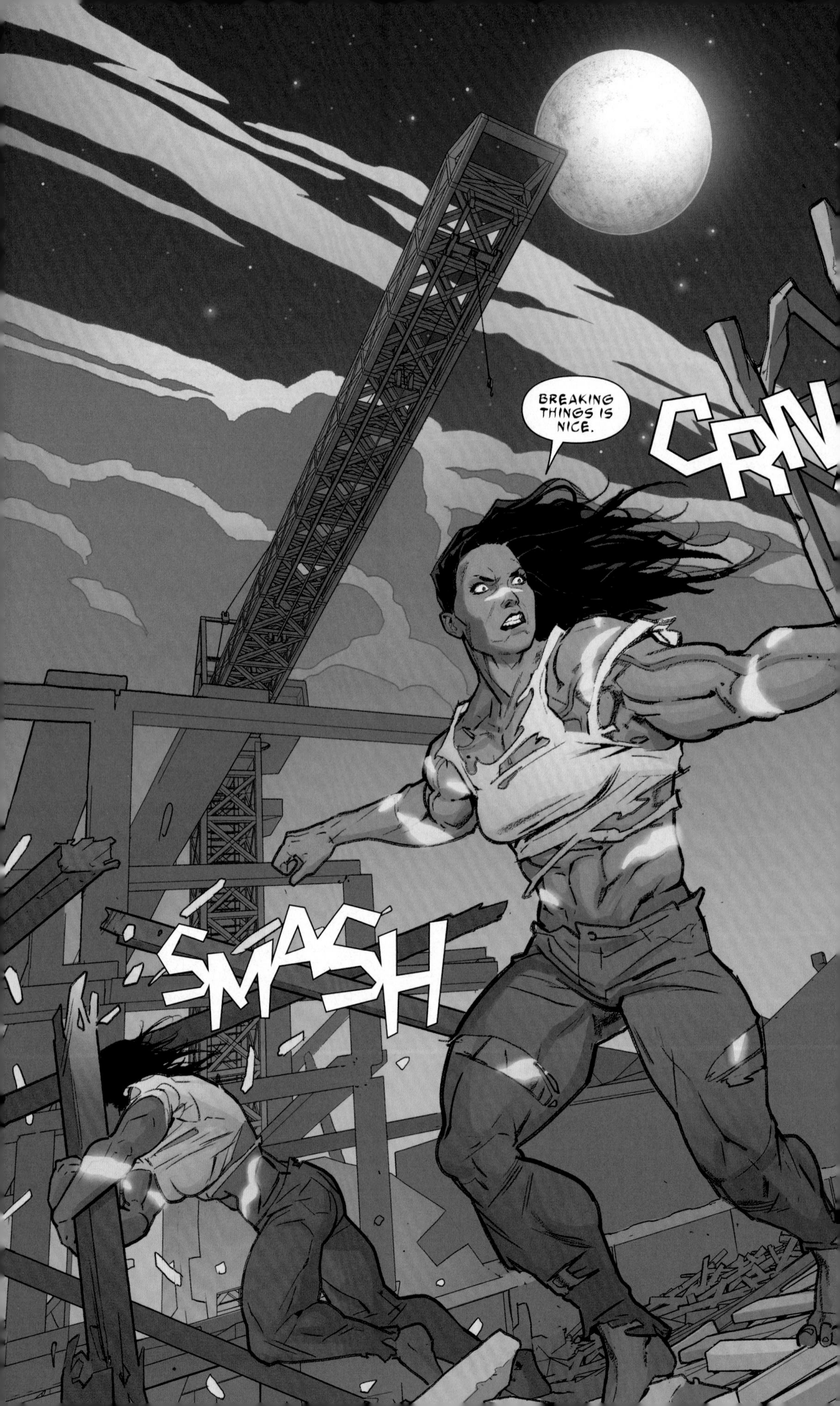
BREAKING THINGS IS NICE.
CRN
SMASH

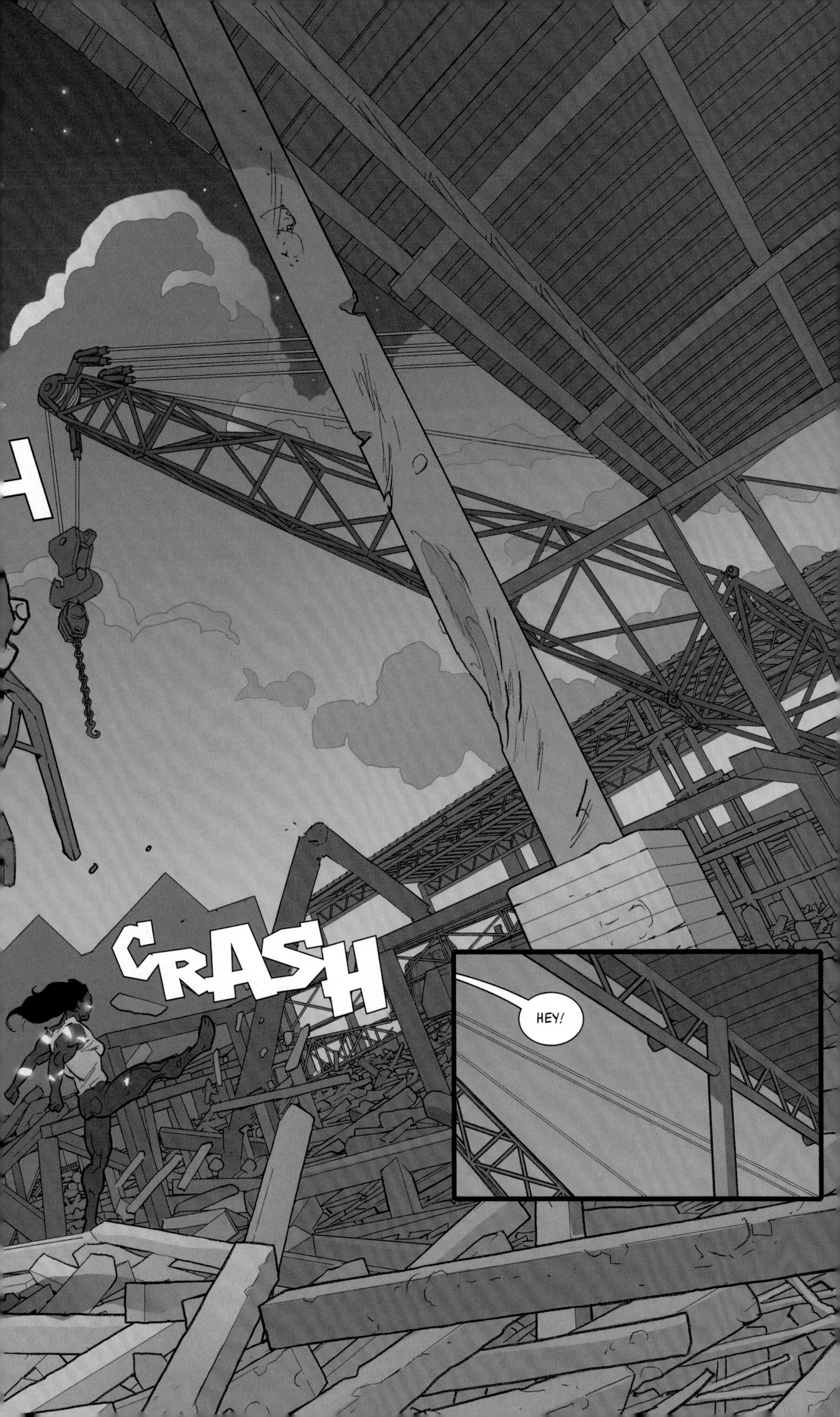
CRASH
HEY!

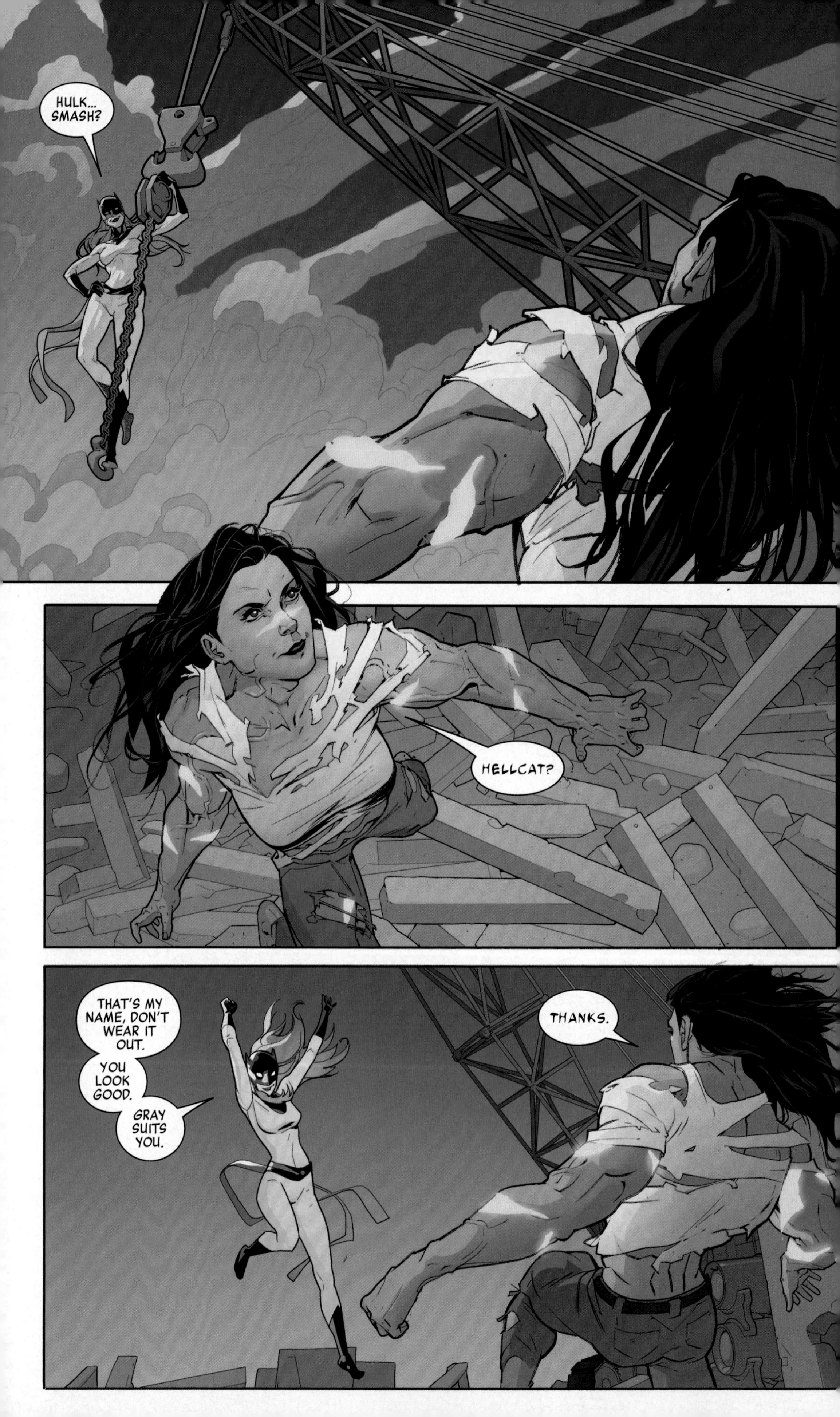
HULK... SMASH?
HELLCAT?
THAT'S MY NAME, DON'T WEAR IT OUT.
YOU LOOK GOOD.
GRAY SUITS YOU.
THANKS.

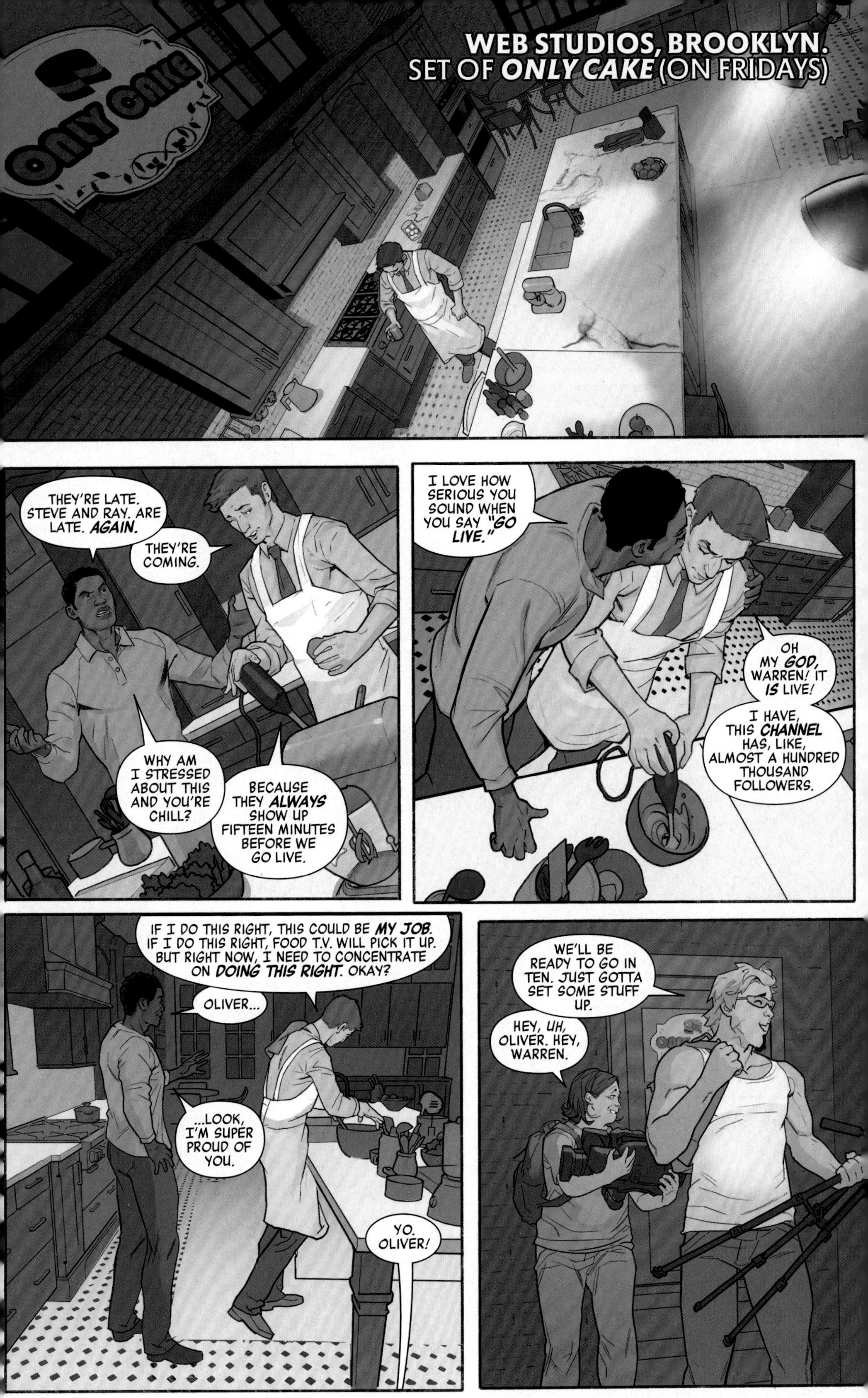
WEB STUDIOS, BROOKLYN.
SET OF ONLY CAKE (ON FRIDAYS)
ONLY CAKE
THEY'RE LATE. STEVE AND RAY. ARE LATE. AGAIN.
THEY'RE COMING.
WHY AM I STRESSED ABOUT THIS AND YOU'RE CHILL?
BECAUSE THEY ALWAYS SHOW UP FIFTEEN MINUTES BEFORE WE GO LIVE.
I LOVE HOW SERIOUS YOU SOUND WHEN YOU SAY "GO LIVE."
OH MY GOD, WARREN! IT IS LIVE!
I HAVE, THIS CHANNEL HAS, LIKE, ALMOST A HUNDRED THOUSAND FOLLOWERS.
IF I DO THIS RIGHT, THIS COULD BE MY JOB. IF I DO THIS RIGHT, FOOD T.V. WILL PICK IT UP. BUT RIGHT NOW, I NEED TO CONCENTRATE ON DOING THIS RIGHT. OKAY?
OLIVER...
...LOOK, I'M SUPER PROUD OF YOU.
YO. OLIVER!
WE'LL BE READY TO GO IN TEN. JUST GOTTA SET SOME STUFF UP.
HEY, UH, OLIVER. HEY, WARREN.

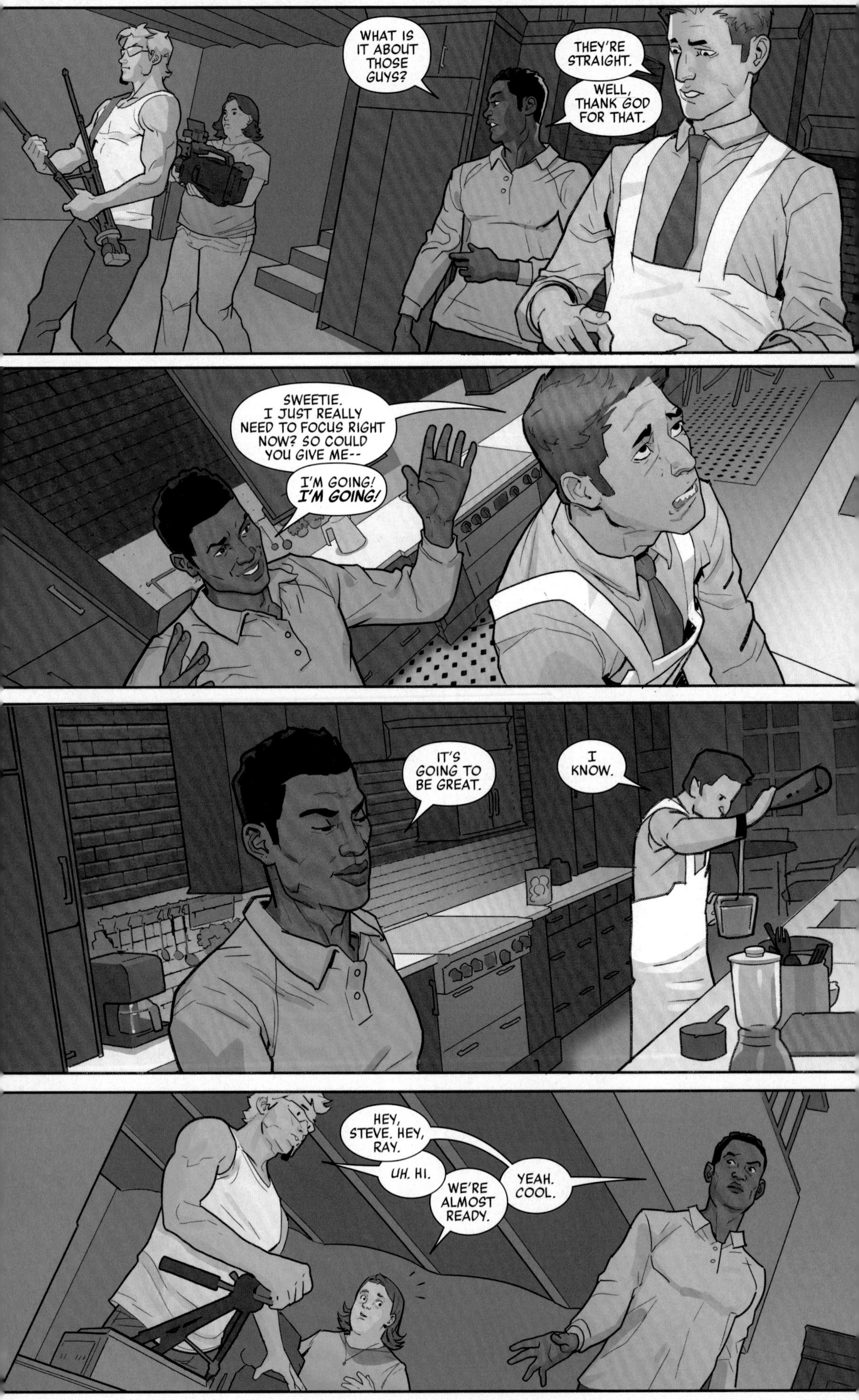
WHAT IS IT ABOUT THOSE GUYS?
THEY'RE STRAIGHT.
WELL, THANK GOD FOR THAT.
SWEETIE. I JUST REALLY NEED TO FOCUS RIGHT NOW? SO COULD YOU GIVE ME--
I'M GOING! **I'M GOING!**
IT'S GOING TO BE GREAT.
I KNOW.
HEY, STEVE. HEY, RAY.
UH. HI.
WE'RE ALMOST READY.
YEAH. COOL.

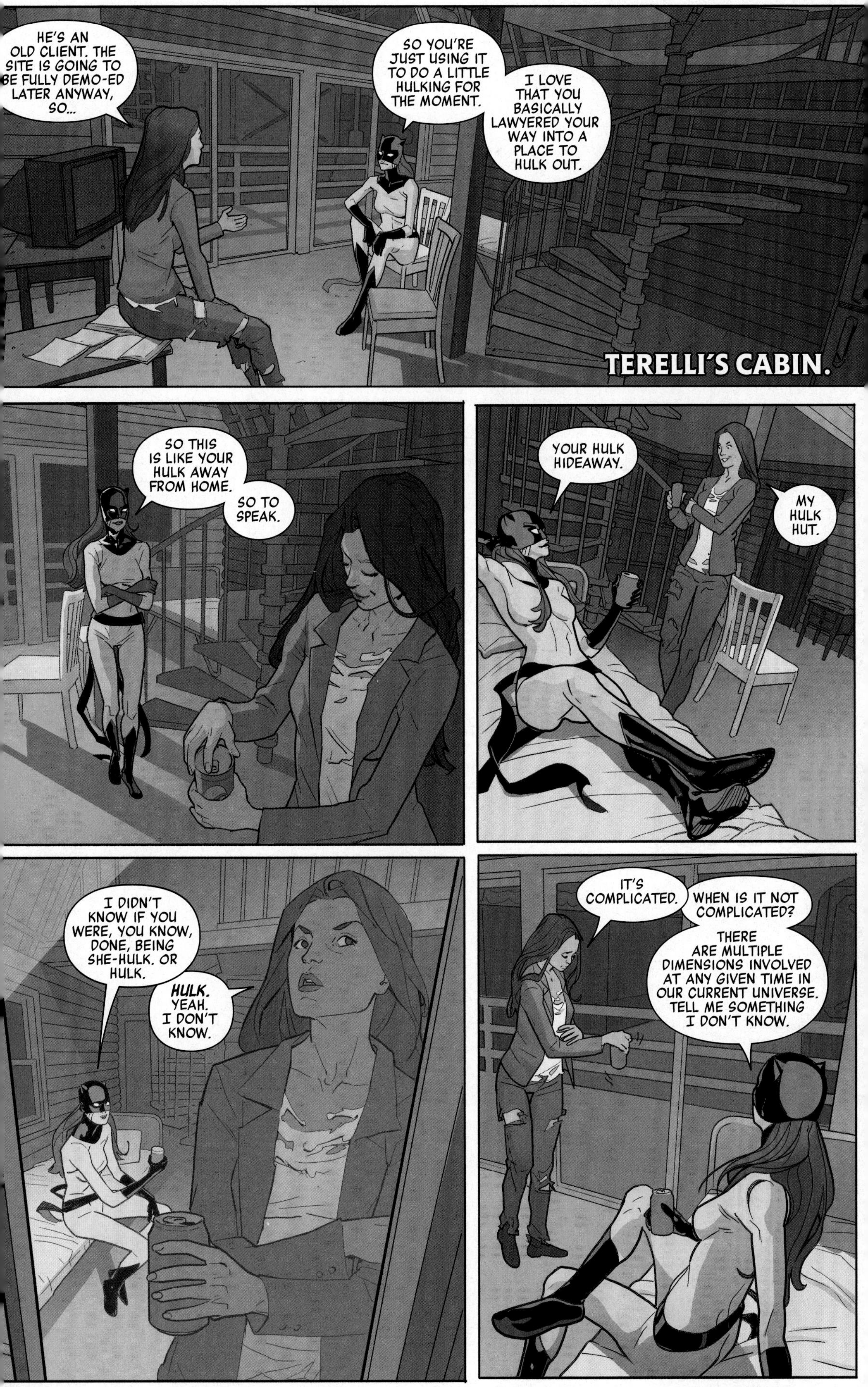
HE'S AN OLD CLIENT. THE SITE IS GOING TO BE FULLY DEMO-ED LATER ANYWAY, SO...
SO YOU'RE JUST USING IT TO DO A LITTLE HULKING FOR THE MOMENT.
I LOVE THAT YOU BASICALLY LAWYERED YOUR WAY INTO A PLACE TO HULK OUT.
TERELLI'S CABIN.
SO THIS IS LIKE YOUR HULK AWAY FROM HOME.
SO TO SPEAK.
YOUR HULK HIDEAWAY.
MY HULK HUT.
I DIDN'T KNOW IF YOU WERE, YOU KNOW, DONE, BEING SHE-HULK. OR HULK.
HULK. YEAH. I DON'T KNOW.
IT'S COMPLICATED.
WHEN IS IT NOT COMPLICATED?
THERE ARE MULTIPLE DIMENSIONS INVOLVED AT ANY GIVEN TIME IN OUR CURRENT UNIVERSE. TELL ME SOMETHING I DON'T KNOW.

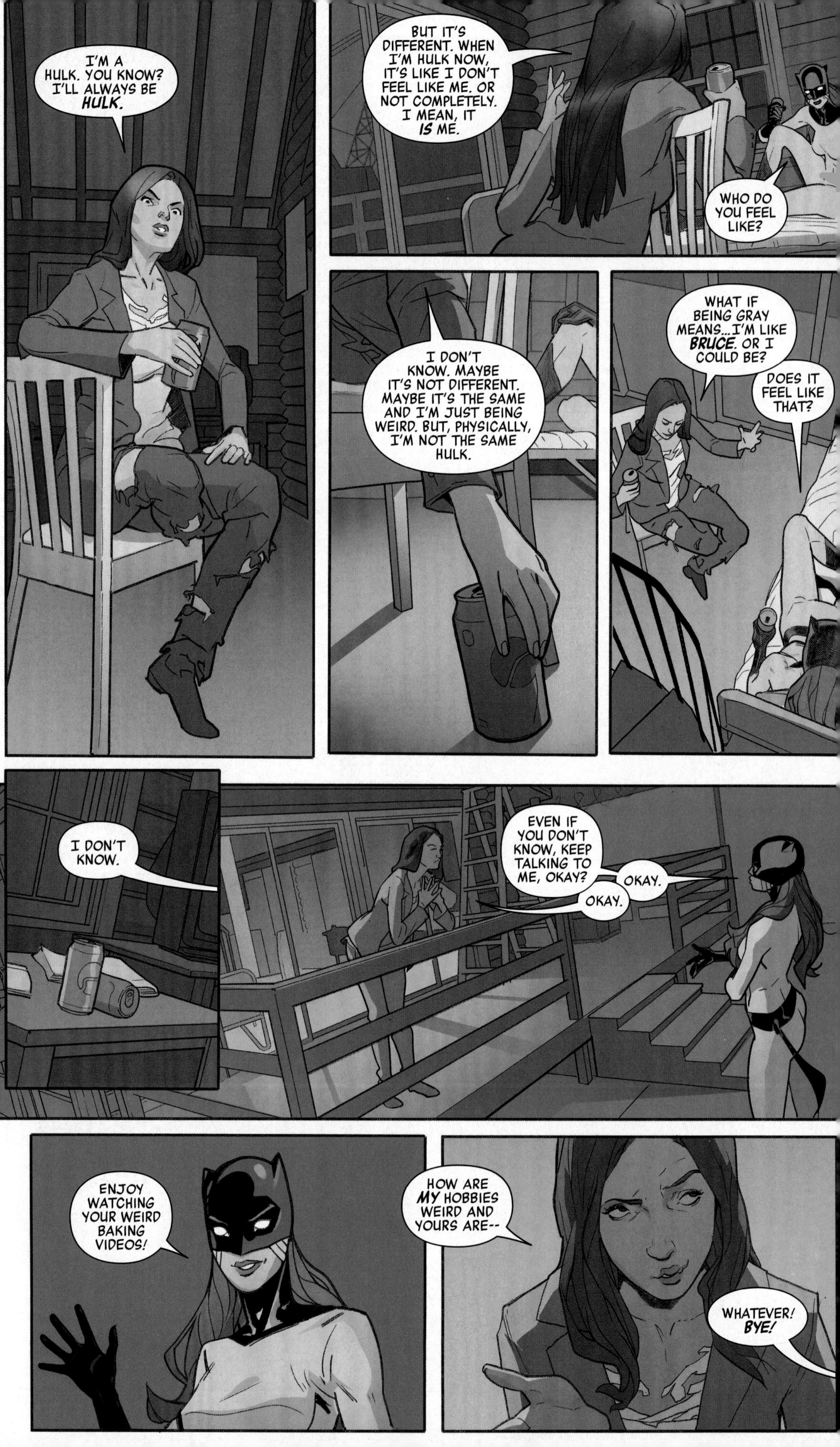
I'M A HULK. YOU KNOW? I'LL ALWAYS BE HULK.
BUT IT'S DIFFERENT. WHEN I'M HULK NOW, IT'S LIKE I DON'T FEEL LIKE ME. OR NOT COMPLETELY. I MEAN, IT IS ME.
WHO DO YOU FEEL LIKE?
I DON'T KNOW. MAYBE IT'S NOT DIFFERENT. MAYBE IT'S THE SAME AND I'M JUST BEING WEIRD. BUT, PHYSICALLY, I'M NOT THE SAME HULK.
WHAT IF BEING GRAY MEANS...I'M LIKE BRUCE. OR I COULD BE?
DOES IT FEEL LIKE THAT?
I DON'T KNOW.
EVEN IF YOU DON'T KNOW, KEEP TALKING TO ME, OKAY?
OKAY.
OKAY.
ENJOY WATCHING YOUR WEIRD BAKING VIDEOS!
HOW ARE MY HOBBIES WEIRD AND YOURS ARE--
WHATEVER! BYE!

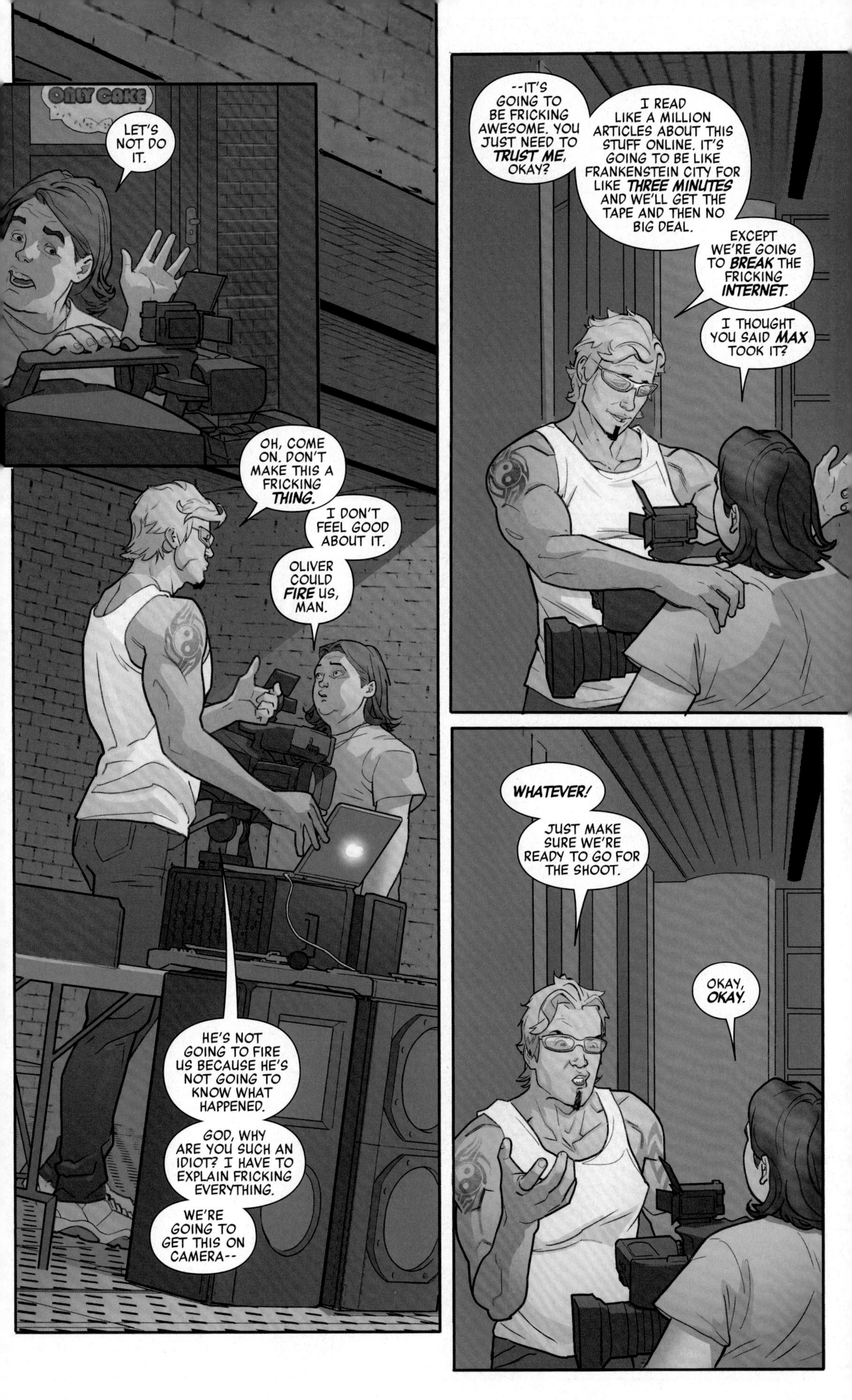
ONLY CAKE
LET'S NOT DO IT.
OH, COME ON. DON'T MAKE THIS A FRICKING THING.
I DON'T FEEL GOOD ABOUT IT.
OLIVER COULD FIRE US, MAN.
HE'S NOT GOING TO FIRE US BECAUSE HE'S NOT GOING TO KNOW WHAT HAPPENED.
GOD, WHY ARE YOU SUCH AN IDIOT? I HAVE TO EXPLAIN FRICKING EVERYTHING.
WE'RE GOING TO GET THIS ON CAMERA--
--IT'S GOING TO BE FRICKING AWESOME. YOU JUST NEED TO TRUST ME, OKAY?
I READ LIKE A MILLION ARTICLES ABOUT THIS STUFF ONLINE. IT'S GOING TO BE LIKE FRANKENSTEIN CITY FOR LIKE THREE MINUTES AND WE'LL GET THE TAPE AND THEN NO BIG DEAL.
EXCEPT WE'RE GOING TO BREAK THE FRICKING INTERNET.
I THOUGHT YOU SAID MAX TOOK IT?
WHATEVER!
JUST MAKE SURE WE'RE READY TO GO FOR THE SHOOT.
OKAY, OKAY.

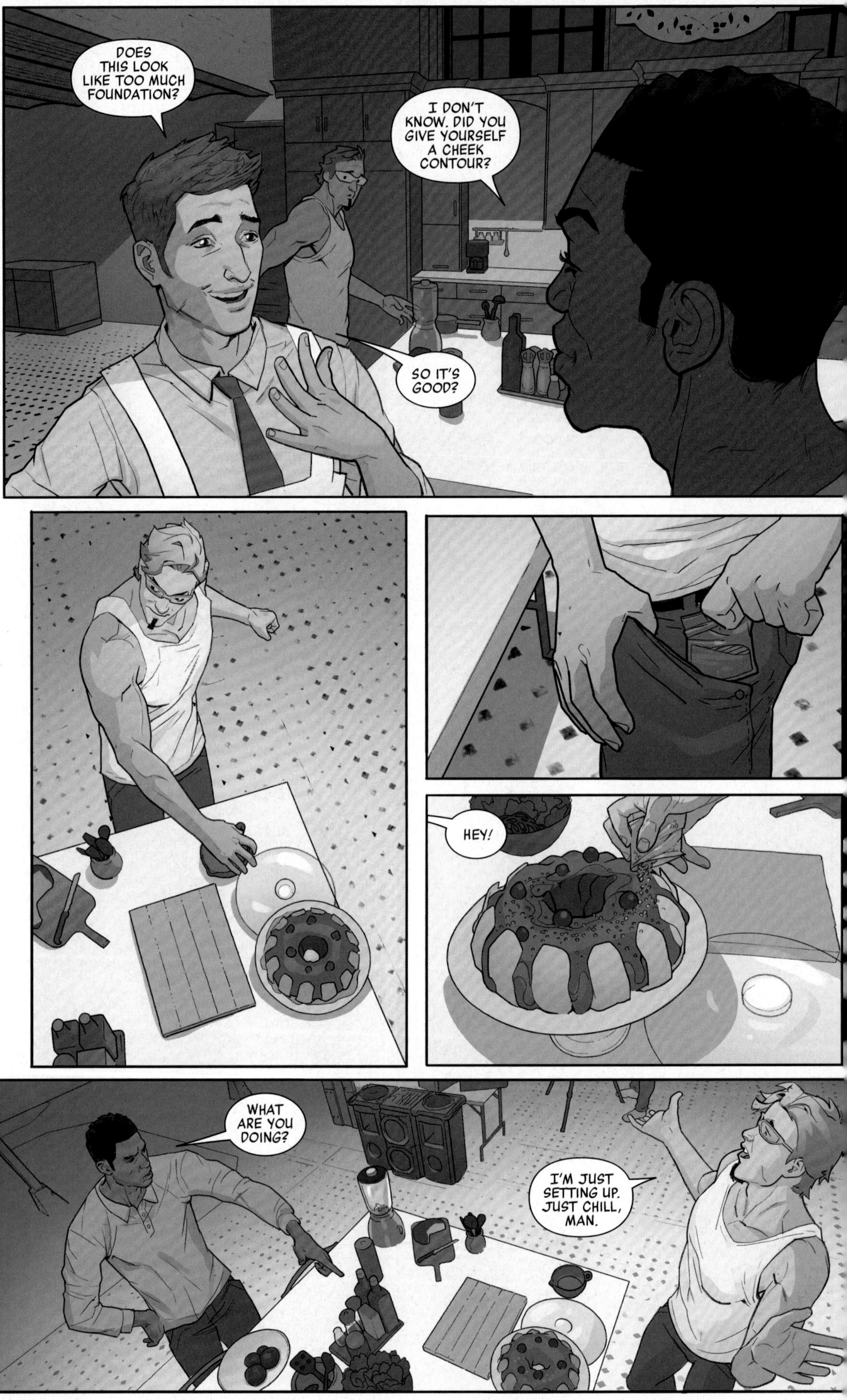
DOES THIS LOOK LIKE TOO MUCH FOUNDATION?
I DON'T KNOW. DID YOU GIVE YOURSELF A CHEEK CONTOUR?
SO IT'S GOOD?
HEY!
WHAT ARE YOU DOING?
I'M JUST SETTING UP. JUST CHILL, MAN.

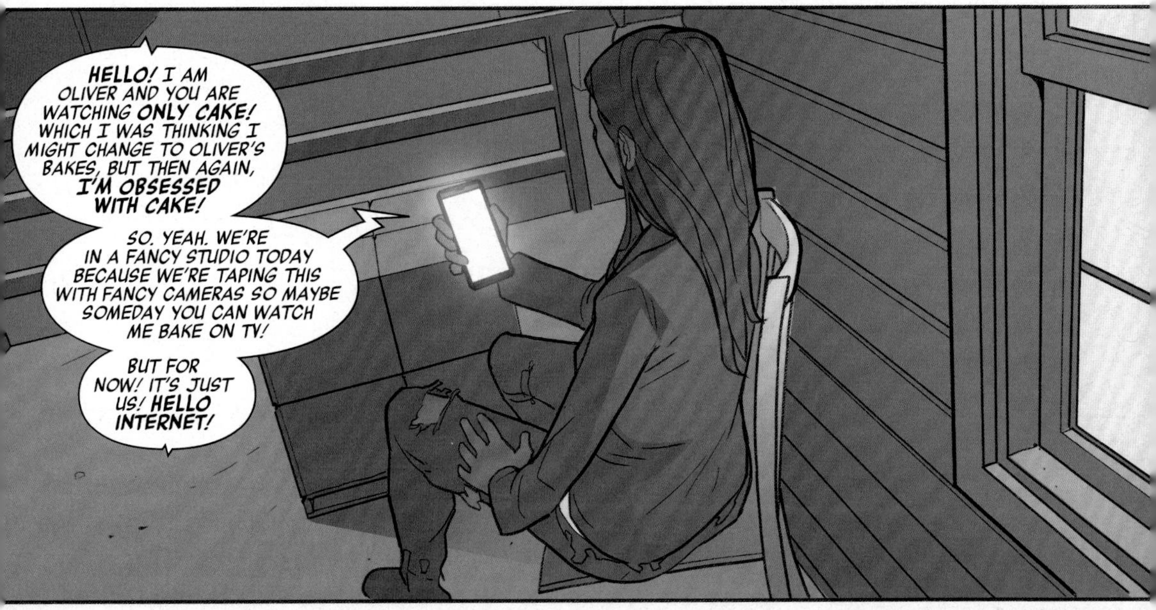
HELLO! I AM OLIVER AND YOU ARE WATCHING ONLY CAKE! WHICH I WAS THINKING I MIGHT CHANGE TO OLIVER'S BAKES, BUT THEN AGAIN, I'M OBSESSED WITH CAKE!
SO. YEAH. WE'RE IN A FANCY STUDIO TODAY BECAUSE WE'RE TAPING THIS WITH FANCY CAMERAS SO MAYBE SOMEDAY YOU CAN WATCH ME BAKE ON TV!
BUT FOR NOW! IT'S JUST US! HELLO INTERNET!

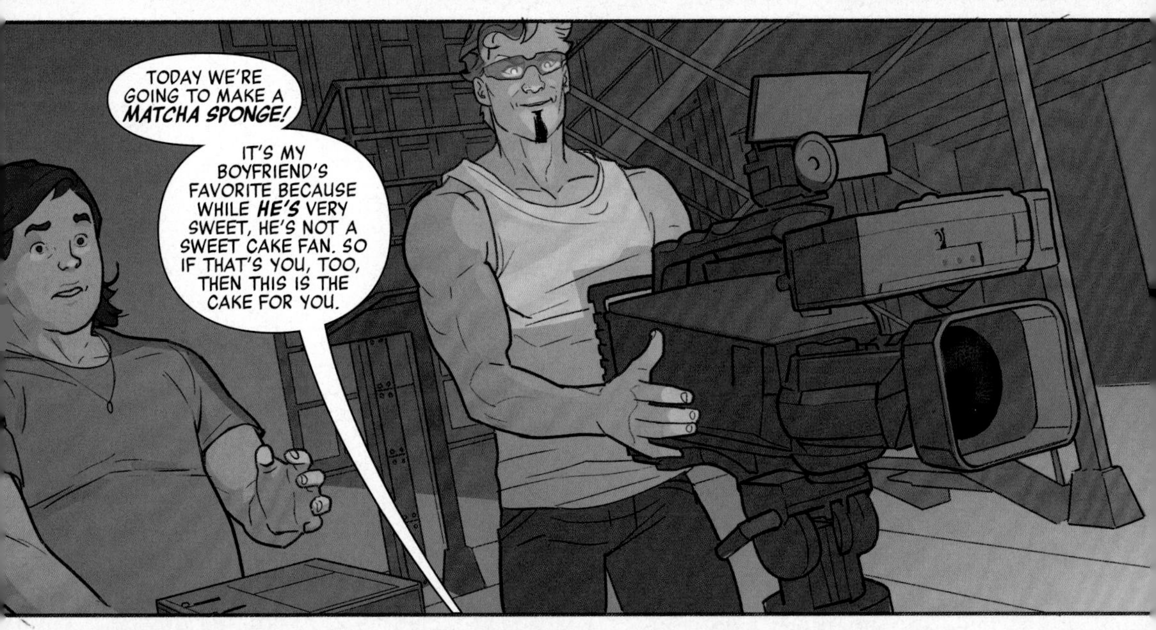
TODAY WE'RE GOING TO MAKE A MATCHA SPONGE!
IT'S MY BOYFRIEND'S FAVORITE BECAUSE WHILE HE'S VERY SWEET, HE'S NOT A SWEET CAKE FAN. SO IF THAT'S YOU, TOO, THEN THIS IS THE CAKE FOR YOU.

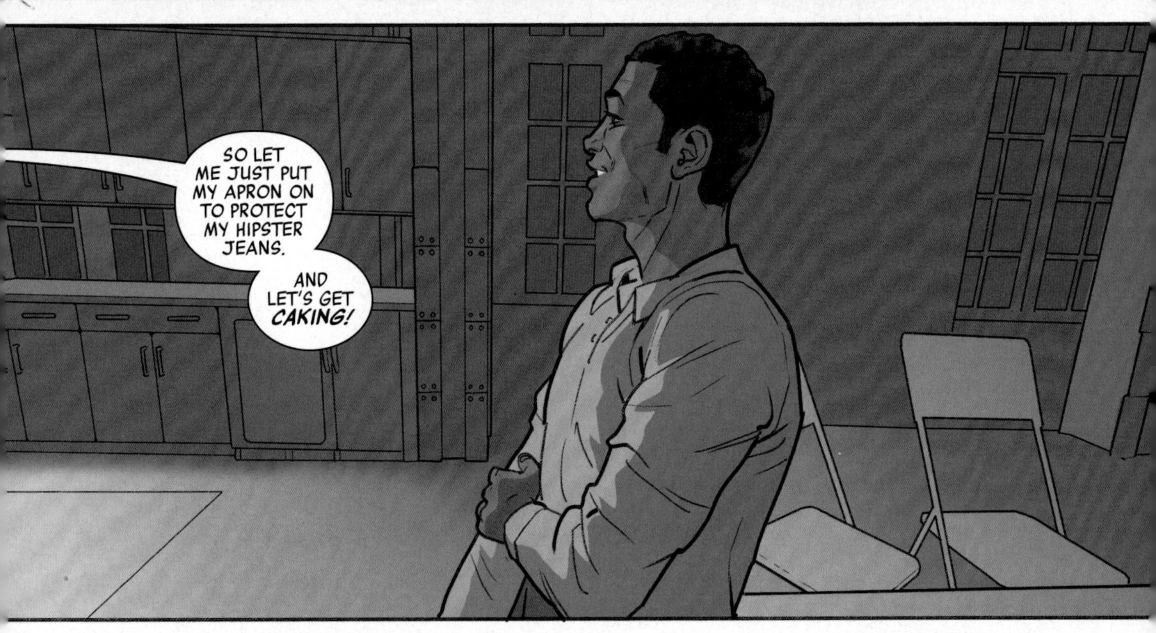
SO LET ME JUST PUT MY APRON ON TO PROTECT MY HIPSTER JEANS.
AND LET'S GET CAKING!

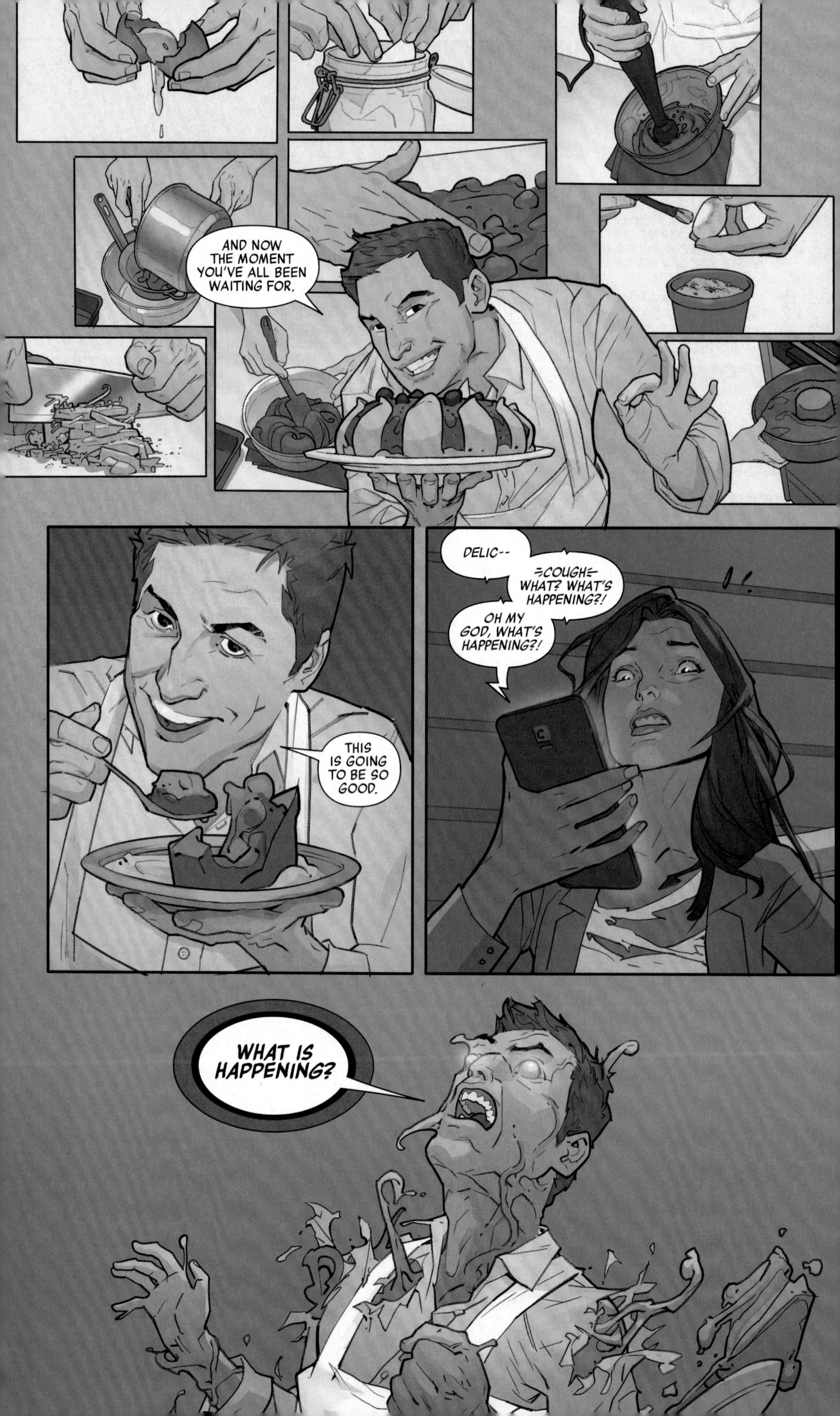
AND NOW THE MOMENT YOU'VE ALL BEEN WAITING FOR.
THIS IS GOING TO BE SO GOOD.
DELIC--
=COUGH= WHAT? WHAT'S HAPPENING?!
OH MY GOD, WHAT'S HAPPENING?!
WHAT IS HAPPENING?

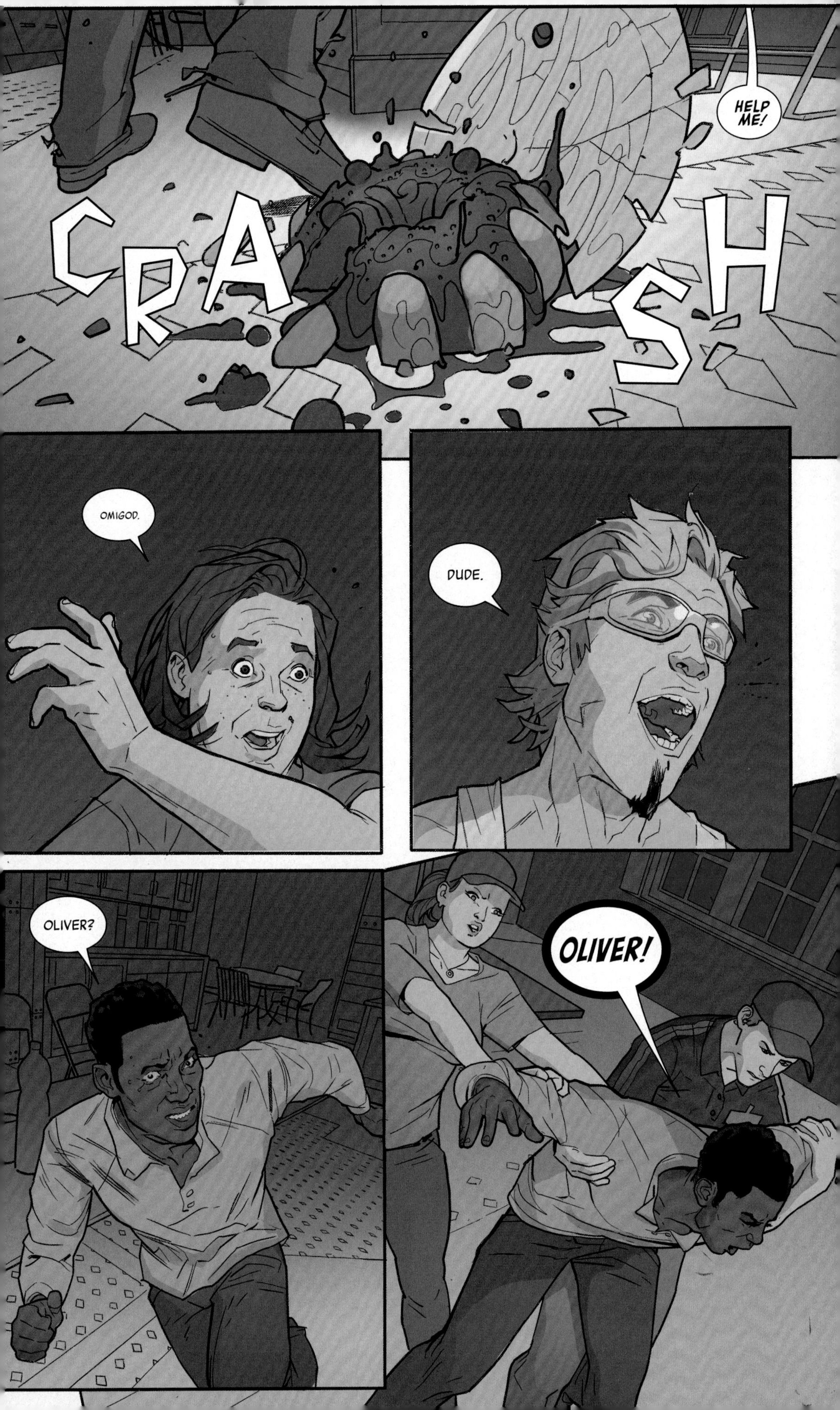
HELP ME!
CRASH
OMIGOD.
DUDE.
OLIVER?
OLIVER!

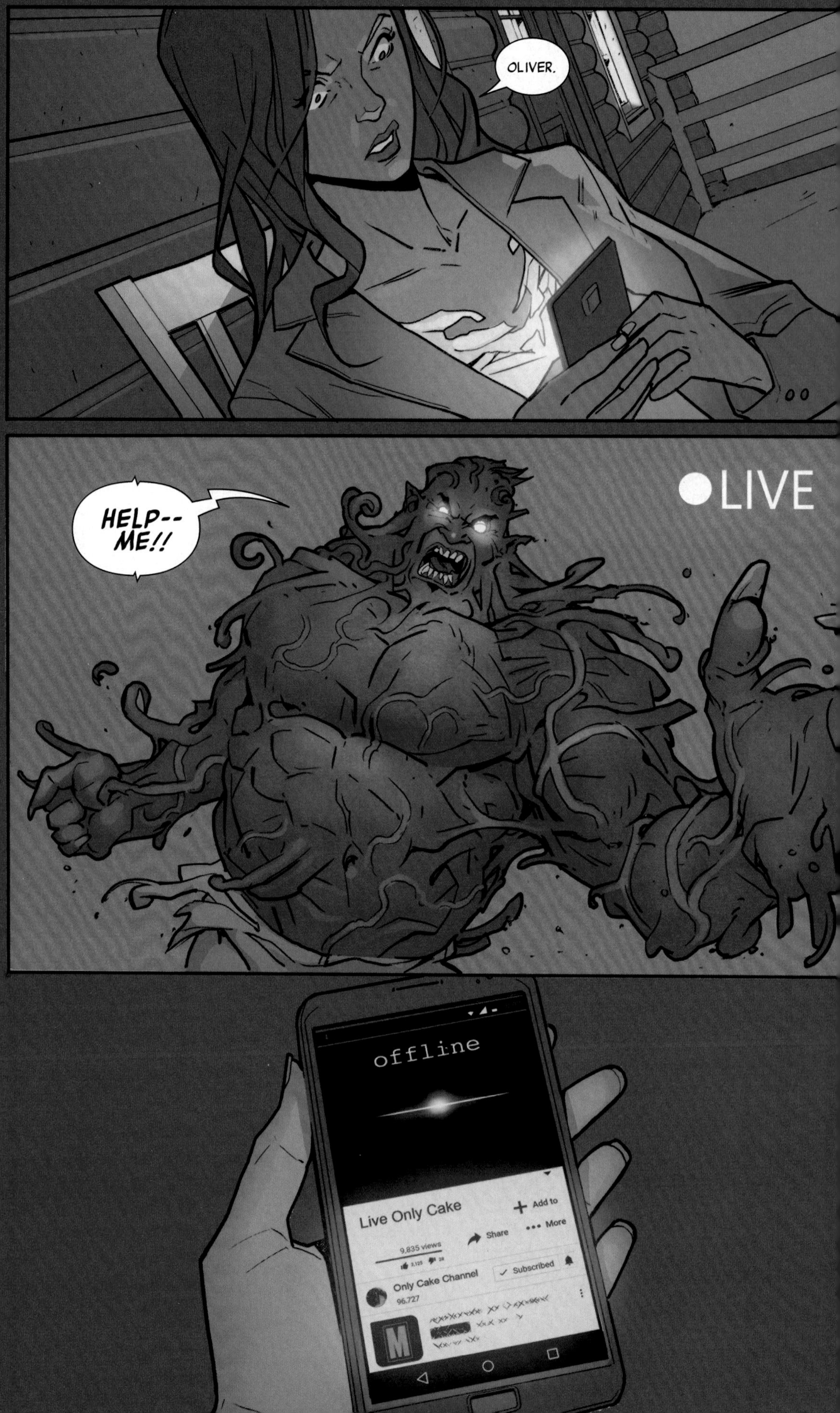
OLIVER.
HELP-- ME!!
LIVE
offline
Live Only Cake
Add to
Share
More
9,835 views
Subscribed
Only Cake Channel
96,727

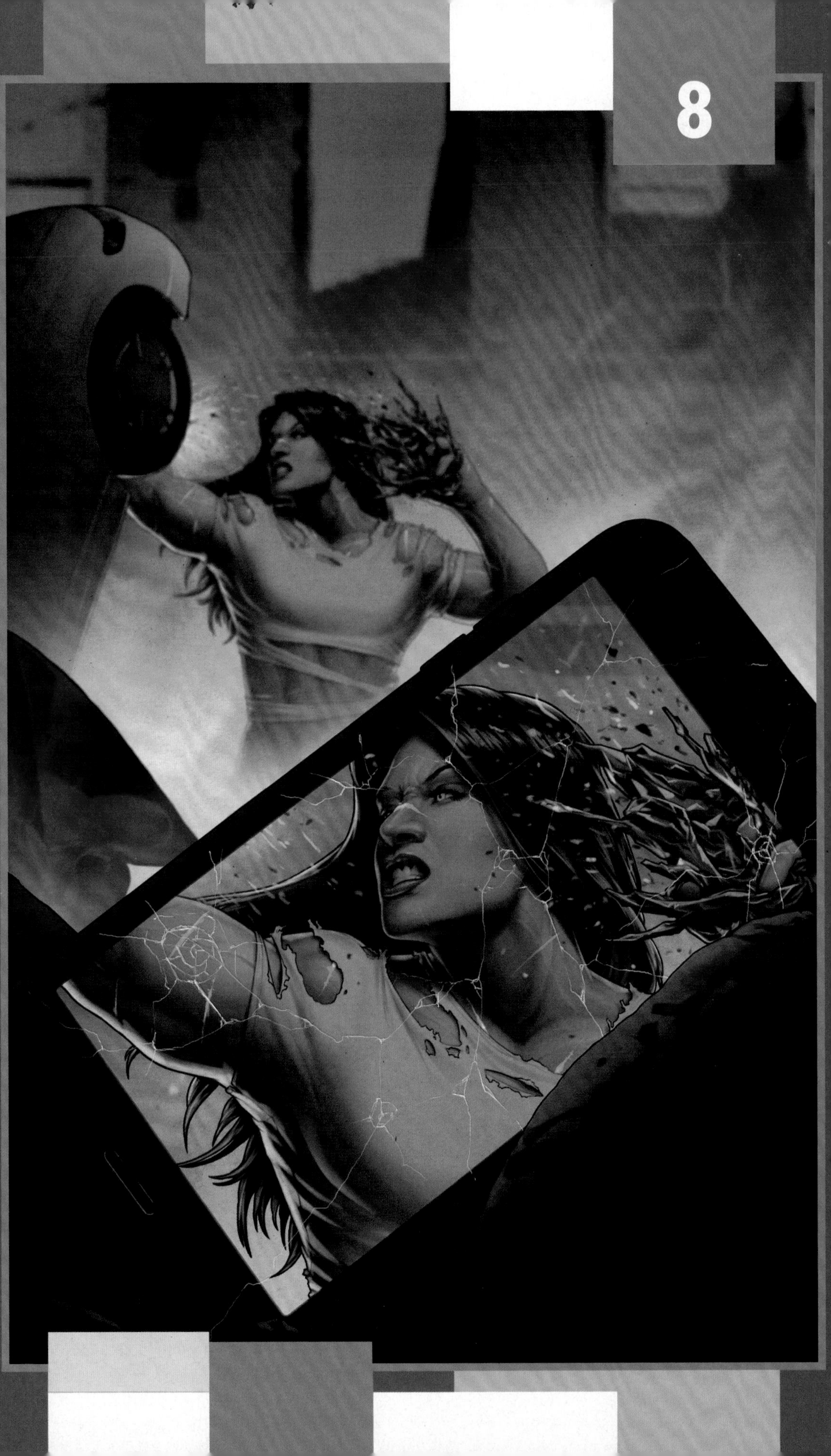
8

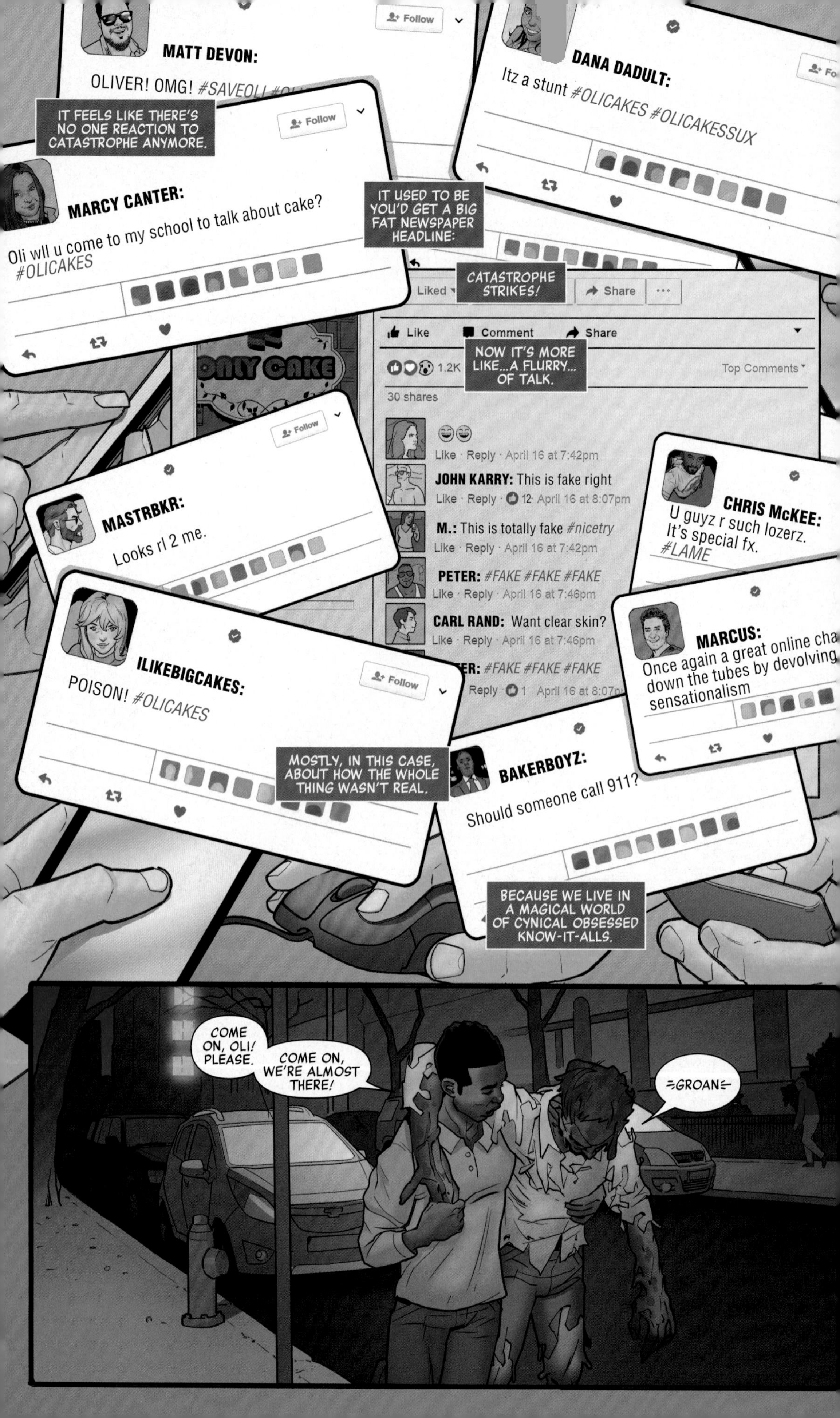

MATT DEVON:
OLIVER! OMG! #SAVEOLI
DANA DADULT:
Itz a stunt #OLICAKES #OLICAKESSUX
IT FEELS LIKE THERE'S NO ONE REACTION TO CATASTROPHE ANYMORE.
MARCY CANTER:
Oli wll u come to my school to talk about cake? #OLICAKES
IT USED TO BE YOU'D GET A BIG FAT NEWSPAPER HEADLINE:
CATASTROPHE STRIKES!
NOW IT'S MORE LIKE...A FLURRY... OF TALK.
ONLY CAKE
1.2K
30 shares
Top Comments
Like · Reply · April 16 at 7:42pm
JOHN KARRY: This is fake right
Like · Reply · 12 April 16 at 8:07pm
M.: This is totally fake #nicetry
Like · Reply · April 16 at 7:42pm
PETER: #FAKE #FAKE #FAKE
Like · Reply · April 16 at 7:46pm
CARL RAND: Want clear skin?
Like · Reply · April 16 at 7:46pm
MASTRBKR:
Looks rl 2 me.
CHRIS McKEE:
U guyz r such lozerz. It's special fx. #LAME
ILIKEBIGCAKES:
POISON! #OLICAKES
MARCUS:
Once again a great online cha down the tubes by devolving sensationalism
MOSTLY, IN THIS CASE, ABOUT HOW THE WHOLE THING WASN'T REAL.
BAKERBOYZ:
Should someone call 911?
BECAUSE WE LIVE IN A MAGICAL WORLD OF CYNICAL OBSESSED KNOW-IT-ALLS.
COME ON, OLI! PLEASE.
COME ON, WE'RE ALMOST THERE!
GROAN

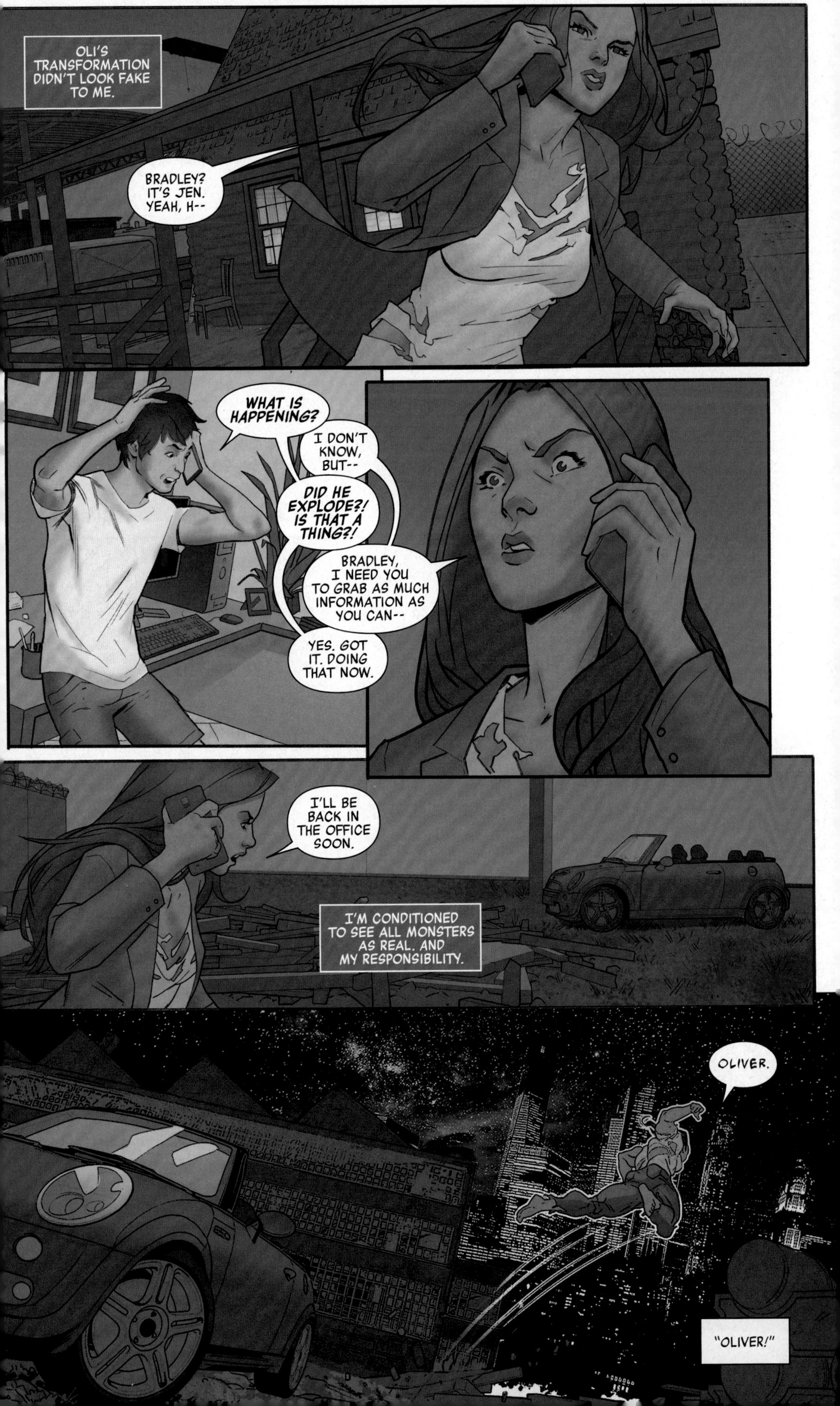
OLI'S TRANSFORMATION DIDN'T LOOK FAKE TO ME.
BRADLEY? IT'S JEN. YEAH, H--
WHAT IS HAPPENING?
I DON'T KNOW, BUT--
DID HE EXPLODE?! IS THAT A THING?!
BRADLEY, I NEED YOU TO GRAB AS MUCH INFORMATION AS YOU CAN--
YES. GOT IT. DOING THAT NOW.
I'LL BE BACK IN THE OFFICE SOON.
I'M CONDITIONED TO SEE ALL MONSTERS AS REAL. AND MY RESPONSIBILITY.
OLIVER.
"OLIVER!"

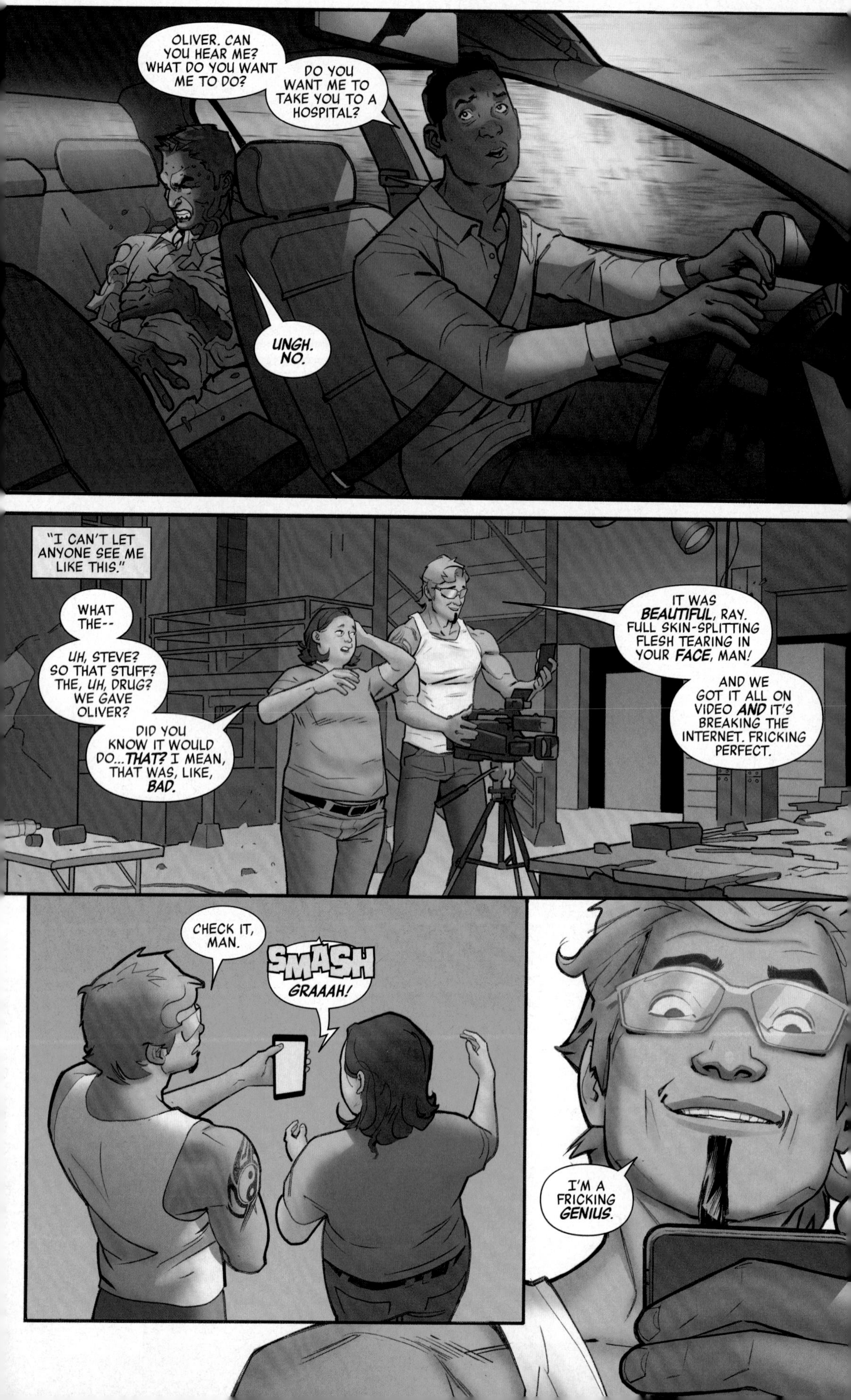
OLIVER. CAN YOU HEAR ME? WHAT DO YOU WANT ME TO DO?
DO YOU WANT ME TO TAKE YOU TO A HOSPITAL?
UNGH. NO.
"I CAN'T LET ANYONE SEE ME LIKE THIS."
WHAT THE--
UH, STEVE? SO THAT STUFF? THE, UH, DRUG? WE GAVE OLIVER?
DID YOU KNOW IT WOULD DO...THAT? I MEAN, THAT WAS, LIKE, BAD.
IT WAS BEAUTIFUL, RAY. FULL SKIN-SPLITTING FLESH TEARING IN YOUR FACE, MAN!
AND WE GOT IT ALL ON VIDEO AND IT'S BREAKING THE INTERNET. FRICKING PERFECT.
CHECK IT, MAN.
SMASH
GRAAAH!
I'M A FRICKING GENIUS.

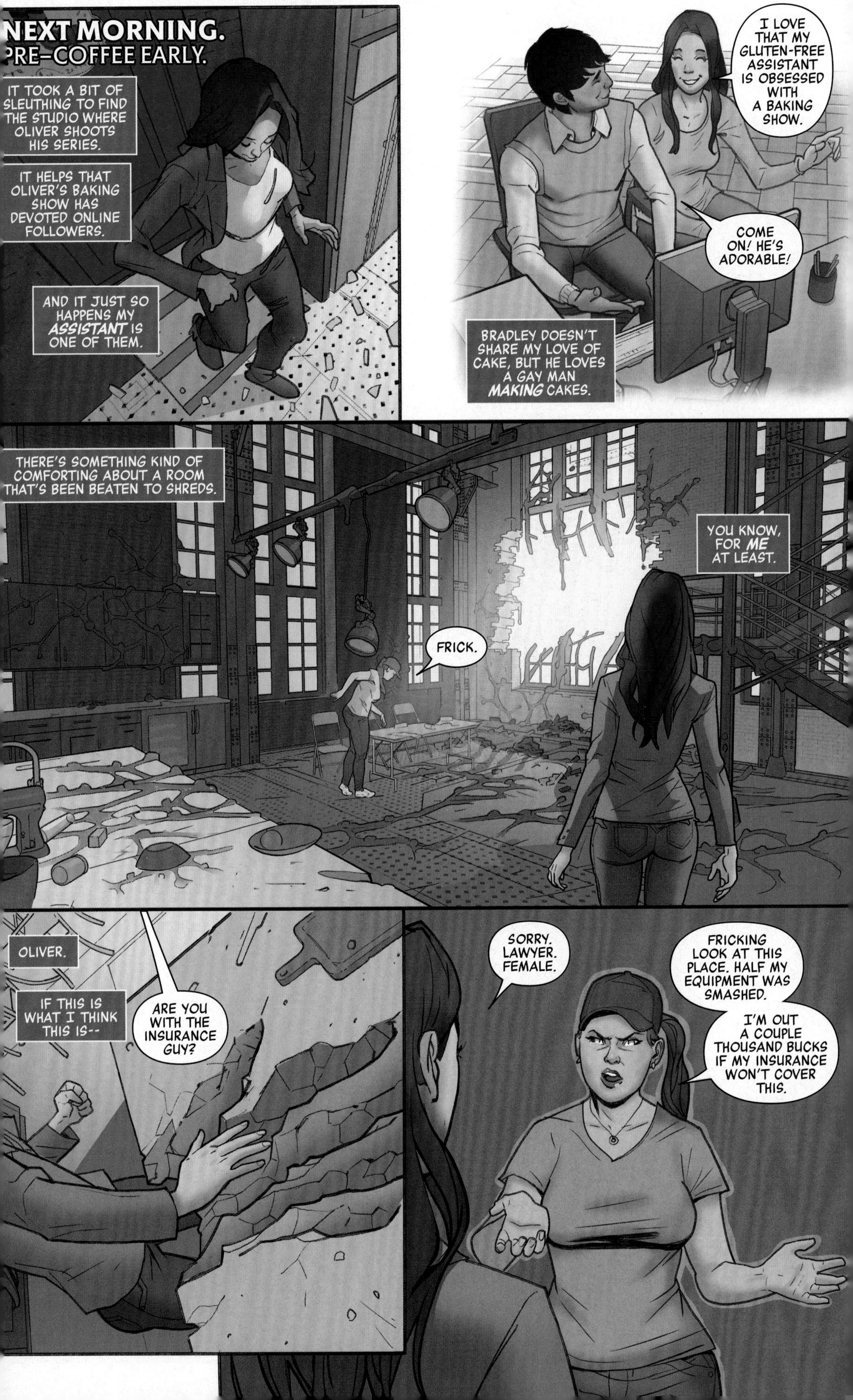

NEXT MORNING.
PRE-COFFEE EARLY.
IT TOOK A BIT OF SLEUTHING TO FIND THE STUDIO WHERE OLIVER SHOOTS HIS SERIES.
IT HELPS THAT OLIVER'S BAKING SHOW HAS DEVOTED ONLINE FOLLOWERS.
AND IT JUST SO HAPPENS MY ASSISTANT IS ONE OF THEM.
I LOVE THAT MY GLUTEN-FREE ASSISTANT IS OBSESSED WITH A BAKING SHOW.
COME ON! HE'S ADORABLE!
BRADLEY DOESN'T SHARE MY LOVE OF CAKE, BUT HE LOVES A GAY MAN MAKING CAKES.
THERE'S SOMETHING KIND OF COMFORTING ABOUT A ROOM THAT'S BEEN BEATEN TO SHREDS.
YOU KNOW, FOR ME AT LEAST.
FRICK.
OLIVER.
IF THIS IS WHAT I THINK THIS IS--
ARE YOU WITH THE INSURANCE GUY?
SORRY. LAWYER. FEMALE.
FRICKING LOOK AT THIS PLACE. HALF MY EQUIPMENT WAS SMASHED.
I'M OUT A COUPLE THOUSAND BUCKS IF MY INSURANCE WON'T COVER THIS.

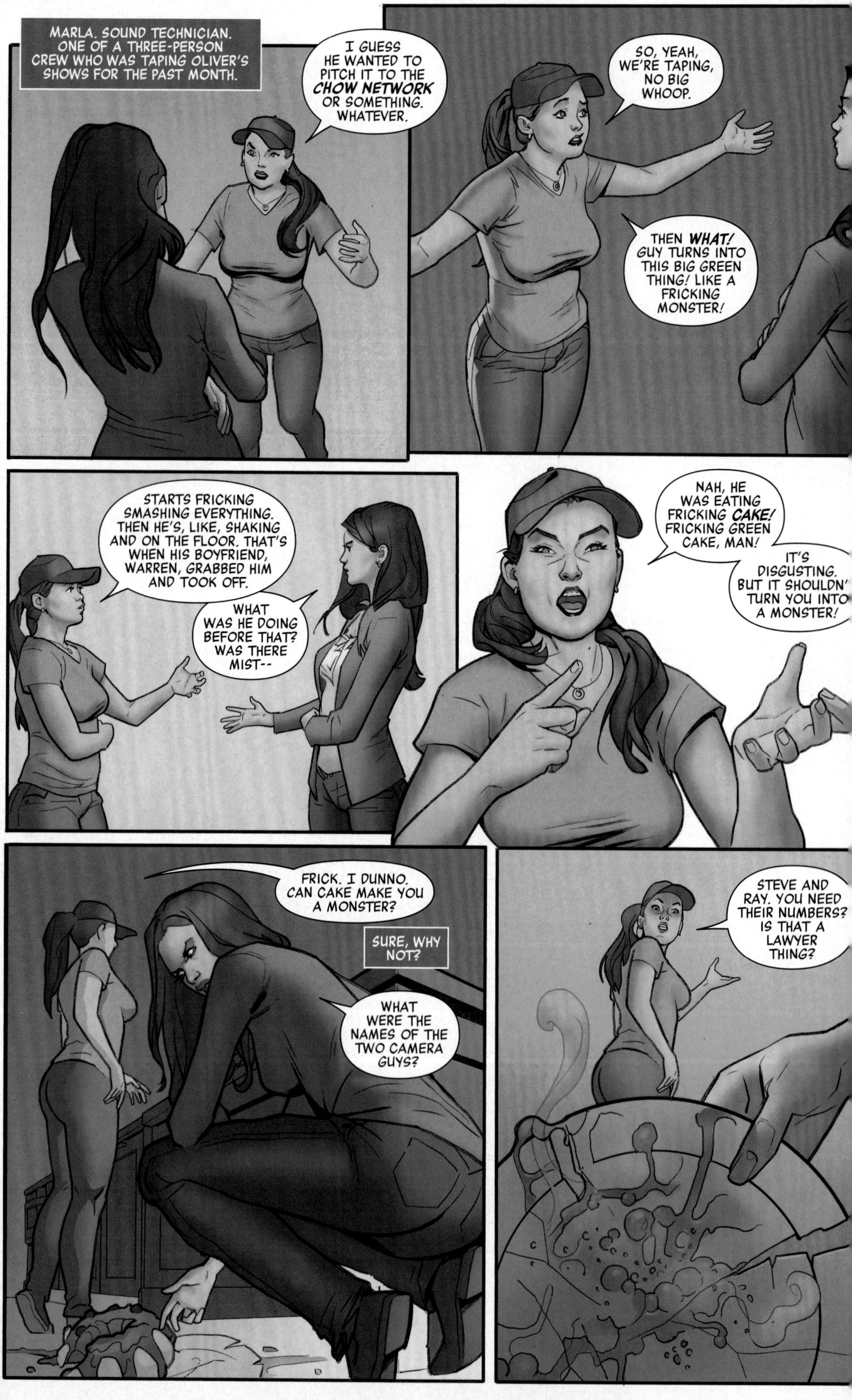
MARLA. SOUND TECHNICIAN. ONE OF A THREE-PERSON CREW WHO WAS TAPING OLIVER'S SHOWS FOR THE PAST MONTH.
I GUESS HE WANTED TO PITCH IT TO THE CHOW NETWORK OR SOMETHING. WHATEVER.
SO, YEAH, WE'RE TAPING, NO BIG WHOOP.
THEN WHAT! GUY TURNS INTO THIS BIG GREEN THING! LIKE A FRICKING MONSTER!
STARTS FRICKING SMASHING EVERYTHING. THEN HE'S, LIKE, SHAKING AND ON THE FLOOR. THAT'S WHEN HIS BOYFRIEND, WARREN, GRABBED HIM AND TOOK OFF.
WHAT WAS HE DOING BEFORE THAT? WAS THERE MIST--
NAH, HE WAS EATING FRICKING CAKE! FRICKING GREEN CAKE, MAN!
IT'S DISGUSTING. BUT IT SHOULDN' TURN YOU INTO A MONSTER!
FRICK. I DUNNO. CAN CAKE MAKE YOU A MONSTER?
SURE, WHY NOT?
WHAT WERE THE NAMES OF THE TWO CAMERA GUYS?
STEVE AND RAY. YOU NEED THEIR NUMBERS? IS THAT A LAWYER THING?

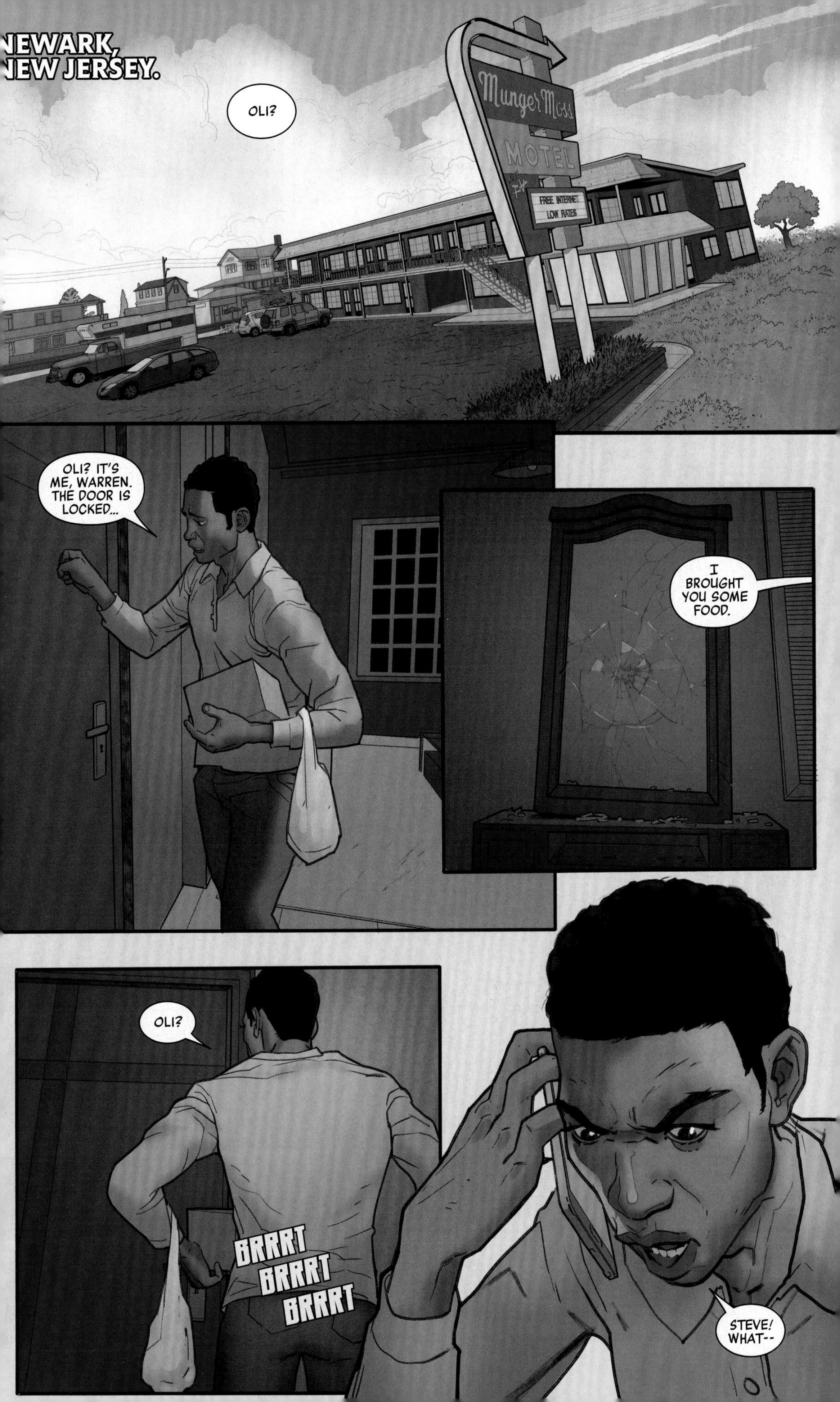
NEWARK, NEW JERSEY.
OLI?
Munger Moss
MOTEL
FREE INTERNET
LOW RATES
OLI? IT'S ME, WARREN. THE DOOR IS LOCKED...
I BROUGHT YOU SOME FOOD.
OLI?
BRRRT
BRRRT
BRRRT
STEVE! WHAT--

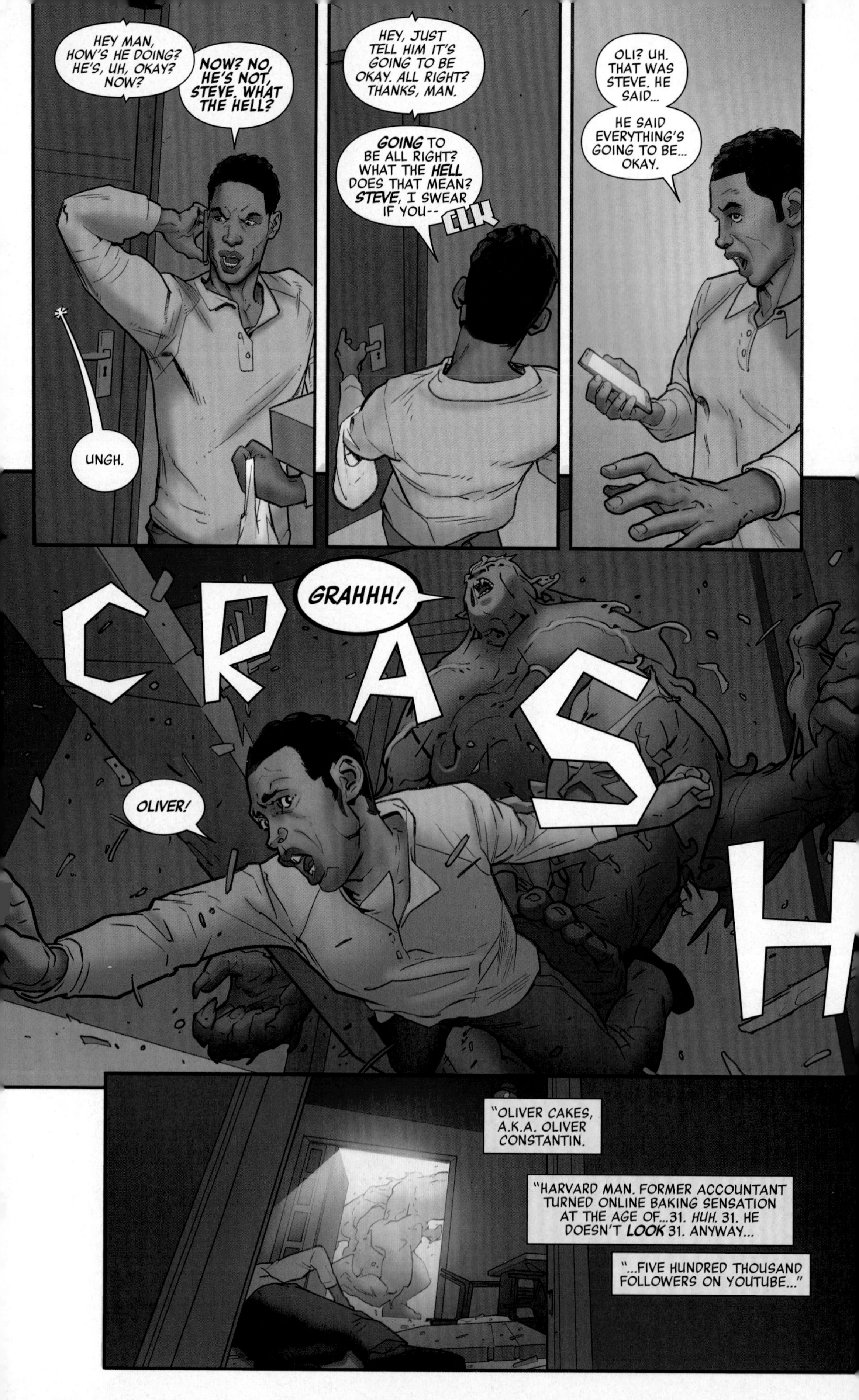

HEY MAN, HOW'S HE DOING? HE'S, UH, OKAY? NOW?
NOW? NO, HE'S NOT, STEVE. WHAT THE HELL?
UNGH.
HEY, JUST TELL HIM IT'S GOING TO BE OKAY. ALL RIGHT? THANKS, MAN.
GOING TO BE ALL RIGHT? WHAT THE HELL DOES THAT MEAN? STEVE, I SWEAR IF YOU--
CLK
OLI? UH. THAT WAS STEVE. HE SAID...
HE SAID EVERYTHING'S GOING TO BE... OKAY.
CRASH
GRAHHH!
OLIVER!
"OLIVER CAKES, A.K.A. OLIVER CONSTANTIN.
"HARVARD MAN. FORMER ACCOUNTANT TURNED ONLINE BAKING SENSATION AT THE AGE OF...31. HUH. 31. HE DOESN'T LOOK 31. ANYWAY...
"...FIVE HUNDRED THOUSAND FOLLOWERS ON YOUTUBE..."

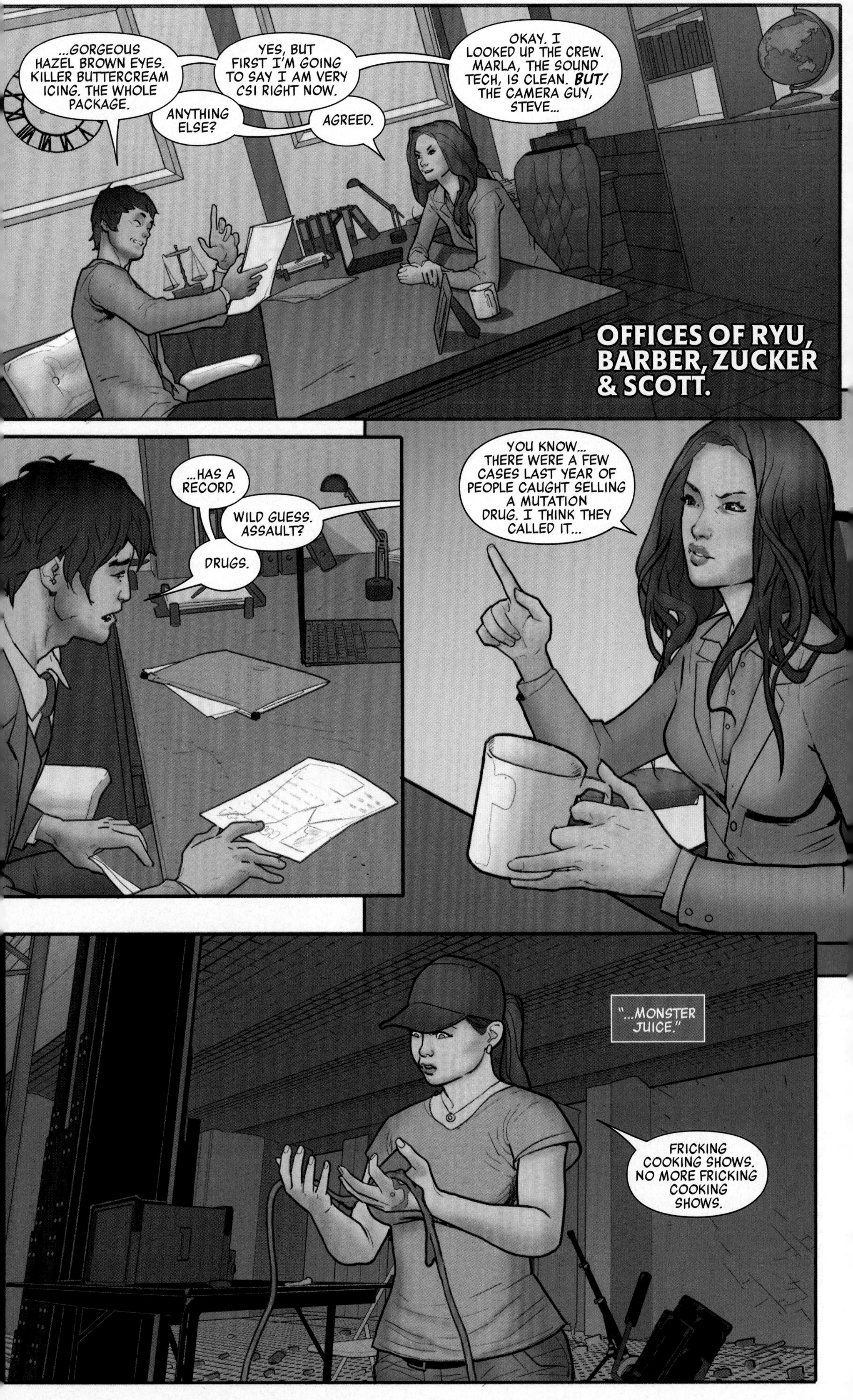
...GORGEOUS HAZEL BROWN EYES. KILLER BUTTERCREAM ICING. THE WHOLE PACKAGE.
ANYTHING ELSE?
YES, BUT FIRST I'M GOING TO SAY I AM VERY CSI RIGHT NOW.
AGREED.
OKAY. I LOOKED UP THE CREW. MARLA, THE SOUND TECH, IS CLEAN. BUT! THE CAMERA GUY, STEVE...
OFFICES OF RYU, BARBER, ZUCKER & SCOTT.
...HAS A RECORD.
WILD GUESS. ASSAULT?
DRUGS.
YOU KNOW... THERE WERE A FEW CASES LAST YEAR OF PEOPLE CAUGHT SELLING A MUTATION DRUG. I THINK THEY CALLED IT...
"...MONSTER JUICE."
FRICKING COOKING SHOWS. NO MORE FRICKING COOKING SHOWS.

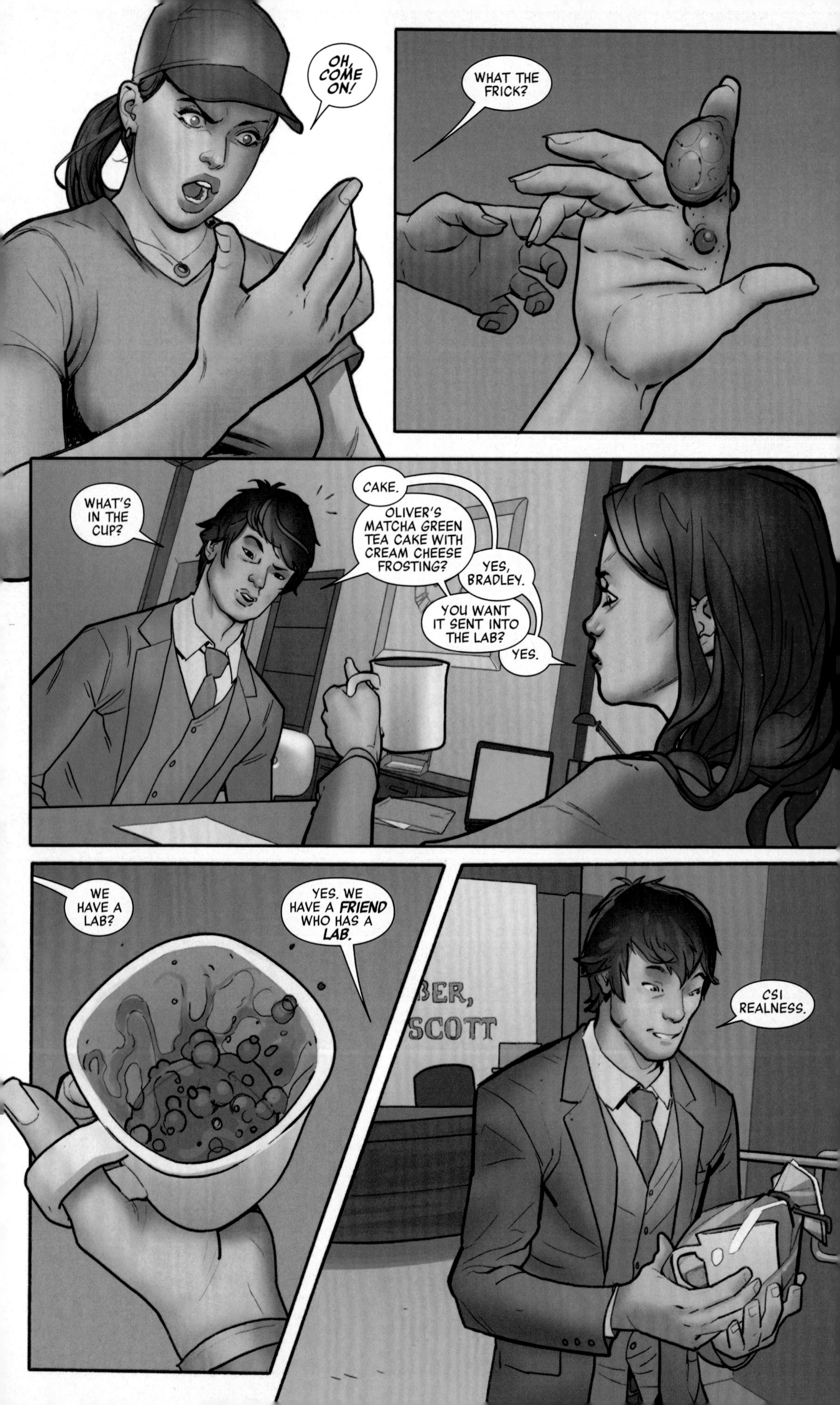

OH, COME ON!
WHAT THE FRICK?
WHAT'S IN THE CUP?
CAKE.
OLIVER'S MATCHA GREEN TEA CAKE WITH CREAM CHEESE FROSTING?
YES, BRADLEY.
YOU WANT IT SENT INTO THE LAB?
YES.
WE HAVE A LAB?
YES. WE HAVE A **FRIEND** WHO HAS A **LAB.**
BER,
SCOTT
CSI REALNESS.

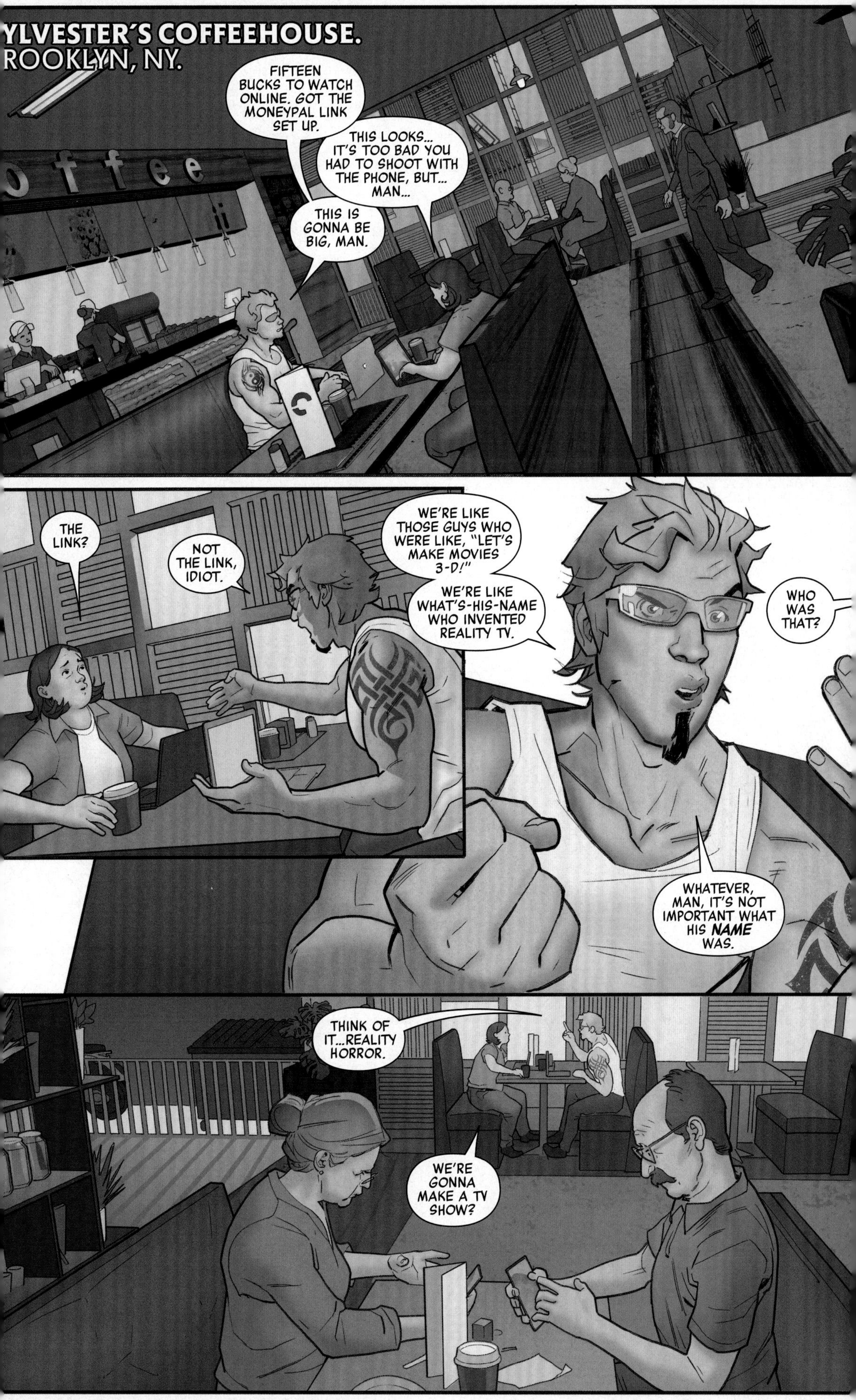
YLVESTER'S COFFEEHOUSE.
ROOKLYN, NY.
FIFTEEN BUCKS TO WATCH ONLINE. GOT THE MONEYPAL LINK SET UP.
THIS LOOKS... IT'S TOO BAD YOU HAD TO SHOOT WITH THE PHONE, BUT... MAN...
THIS IS GONNA BE BIG, MAN.
THE LINK?
NOT THE LINK, IDIOT.
WE'RE LIKE THOSE GUYS WHO WERE LIKE, "LET'S MAKE MOVIES 3-D!"
WE'RE LIKE WHAT'S-HIS-NAME WHO INVENTED REALITY TV.
WHO WAS THAT?
WHATEVER, MAN, IT'S NOT IMPORTANT WHAT HIS ***NAME*** WAS.
THINK OF IT...REALITY HORROR.
WE'RE GONNA MAKE A TV SHOW?

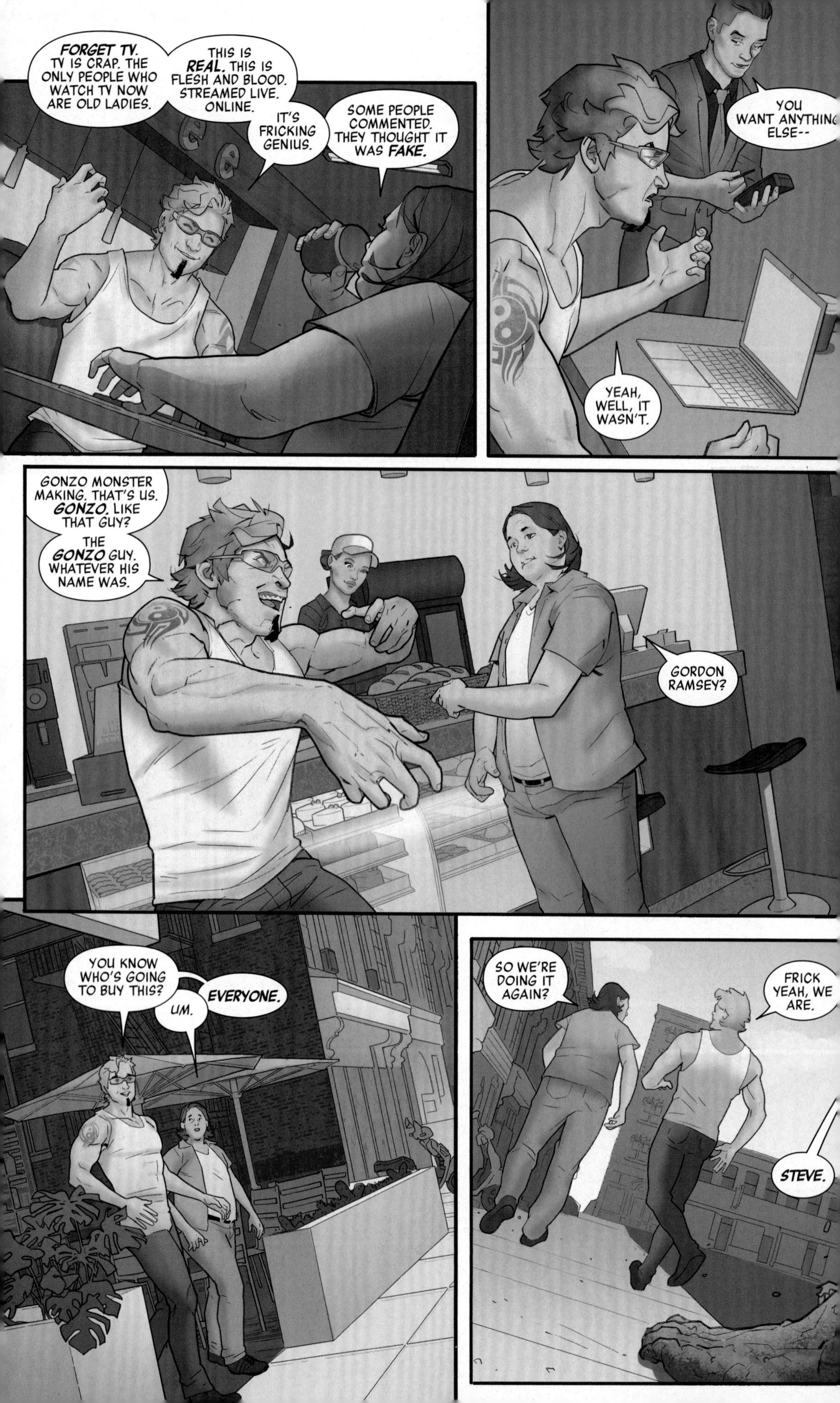
FORGET TV. TV IS CRAP. THE ONLY PEOPLE WHO WATCH TV NOW ARE OLD LADIES.
THIS IS REAL. THIS IS FLESH AND BLOOD. STREAMED LIVE. ONLINE.
IT'S FRICKING GENIUS.
SOME PEOPLE COMMENTED. THEY THOUGHT IT WAS FAKE.
YOU WANT ANYTHING ELSE--
YEAH, WELL, IT WASN'T.
GONZO MONSTER MAKING. THAT'S US. GONZO. LIKE THAT GUY?
THE GONZO GUY. WHATEVER HIS NAME WAS.
GORDON RAMSEY?
YOU KNOW WHO'S GOING TO BUY THIS?
EVERYONE.
UM.
SO WE'RE DOING IT AGAIN?
FRICK YEAH, WE ARE.
STEVE.

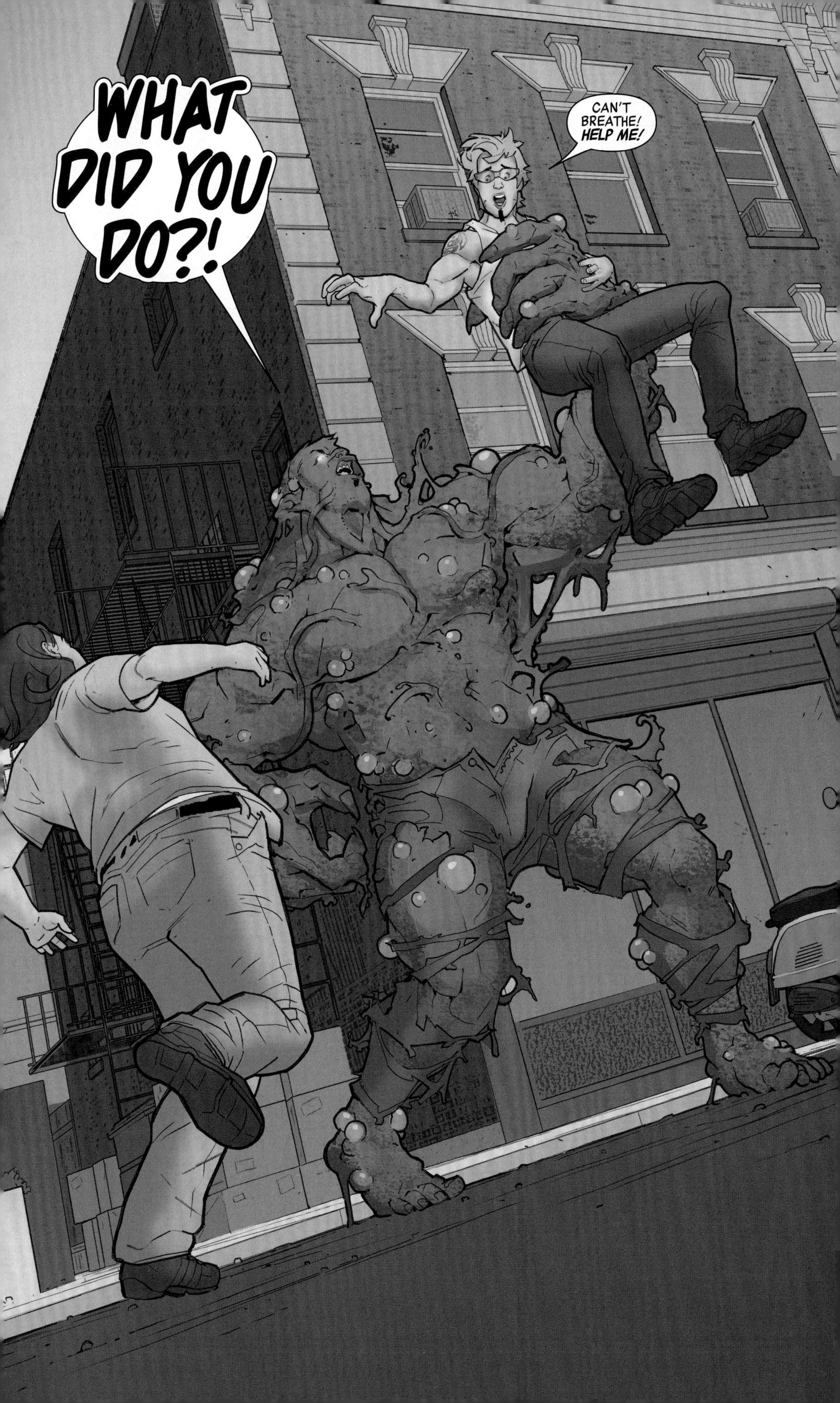
WHAT DID YOU DO?!
CAN'T BREATHE! HELP ME!

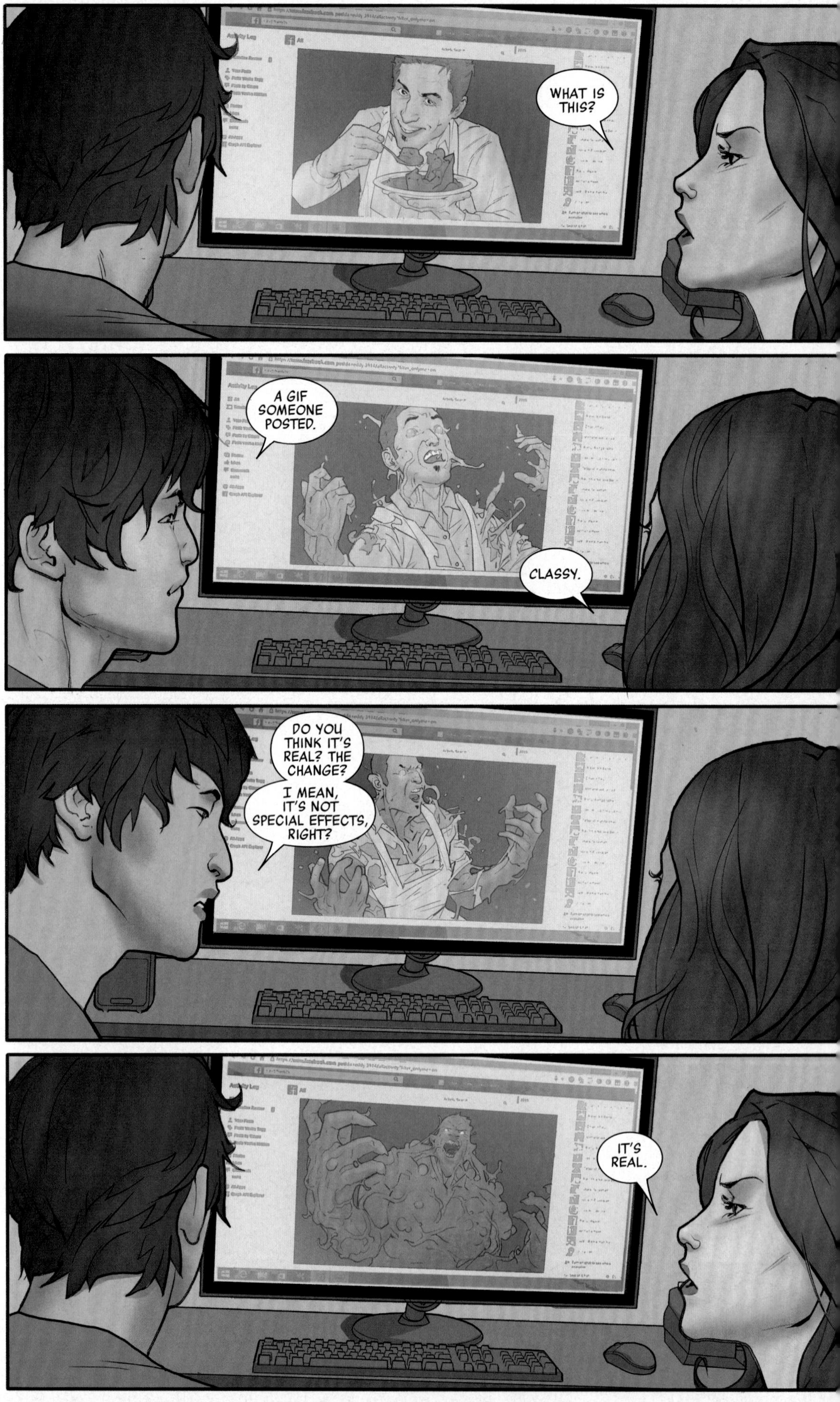
WHAT IS THIS?
A GIF SOMEONE POSTED.
CLASSY.
DO YOU THINK IT'S REAL? THE CHANGE?
I MEAN, IT'S NOT SPECIAL EFFECTS, RIGHT?
IT'S REAL.

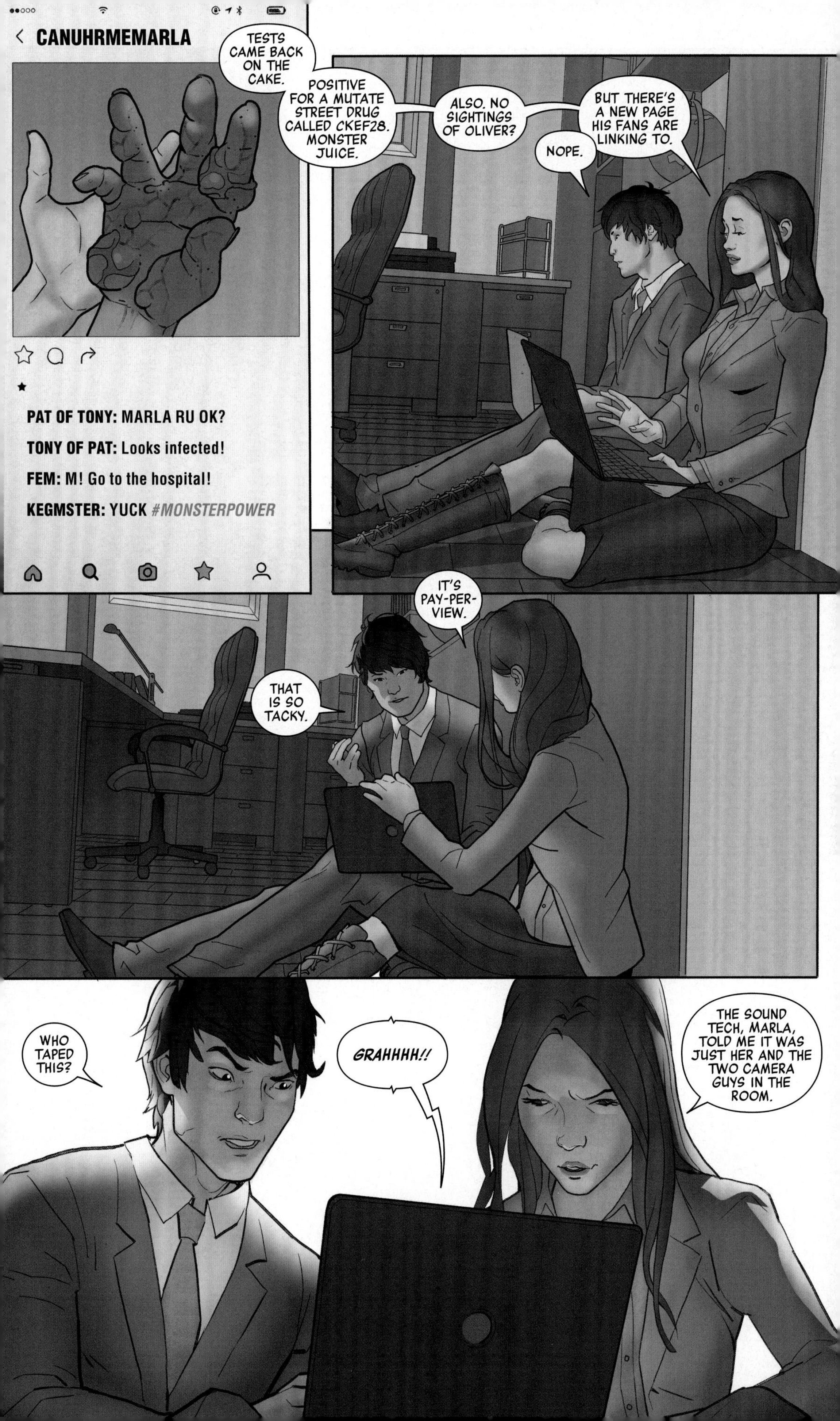

CANUHRMEMARLA
PAT OF TONY: MARLA RU OK?
TONY OF PAT: Looks infected!
FEM: M! Go to the hospital!
KEGMSTER: YUCK #MONSTERPOWER
TESTS CAME BACK ON THE CAKE.
POSITIVE FOR A MUTATE STREET DRUG CALLED CKEF28. MONSTER JUICE.
ALSO. NO SIGHTINGS OF OLIVER?
NOPE.
BUT THERE'S A NEW PAGE HIS FANS ARE LINKING TO.
IT'S PAY-PER-VIEW.
THAT IS SO TACKY.
WHO TAPED THIS?
GRAHHHH!!
THE SOUND TECH, MARLA, TOLD ME IT WAS JUST HER AND THE TWO CAMERA GUYS IN THE ROOM.

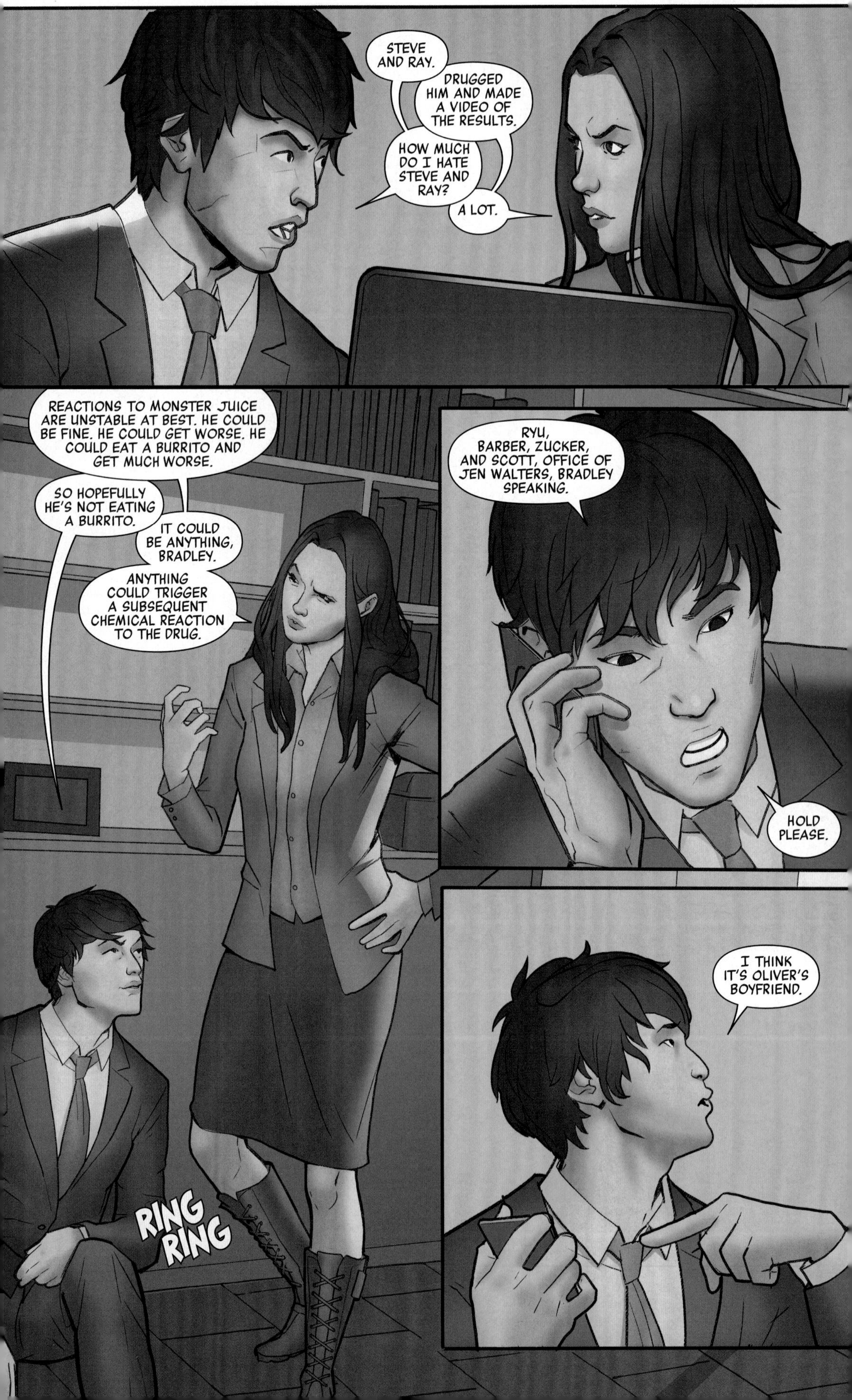
STEVE AND RAY.
DRUGGED HIM AND MADE A VIDEO OF THE RESULTS.
HOW MUCH DO I HATE STEVE AND RAY?
A LOT.
REACTIONS TO MONSTER JUICE ARE UNSTABLE AT BEST. HE COULD BE FINE. HE COULD GET WORSE. HE COULD EAT A BURRITO AND GET MUCH WORSE.
SO HOPEFULLY HE'S NOT EATING A BURRITO.
IT COULD BE ANYTHING, BRADLEY.
ANYTHING COULD TRIGGER A SUBSEQUENT CHEMICAL REACTION TO THE DRUG.
RING RING
RYU, BARBER, ZUCKER, AND SCOTT, OFFICE OF JEN WALTERS, BRADLEY SPEAKING.
HOLD PLEASE.
I THINK IT'S OLIVER'S BOYFRIEND.

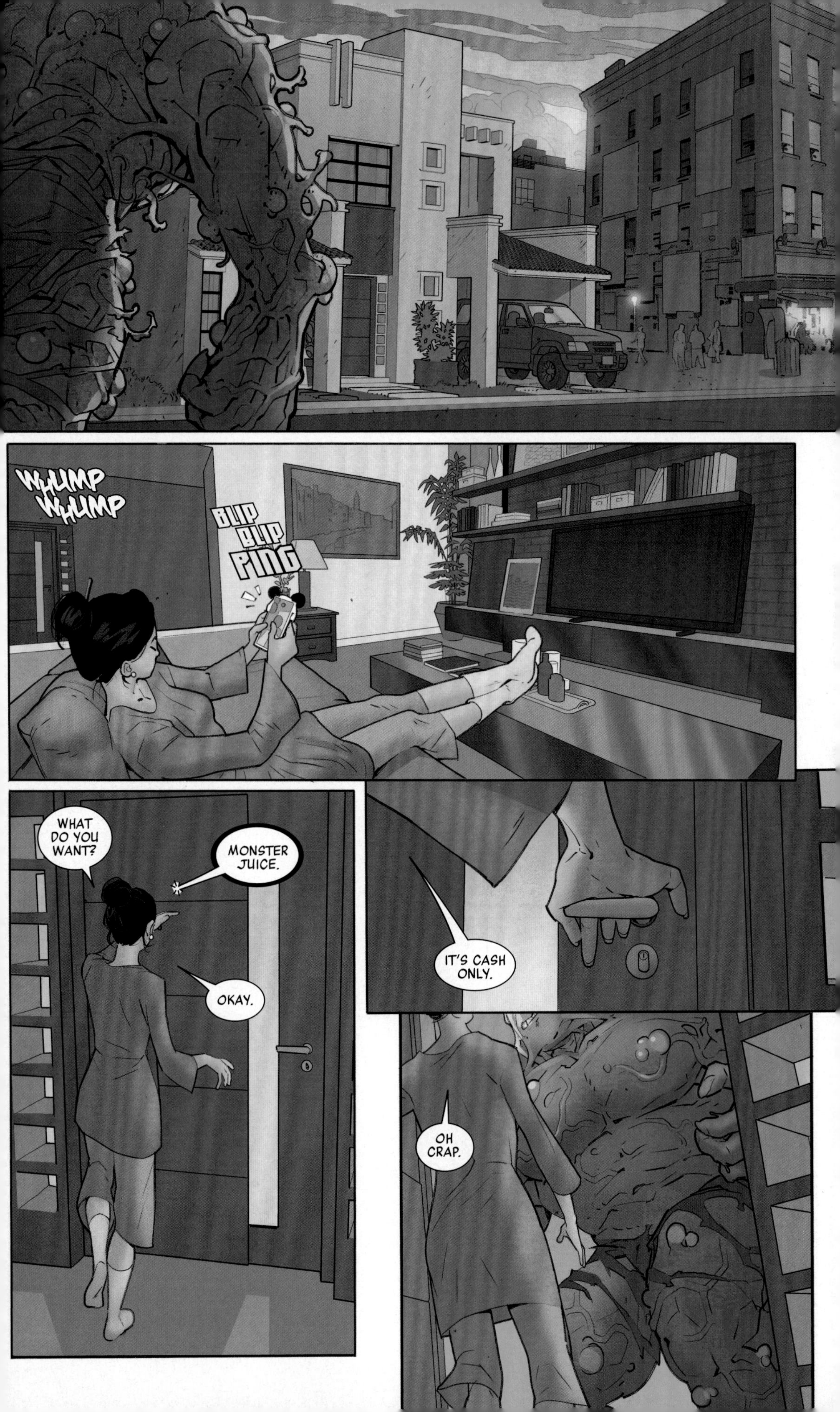
WHUMP WHUMP
BLIP BLIP PING
WHAT DO YOU WANT?
MONSTER JUICE.
OKAY.
IT'S CASH ONLY.
OH CRAP.

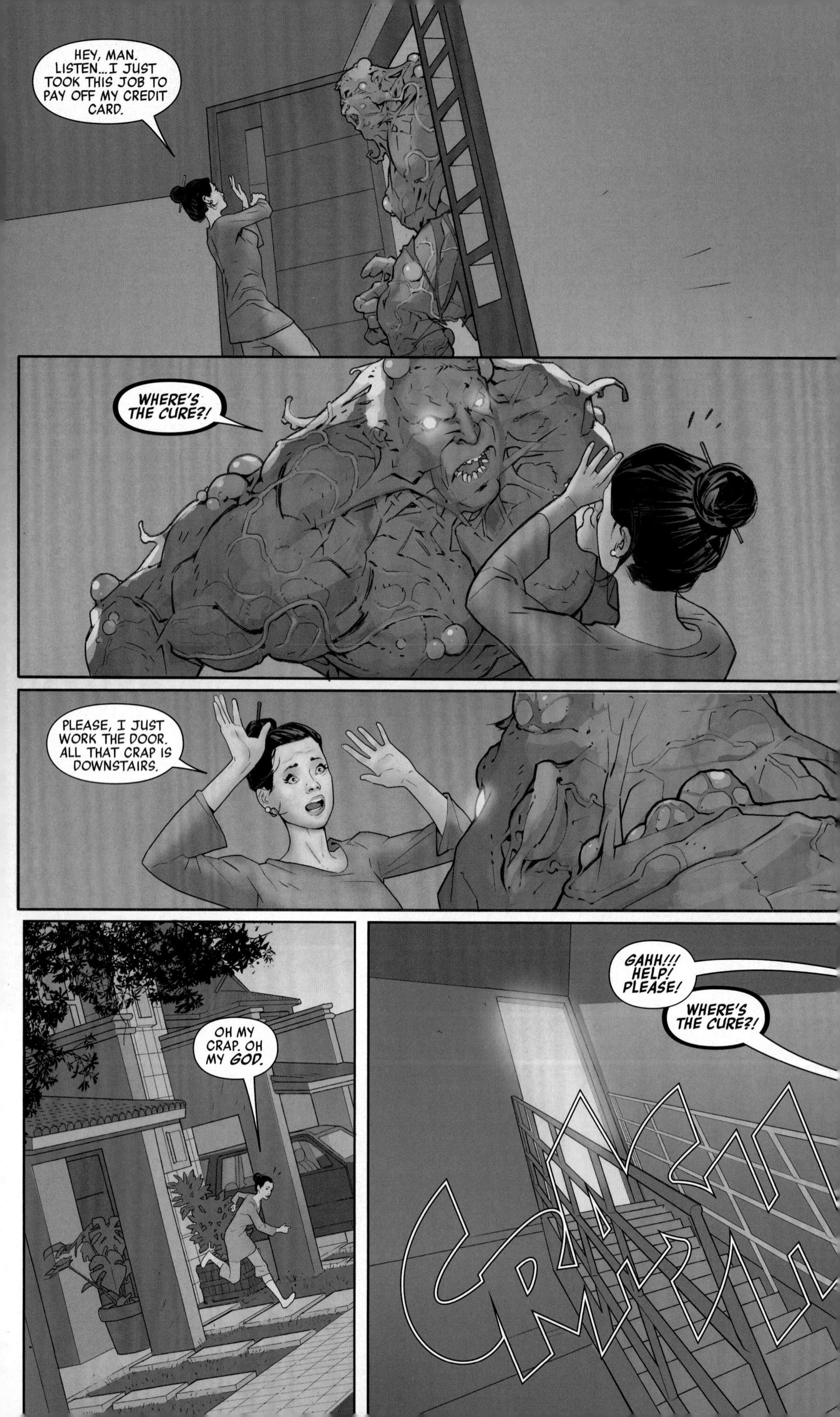
HEY, MAN. LISTEN... I JUST TOOK THIS JOB TO PAY OFF MY CREDIT CARD.
WHERE'S THE CURE?!
PLEASE, I JUST WORK THE DOOR. ALL THAT CRAP IS DOWNSTAIRS.
OH MY CRAP. OH MY GOD.
GAHH!!! HELP! PLEASE!
WHERE'S THE CURE?!

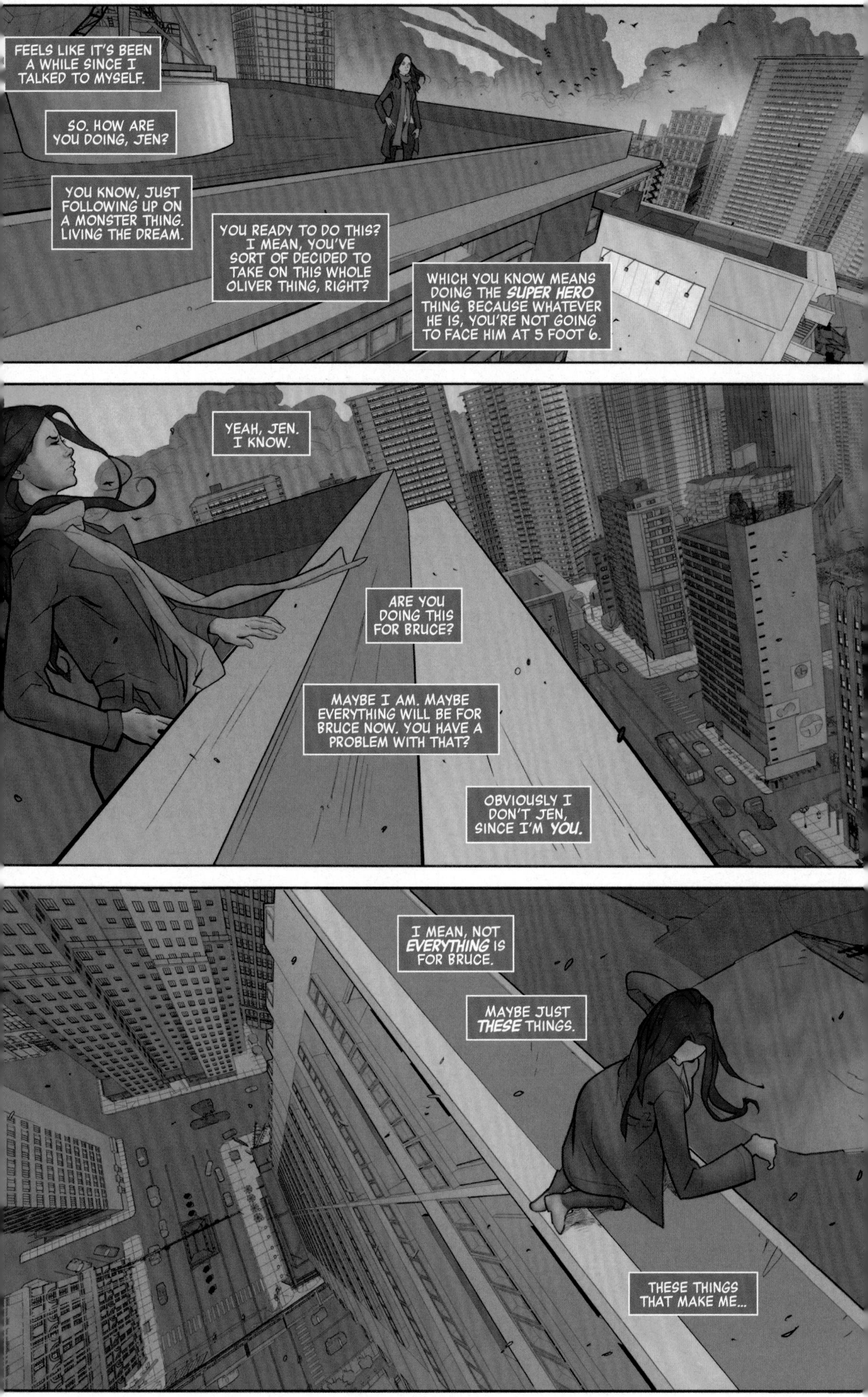

FEELS LIKE IT'S BEEN A WHILE SINCE I TALKED TO MYSELF.
SO. HOW ARE YOU DOING, JEN?
YOU KNOW, JUST FOLLOWING UP ON A MONSTER THING. LIVING THE DREAM.
YOU READY TO DO THIS? I MEAN, YOU'VE SORT OF DECIDED TO TAKE ON THIS WHOLE OLIVER THING, RIGHT?
WHICH YOU KNOW MEANS DOING THE SUPER HERO THING. BECAUSE WHATEVER HE IS, YOU'RE NOT GOING TO FACE HIM AT 5 FOOT 6.
YEAH, JEN. I KNOW.
ARE YOU DOING THIS FOR BRUCE?
MAYBE I AM. MAYBE EVERYTHING WILL BE FOR BRUCE NOW. YOU HAVE A PROBLEM WITH THAT?
OBVIOUSLY I DON'T JEN, SINCE I'M YOU.
I MEAN, NOT EVERYTHING IS FOR BRUCE.
MAYBE JUST THESE THINGS.
THESE THINGS THAT MAKE ME...

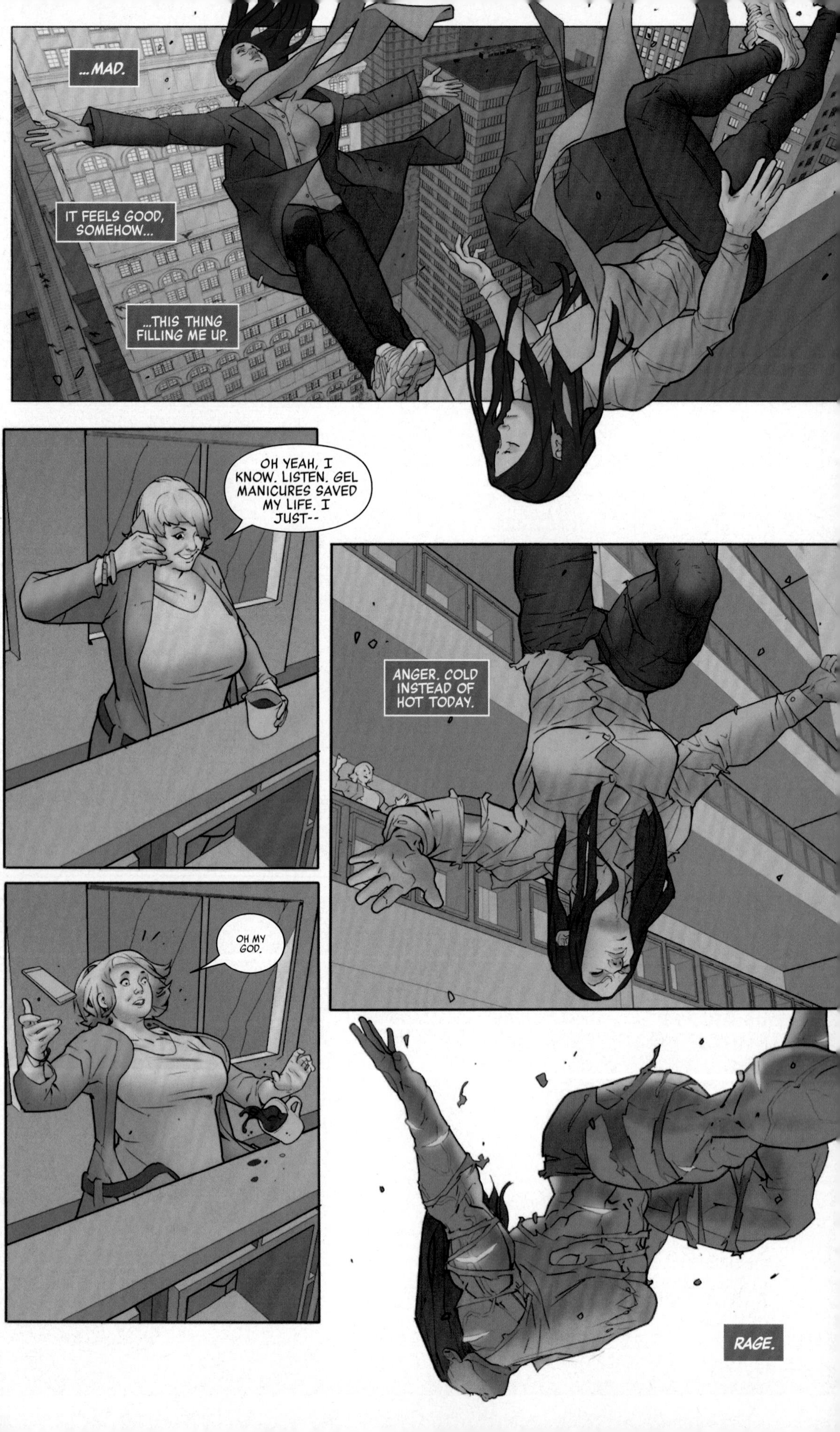
...MAD.
IT FEELS GOOD, SOMEHOW...
...THIS THING FILLING ME UP.
OH YEAH, I KNOW. LISTEN. GEL MANICURES SAVED MY LIFE. I JUST--
ANGER. COLD INSTEAD OF HOT TODAY.
OH MY GOD.
RAGE.

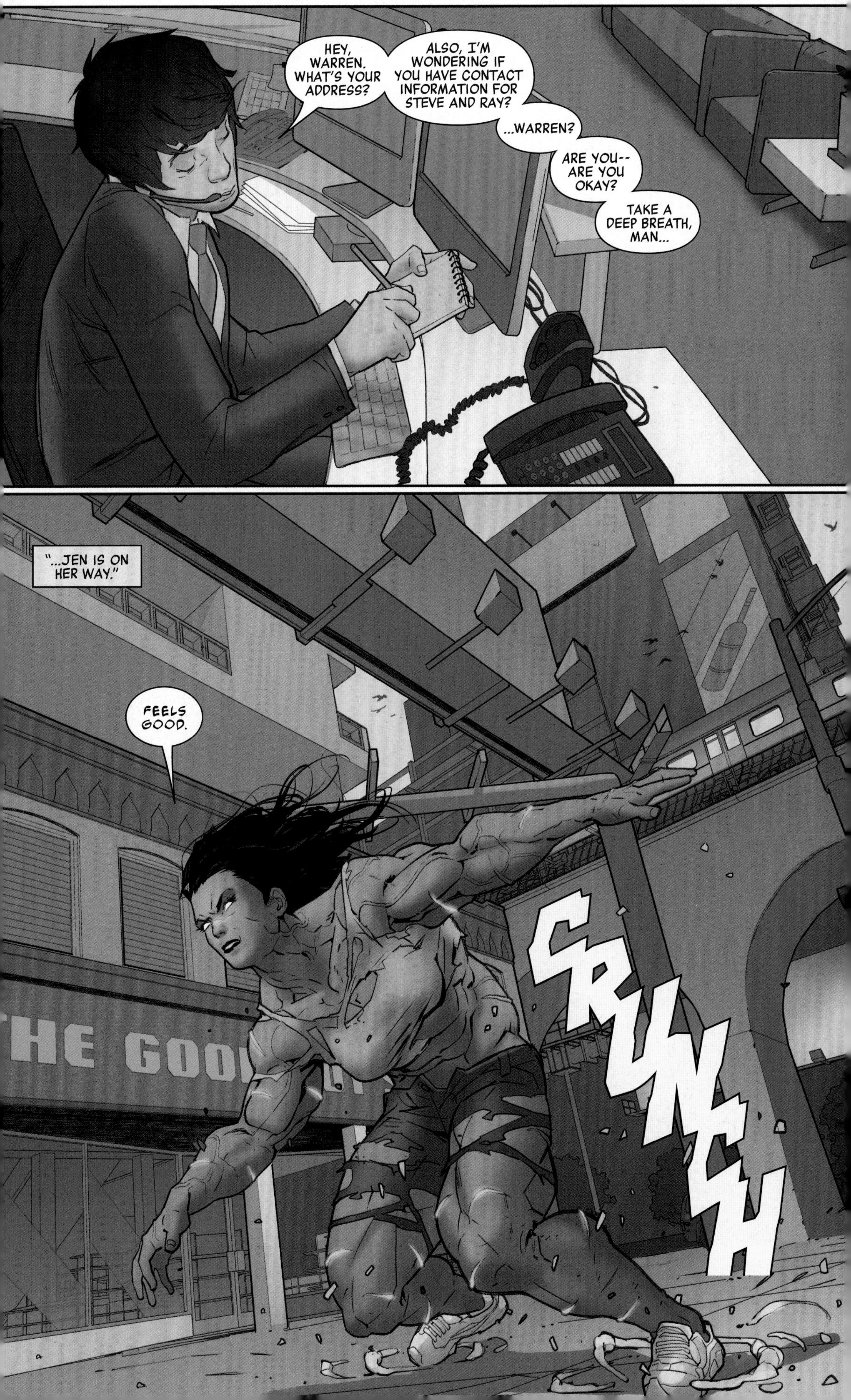
HEY, WARREN. WHAT'S YOUR ADDRESS?
ALSO, I'M WONDERING IF YOU HAVE CONTACT INFORMATION FOR STEVE AND RAY?
...WARREN?
ARE YOU-- ARE YOU OKAY?
TAKE A DEEP BREATH, MAN...
"...JEN IS ON HER WAY."
FEELS GOOD.
CRUNCH

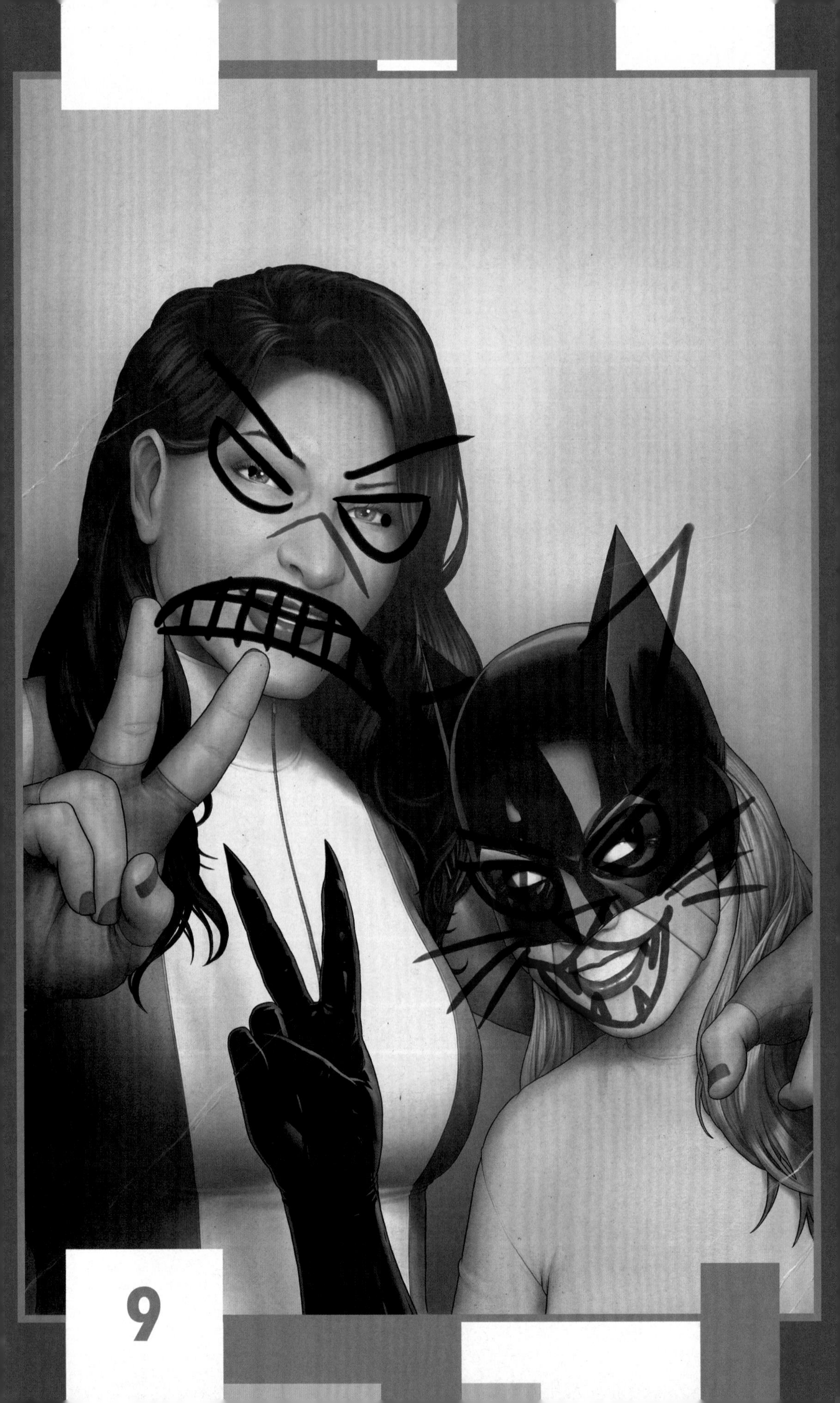
9

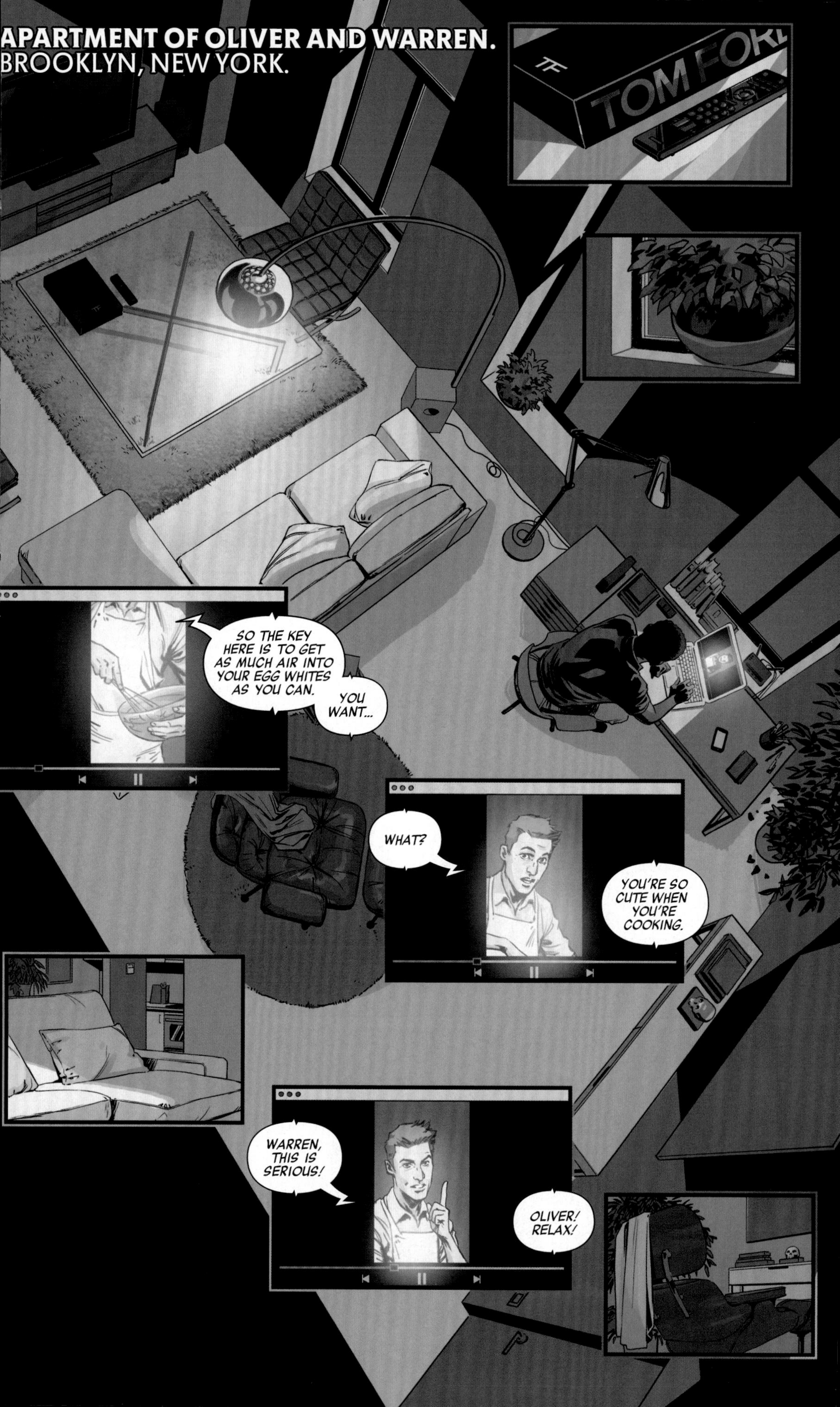

APARTMENT OF OLIVER AND WARREN.
BROOKLYN, NEW YORK.
TOM FORD
TF
SO THE KEY HERE IS TO GET AS MUCH AIR INTO YOUR EGG WHITES AS YOU CAN.
YOU WANT...
WHAT?
YOU'RE SO CUTE WHEN YOU'RE COOKING.
WARREN, THIS IS SERIOUS!
OLIVER! RELAX!

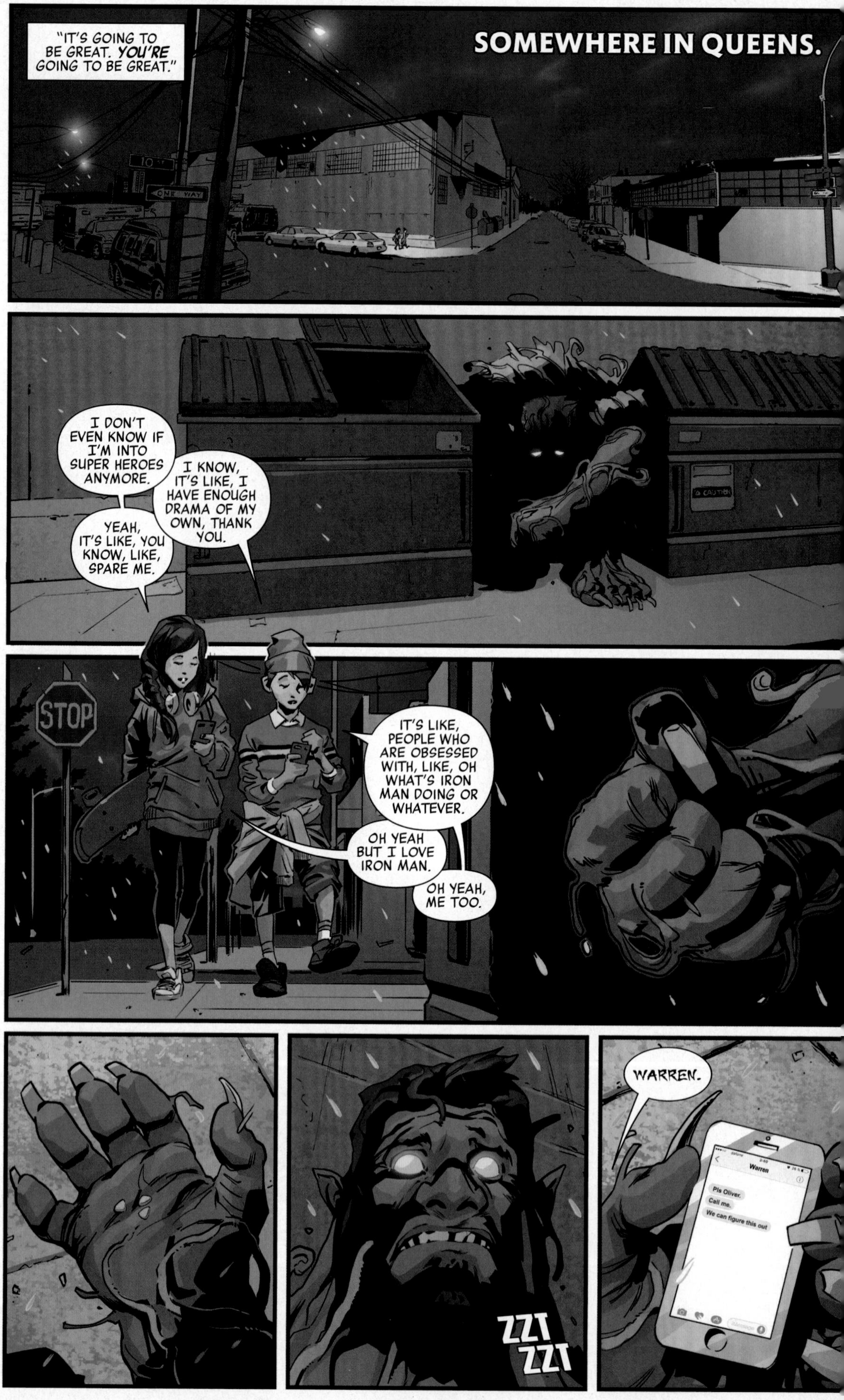
"IT'S GOING TO BE GREAT. YOU'RE GOING TO BE GREAT."
SOMEWHERE IN QUEENS.
ONE WAY
I DON'T EVEN KNOW IF I'M INTO SUPER HEROES ANYMORE.
YEAH, IT'S LIKE, YOU KNOW, LIKE, SPARE ME.
I KNOW, IT'S LIKE, I HAVE ENOUGH DRAMA OF MY OWN, THANK YOU.
CAUTION
STOP
IT'S LIKE, PEOPLE WHO ARE OBSESSED WITH, LIKE, OH WHAT'S IRON MAN DOING OR WHATEVER.
OH YEAH BUT I LOVE IRON MAN.
OH YEAH, ME TOO.
ZZT ZZT
WARREN.
Warren
Pls Oliver.
Call me.
We can figure this out

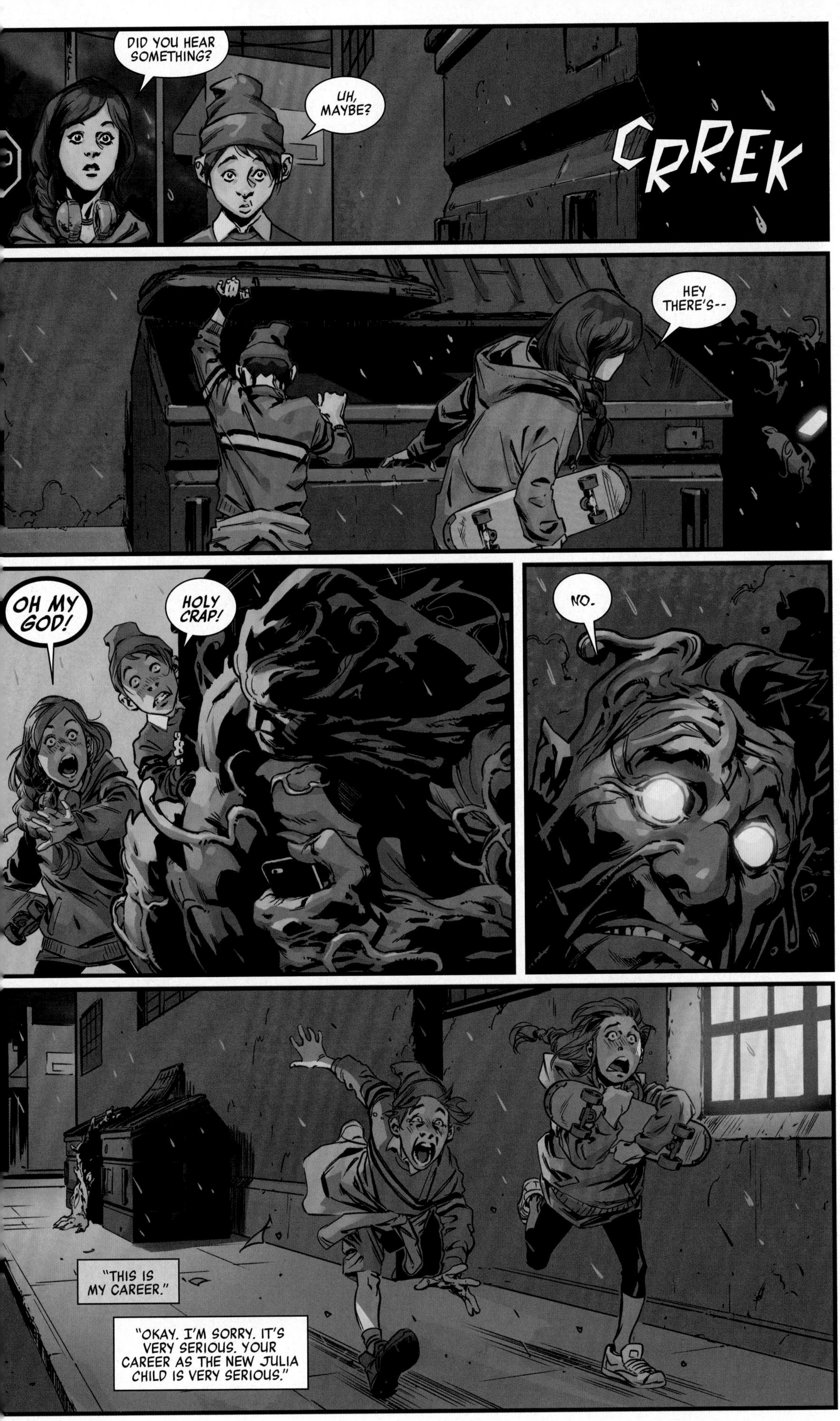
DID YOU HEAR SOMETHING?
UH, MAYBE?
CRREK
HEY THERE'S--
OH MY GOD!
HOLY CRAP!
NO.
"THIS IS MY CAREER."
"OKAY. I'M SORRY. IT'S VERY SERIOUS. YOUR CAREER AS THE NEW JULIA CHILD IS VERY SERIOUS."

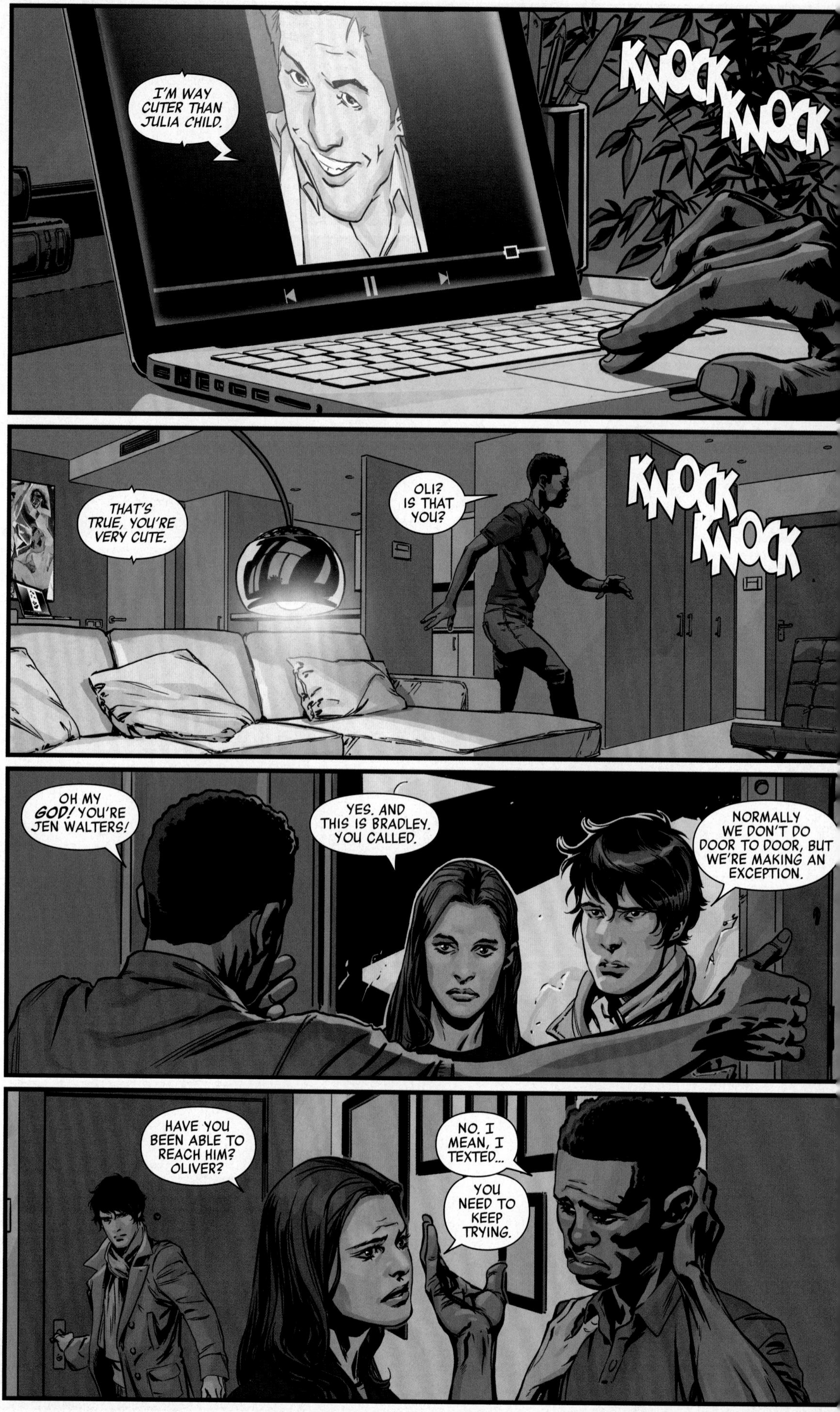
I'M WAY CUTER THAN JULIA CHILD.
KNOCK KNOCK
THAT'S TRUE, YOU'RE VERY CUTE.
OLI? IS THAT YOU?
KNOCK KNOCK
OH MY GOD! YOU'RE JEN WALTERS!
YES. AND THIS IS BRADLEY. YOU CALLED.
NORMALLY WE DON'T DO DOOR TO DOOR, BUT WE'RE MAKING AN EXCEPTION.
HAVE YOU BEEN ABLE TO REACH HIM? OLIVER?
NO. I MEAN, I TEXTED...
YOU NEED TO KEEP TRYING.

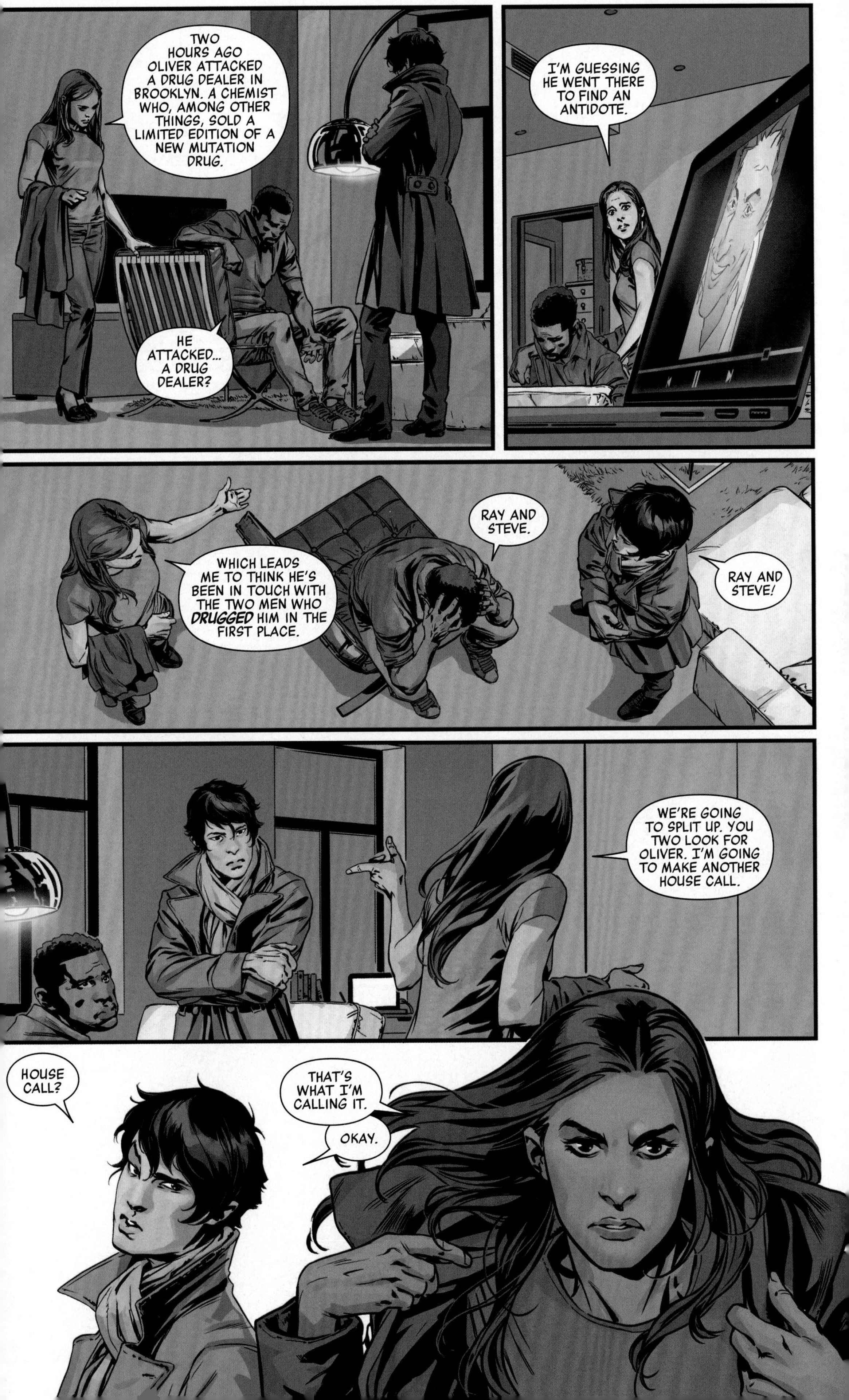
TWO HOURS AGO OLIVER ATTACKED A DRUG DEALER IN BROOKLYN. A CHEMIST WHO, AMONG OTHER THINGS, SOLD A LIMITED EDITION OF A NEW MUTATION DRUG.
HE ATTACKED... A DRUG DEALER?
I'M GUESSING HE WENT THERE TO FIND AN ANTIDOTE.
WHICH LEADS ME TO THINK HE'S BEEN IN TOUCH WITH THE TWO MEN WHO *DRUGGED* HIM IN THE FIRST PLACE.
RAY AND STEVE.
RAY AND STEVE!
WE'RE GOING TO SPLIT UP. YOU TWO LOOK FOR OLIVER. I'M GOING TO MAKE ANOTHER HOUSE CALL.
HOUSE CALL?
THAT'S WHAT I'M CALLING IT.
OKAY.

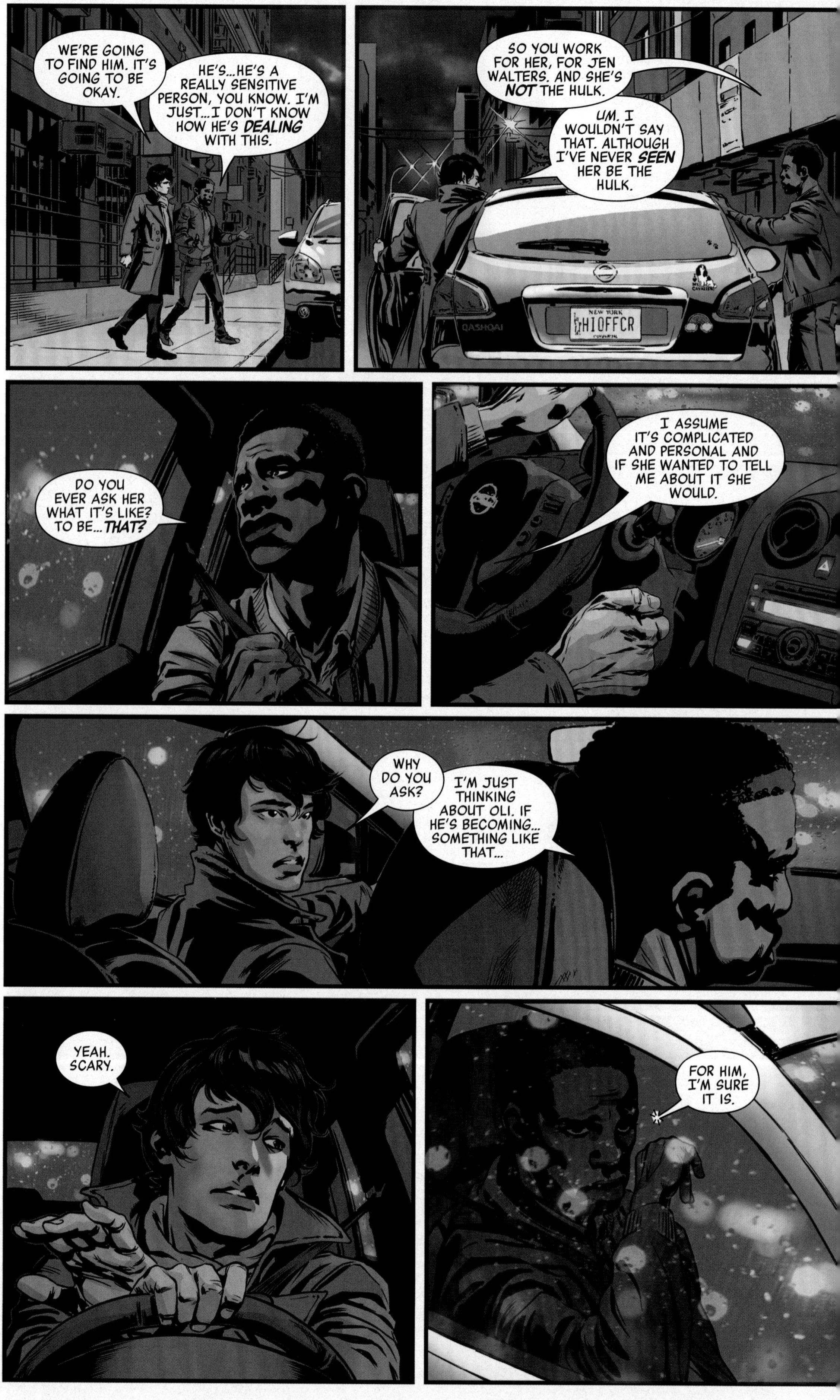
WE'RE GOING TO FIND HIM. IT'S GOING TO BE OKAY.
HE'S...HE'S A REALLY SENSITIVE PERSON, YOU KNOW. I'M JUST...I DON'T KNOW HOW HE'S DEALING WITH THIS.
SO YOU WORK FOR HER, FOR JEN WALTERS. AND SHE'S NOT THE HULK.
UM. I WOULDN'T SAY THAT. ALTHOUGH I'VE NEVER SEEN HER BE THE HULK.
NEW YORK
HIOFFCR
QASHQAI
DO YOU EVER ASK HER WHAT IT'S LIKE? TO BE...THAT?
I ASSUME IT'S COMPLICATED AND PERSONAL AND IF SHE WANTED TO TELL ME ABOUT IT SHE WOULD.
WHY DO YOU ASK?
I'M JUST THINKING ABOUT OLI. IF HE'S BECOMING... SOMETHING LIKE THAT...
YEAH. SCARY.
FOR HIM, I'M SURE IT IS.

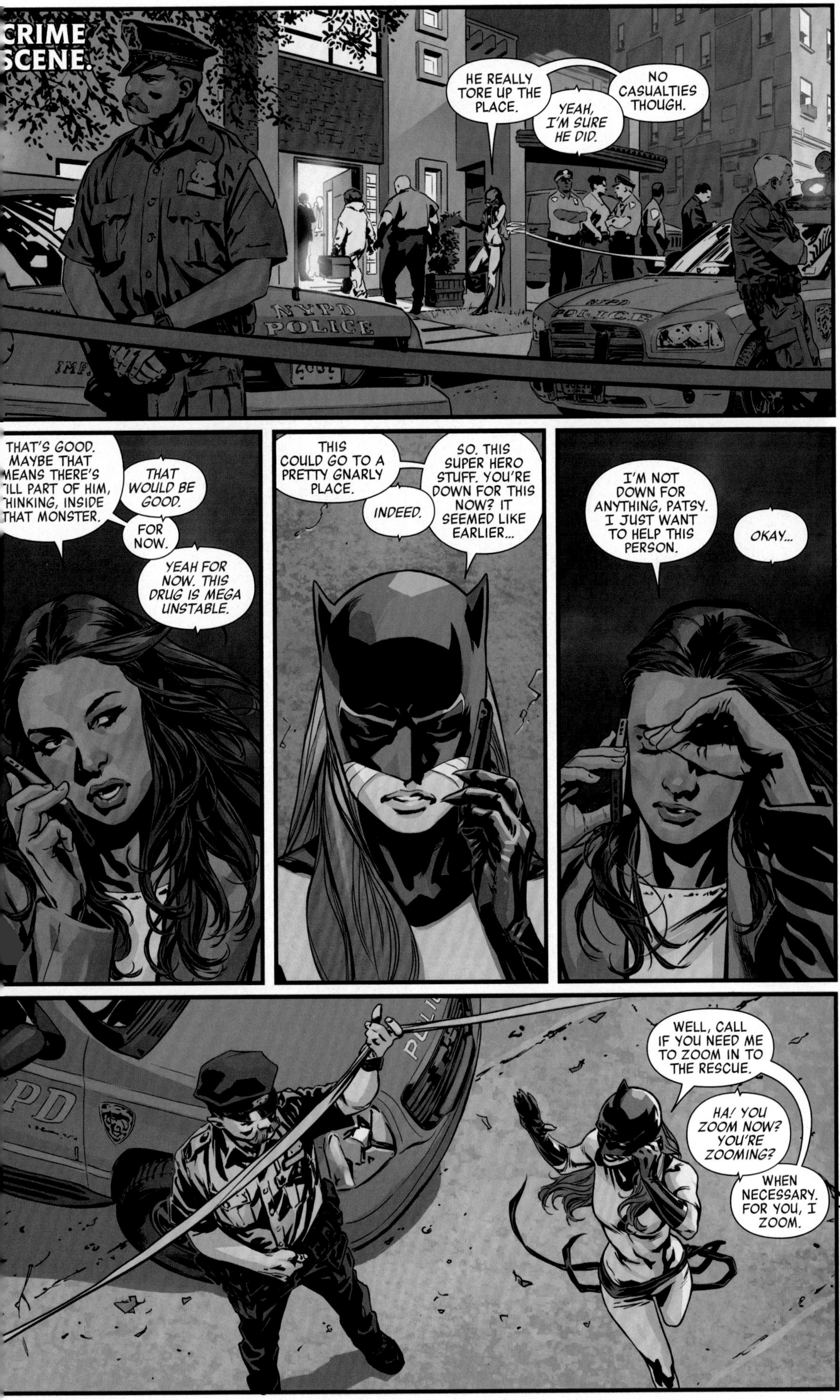

CRIME SCENE.
HE REALLY TORE UP THE PLACE.
YEAH, I'M SURE HE DID.
NO CASUALTIES THOUGH.
NYPD POLICE
THAT'S GOOD. MAYBE THAT MEANS THERE'S STILL PART OF HIM, THINKING, INSIDE THAT MONSTER.
THAT WOULD BE GOOD.
FOR NOW.
YEAH FOR NOW. THIS DRUG IS MEGA UNSTABLE.
THIS COULD GO TO A PRETTY GNARLY PLACE.
INDEED.
SO. THIS SUPER HERO STUFF. YOU'RE DOWN FOR THIS NOW? IT SEEMED LIKE EARLIER...
I'M NOT DOWN FOR ANYTHING, PATSY. I JUST WANT TO HELP THIS PERSON.
OKAY...
WELL, CALL IF YOU NEED ME TO ZOOM IN TO THE RESCUE.
HA! YOU ZOOM NOW? YOU'RE ZOOMING?
WHEN NECESSARY. FOR YOU, I ZOOM.

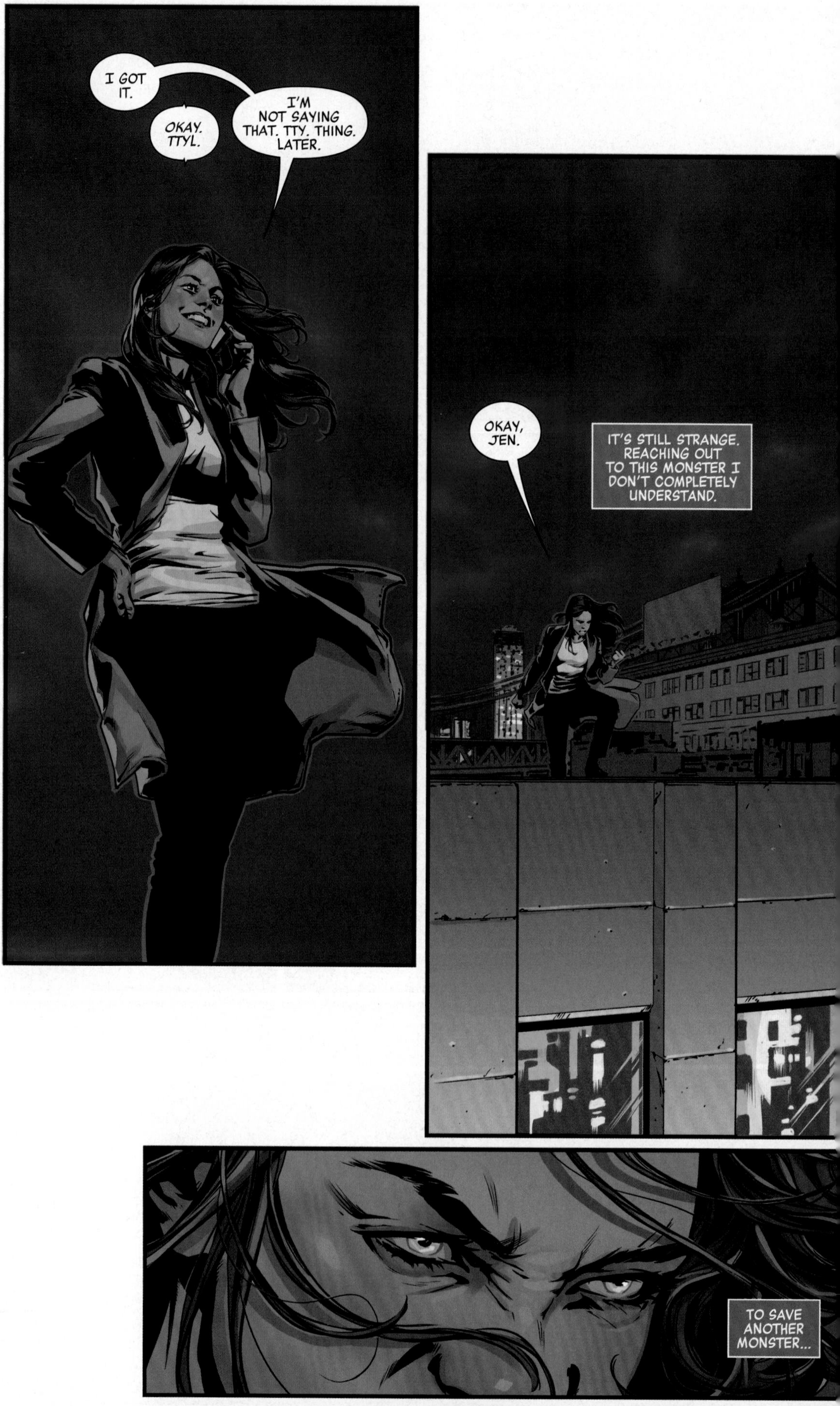
I GOT IT.
I'M NOT SAYING THAT. TTY. THING. LATER.
OKAY. TTYL.
OKAY, JEN.
IT'S STILL STRANGE. REACHING OUT TO THIS MONSTER I DON'T COMPLETELY UNDERSTAND.
TO SAVE ANOTHER MONSTER...

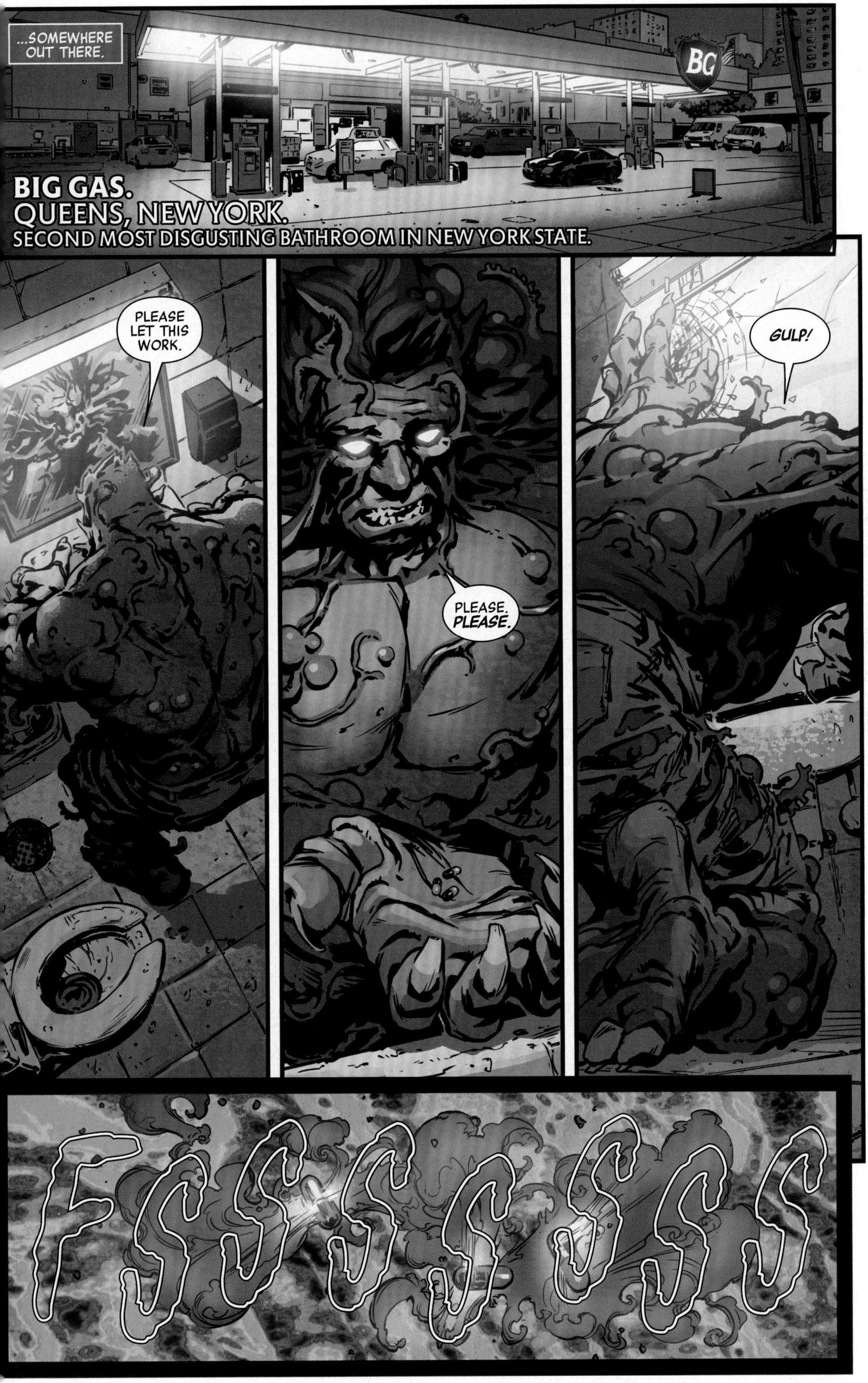

...SOMEWHERE OUT THERE.
BIG GAS.
QUEENS, NEW YORK.
SECOND MOST DISGUSTING BATHROOM IN NEW YORK STATE.
PLEASE LET THIS WORK.
PLEASE. PLEASE.
GULP!
FSSSSSSS

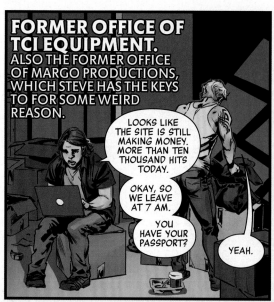

FORMER OFFICE OF TCI EQUIPMENT. ALSO THE FORMER OFFICE OF MARGO PRODUCTIONS, WHICH STEVE HAS THE KEYS TO FOR SOME WEIRD REASON.

LOOKS LIKE THE SITE IS STILL MAKING MONEY. MORE THAN TEN THOUSAND HITS TODAY.

OKAY, SO WE LEAVE AT 7 AM.

YOU HAVE YOUR PASSPORT?

YEAH.

SO, *MANY* FLIGHTS LATER, WE LAND IN MEXICO AT 6:45 PM.

AND YOU HAVE PEOPLE, RIGHT, THAT WE CAN STAY WITH?

YES. I TOLD YOU "YES" ALREADY.

GEEZ, RAY. YOU'RE FREAKING ME OUT, OKAY? RELAX.

STEVE? DO YOU THINK HE CAN FIND US? HERE?

NO, I DON'T. STOP BEING SO FRICKING *PARANOID*.

HE ALMOST *KILLED* YOU.

YEAH, BUT EVEN AS A MONSTER, OLIVER'S NOT KILLING ANYONE.

SO SHUT UP ABOUT IT AND GO TO SLEEP.

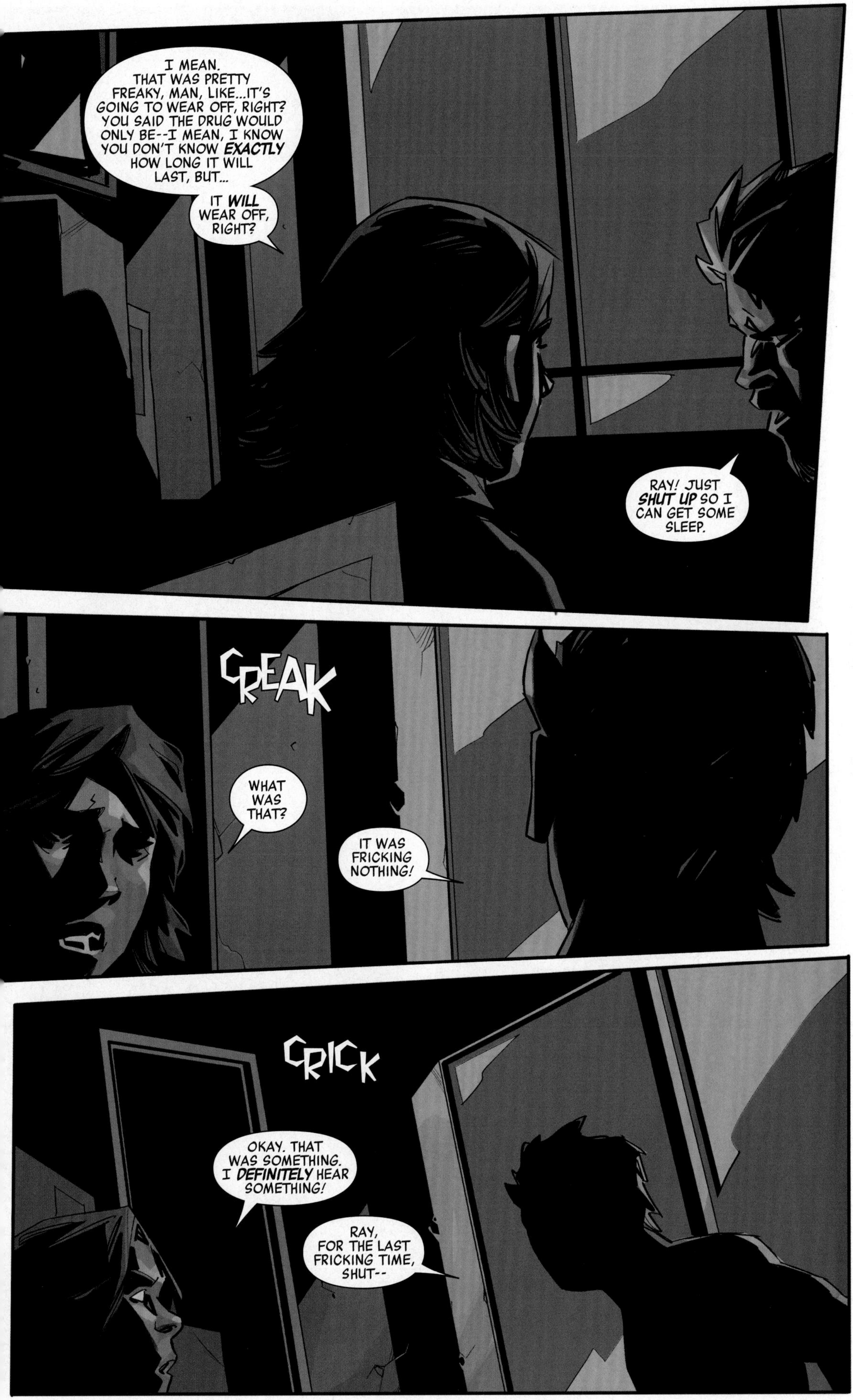
I MEAN. THAT WAS PRETTY FREAKY, MAN, LIKE...IT'S GOING TO WEAR OFF, RIGHT? YOU SAID THE DRUG WOULD ONLY BE--I MEAN, I KNOW YOU DON'T KNOW *EXACTLY* HOW LONG IT WILL LAST, BUT...
IT *WILL* WEAR OFF, RIGHT?
RAY! JUST *SHUT UP* SO I CAN GET SOME SLEEP.
CREAK
WHAT WAS THAT?
IT WAS FRICKING NOTHING!
CRICK
OKAY. THAT WAS SOMETHING. I *DEFINITELY* HEAR SOMETHING!
RAY, FOR THE LAST FRICKING TIME, SHUT--

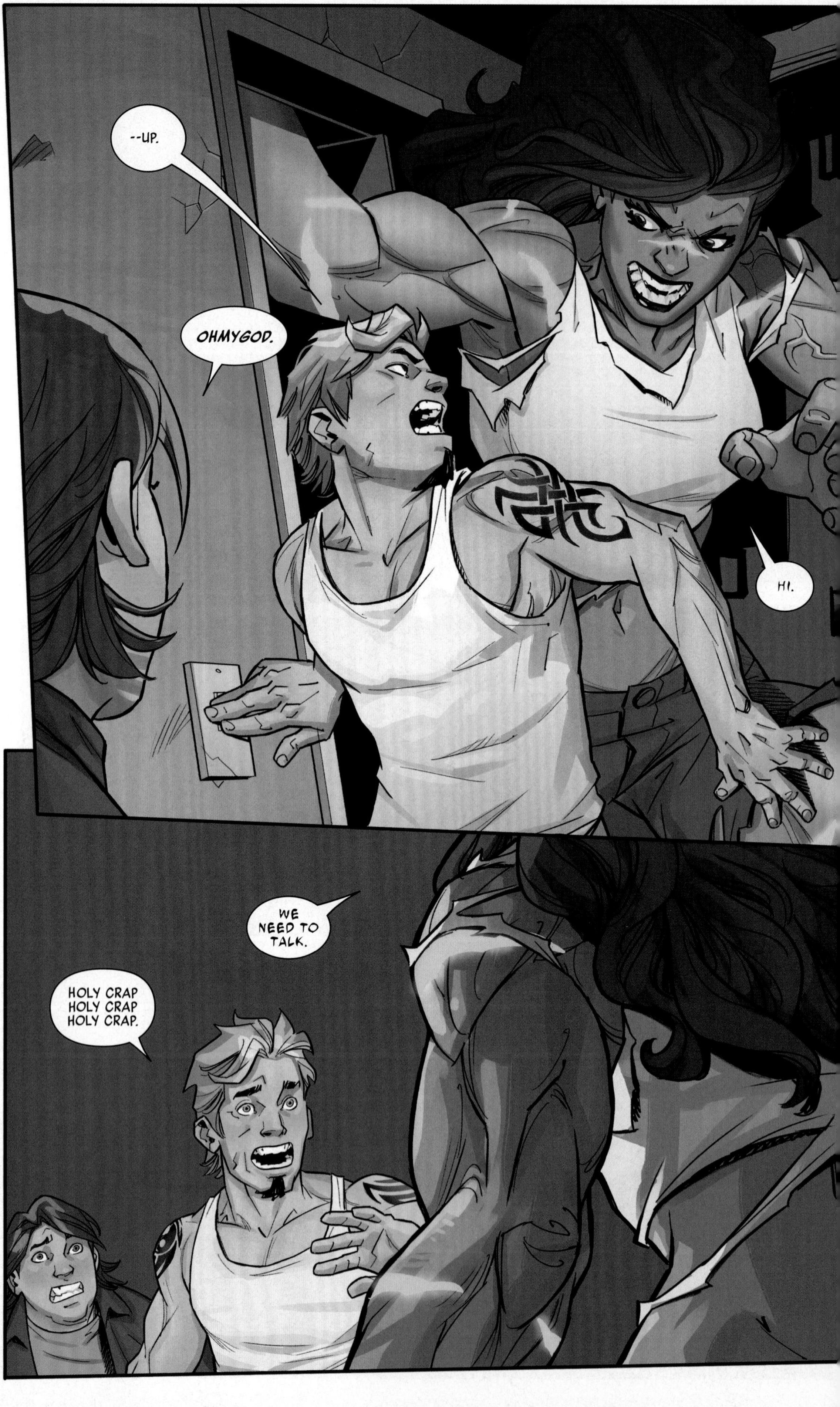
--UP.
OHMYGOD.
HI.
WE NEED TO TALK.
HOLY CRAP HOLY CRAP HOLY CRAP.

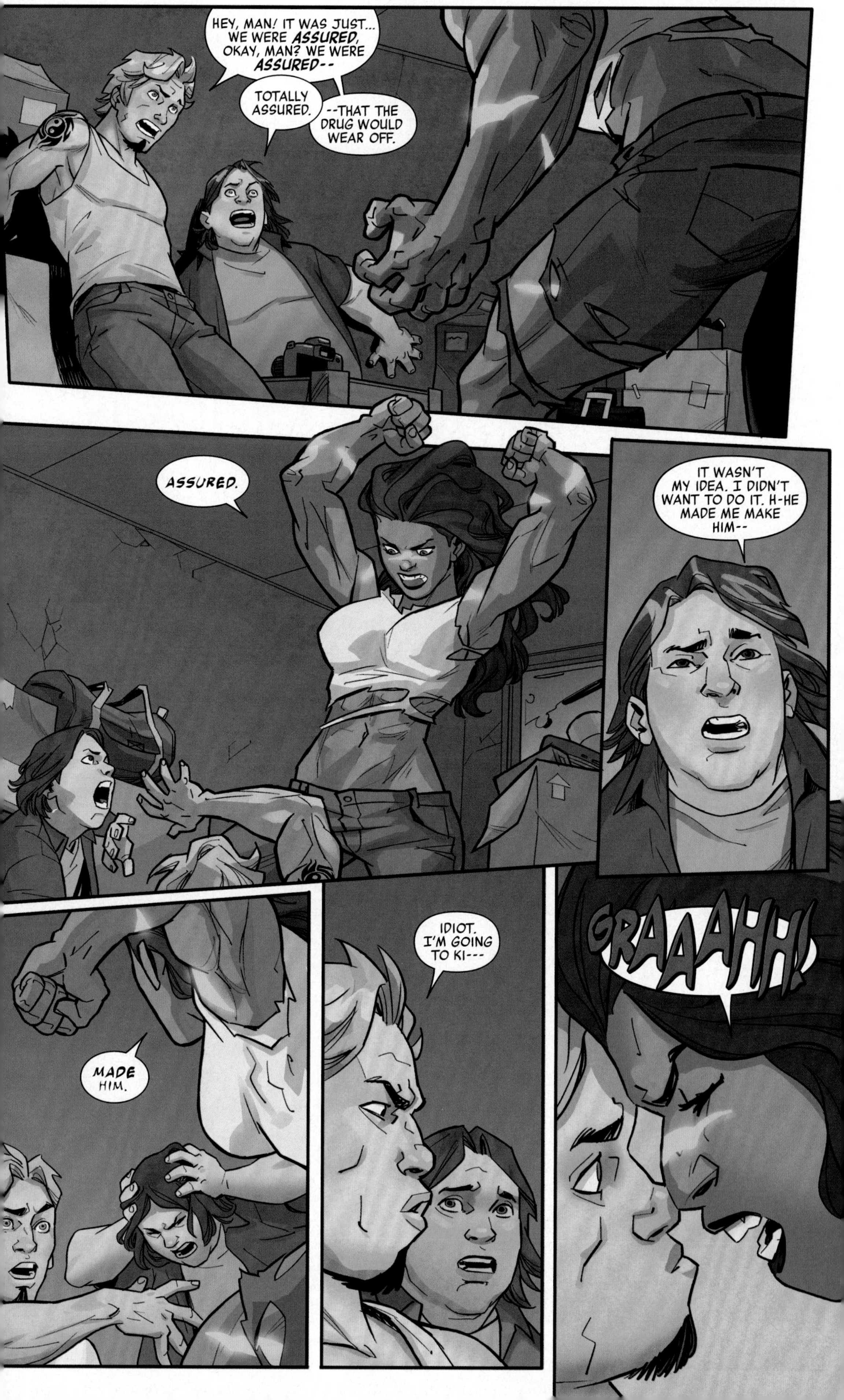
HEY, MAN! IT WAS JUST... WE WERE ASSURED, OKAY, MAN? WE WERE ASSURED--
TOTALLY ASSURED.
--THAT THE DRUG WOULD WEAR OFF.
ASSURED.
IT WASN'T MY IDEA. I DIDN'T WANT TO DO IT. H-HE MADE ME MAKE HIM--
MADE HIM.
IDIOT. I'M GOING TO KI---
GRAAAHH!

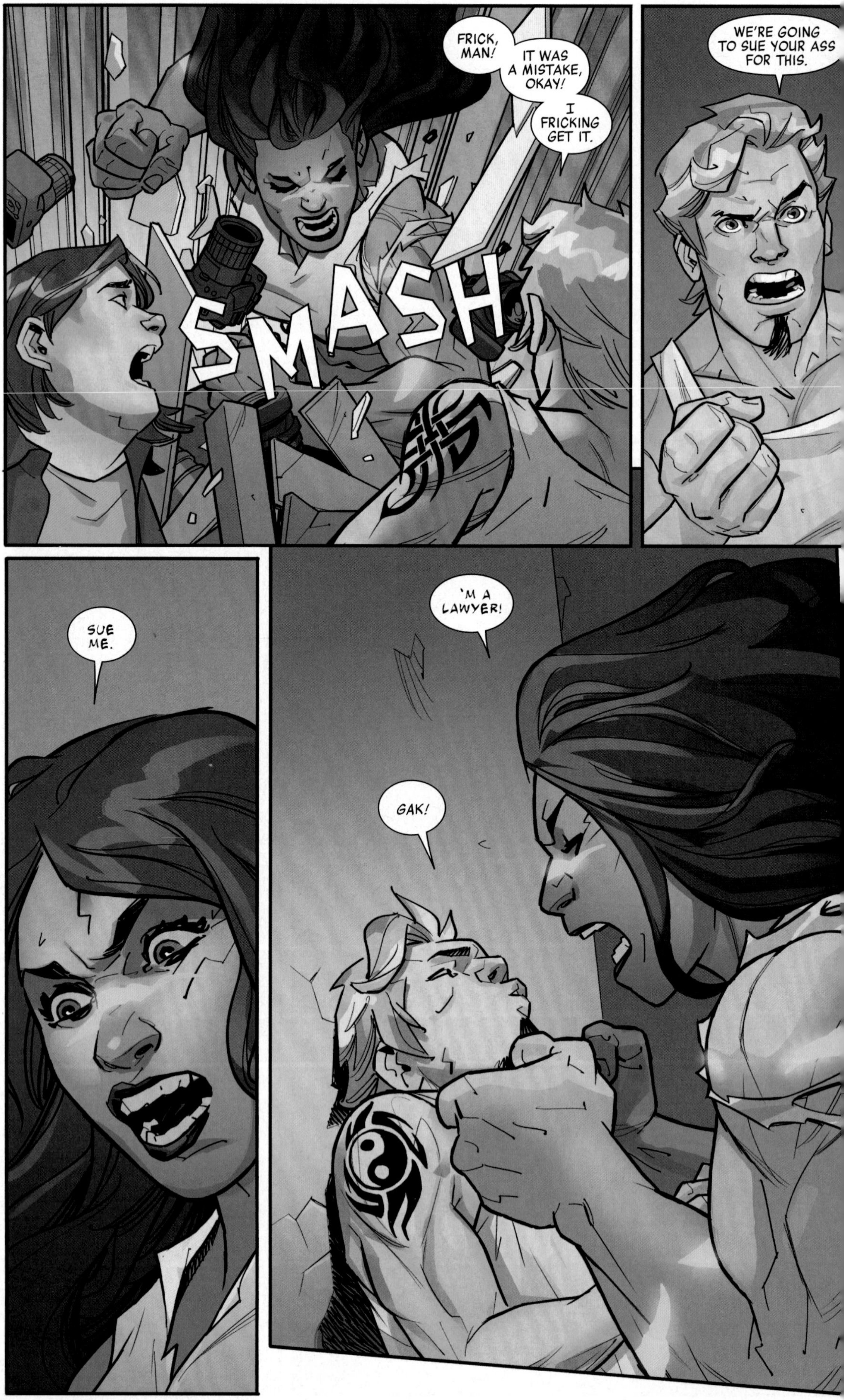
FRICK, MAN!
IT WAS A MISTAKE, OKAY!
I FRICKING GET IT.
SMASH
WE'RE GOING TO SUE YOUR ASS FOR THIS.
SUE ME.
'M A LAWYER!
GAK!

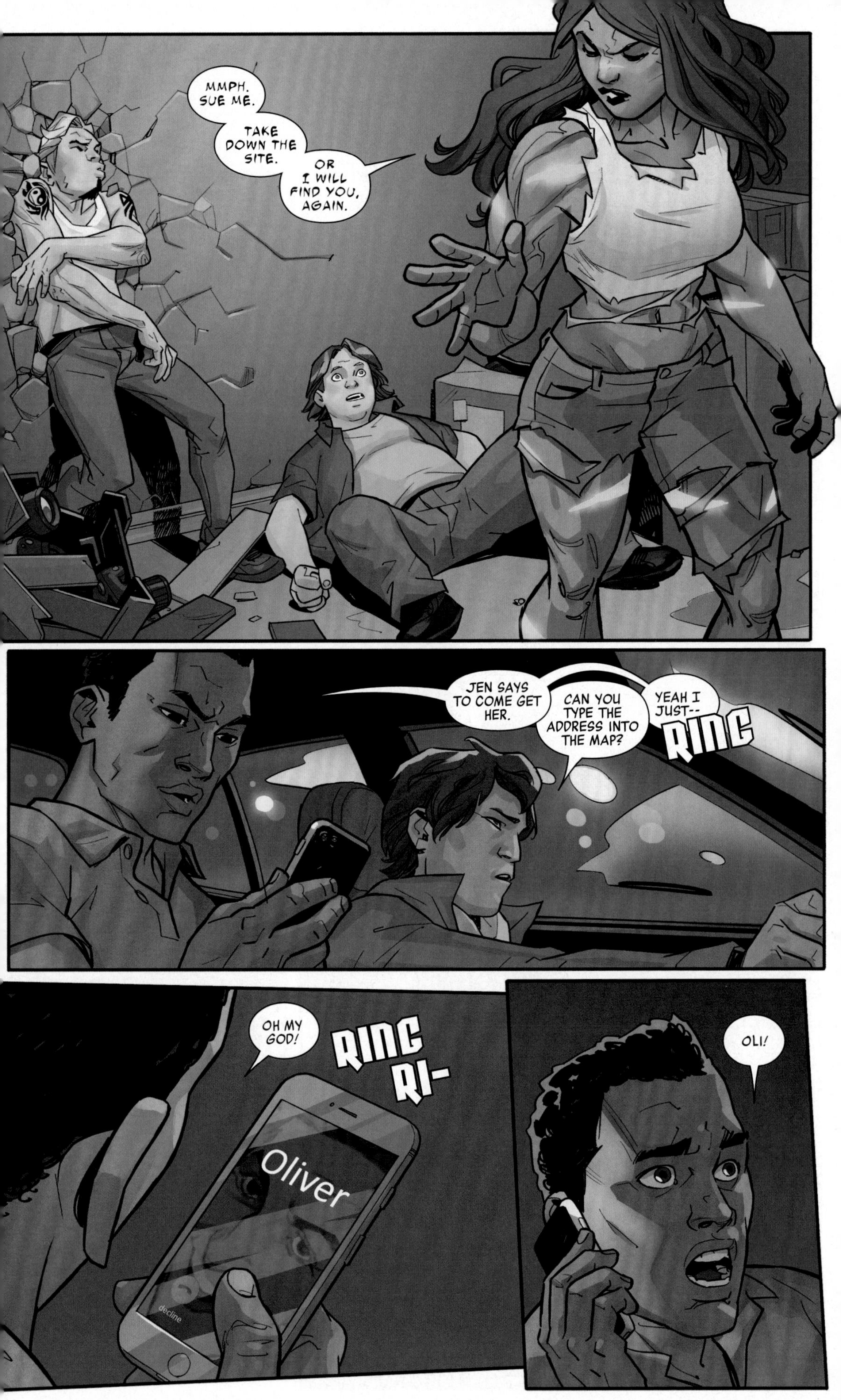
MMPH. SUE ME.
TAKE DOWN THE SITE.
OR I WILL FIND YOU, AGAIN.
JEN SAYS TO COME GET HER.
CAN YOU TYPE THE ADDRESS INTO THE MAP?
YEAH I JUST--
RING
OH MY GOD!
RING RI-
Oliver
decline
OLI!

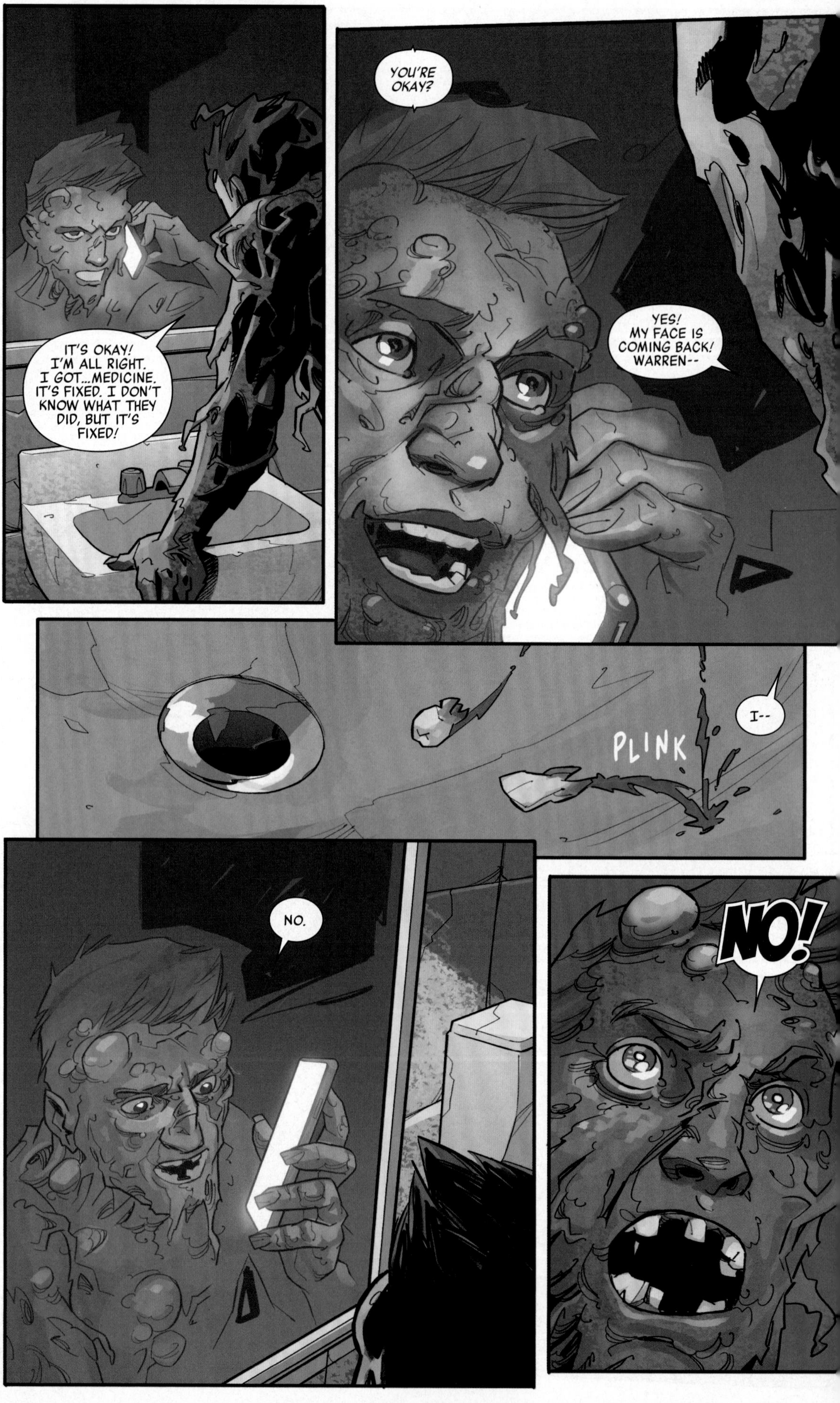

IT'S OKAY! I'M ALL RIGHT. I GOT...MEDICINE. IT'S FIXED. I DON'T KNOW WHAT THEY DID, BUT IT'S FIXED!
YOU'RE OKAY?
YES! MY FACE IS COMING BACK! WARREN--
PLINK
I--
NO.
NO!

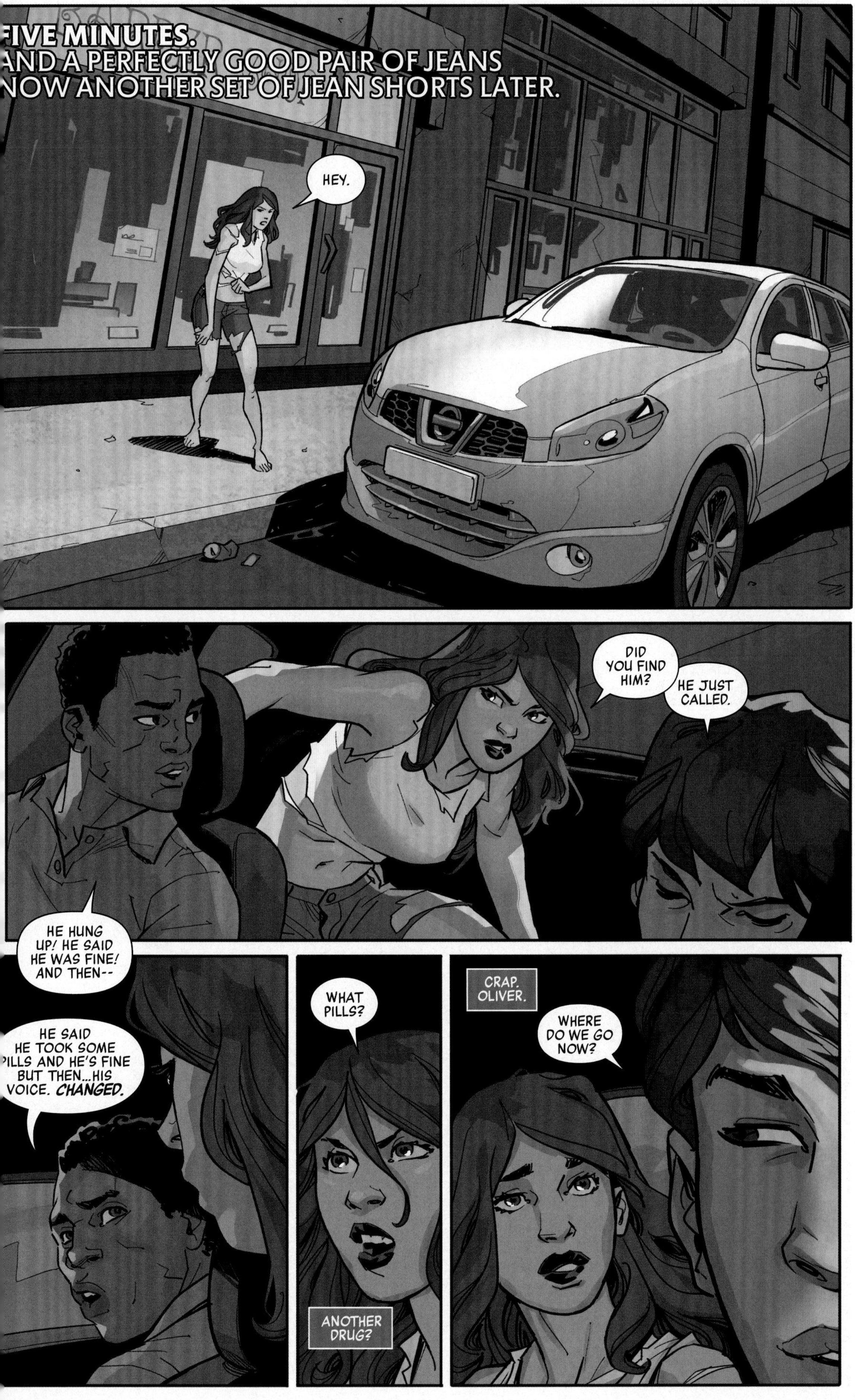
FIVE MINUTES.
AND A PERFECTLY GOOD PAIR OF JEANS
NOW ANOTHER SET OF JEAN SHORTS LATER.
HEY.
DID YOU FIND HIM?
HE JUST CALLED.
HE HUNG UP! HE SAID HE WAS FINE! AND THEN--
HE SAID HE TOOK SOME PILLS AND HE'S FINE BUT THEN...HIS VOICE. *CHANGED.*
WHAT PILLS?
ANOTHER DRUG?
CRAP. OLIVER.
WHERE DO WE GO NOW?

WE FIND HIM.

TRY CALLING HIM AGAIN.

BECAUSE WHATEVER OLIVER IS BECOMING ISN'T SOMETHING THAT CAN STAY HIDDEN FOR LONG.

COME ON, OLIVER. PICK UP. PLEASE.

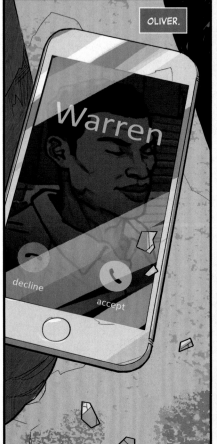

OLIVER.

Warren

decline

accept

WHATEVER YOU ARE BECOMING...

BRRRINC

BRRRINC

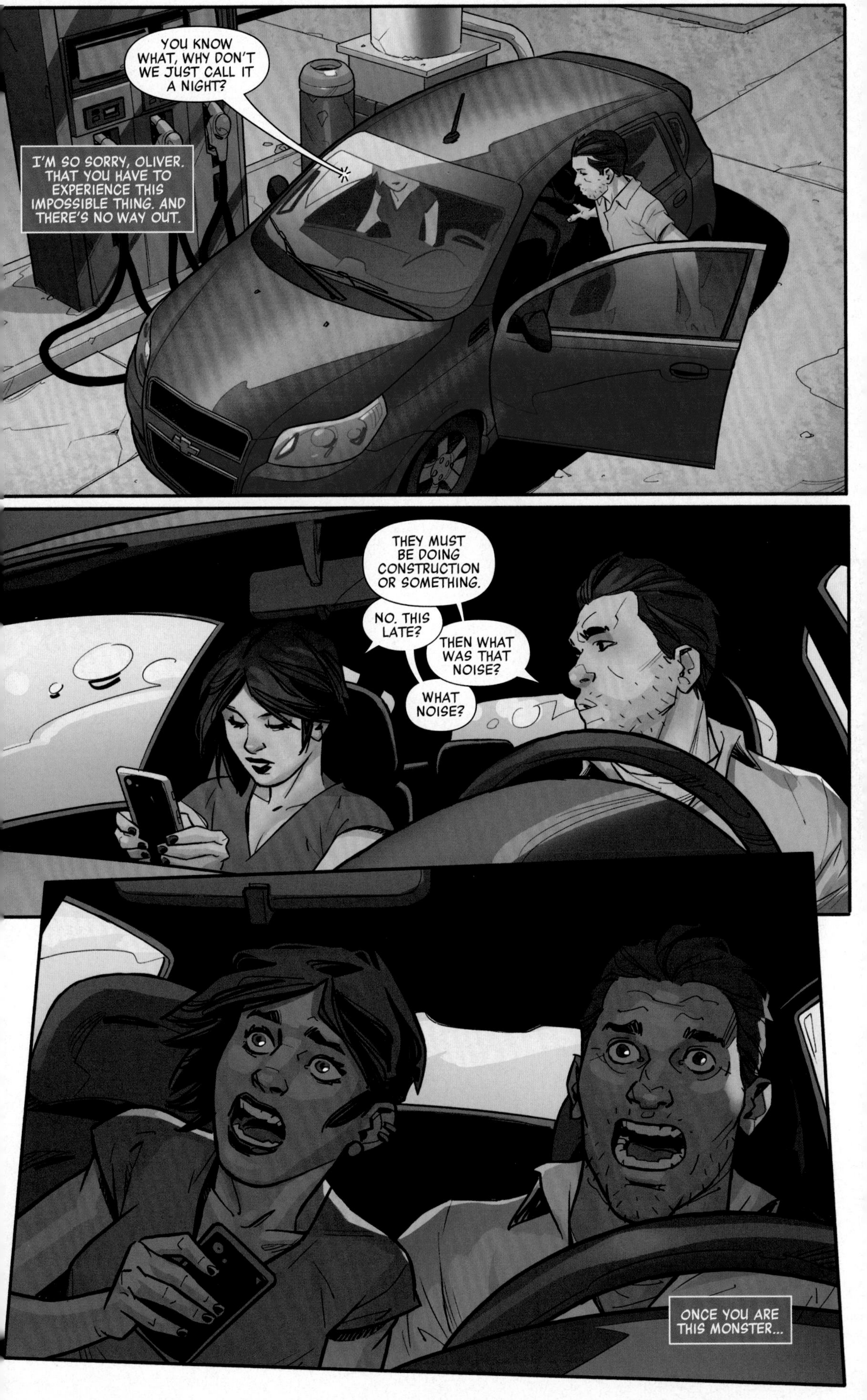
YOU KNOW WHAT, WHY DON'T WE JUST CALL IT A NIGHT?
I'M SO SORRY, OLIVER. THAT YOU HAVE TO EXPERIENCE THIS IMPOSSIBLE THING. AND THERE'S NO WAY OUT.
THEY MUST BE DOING CONSTRUCTION OR SOMETHING.
NO. THIS LATE?
THEN WHAT WAS THAT NOISE?
WHAT NOISE?
ONCE YOU ARE THIS MONSTER...

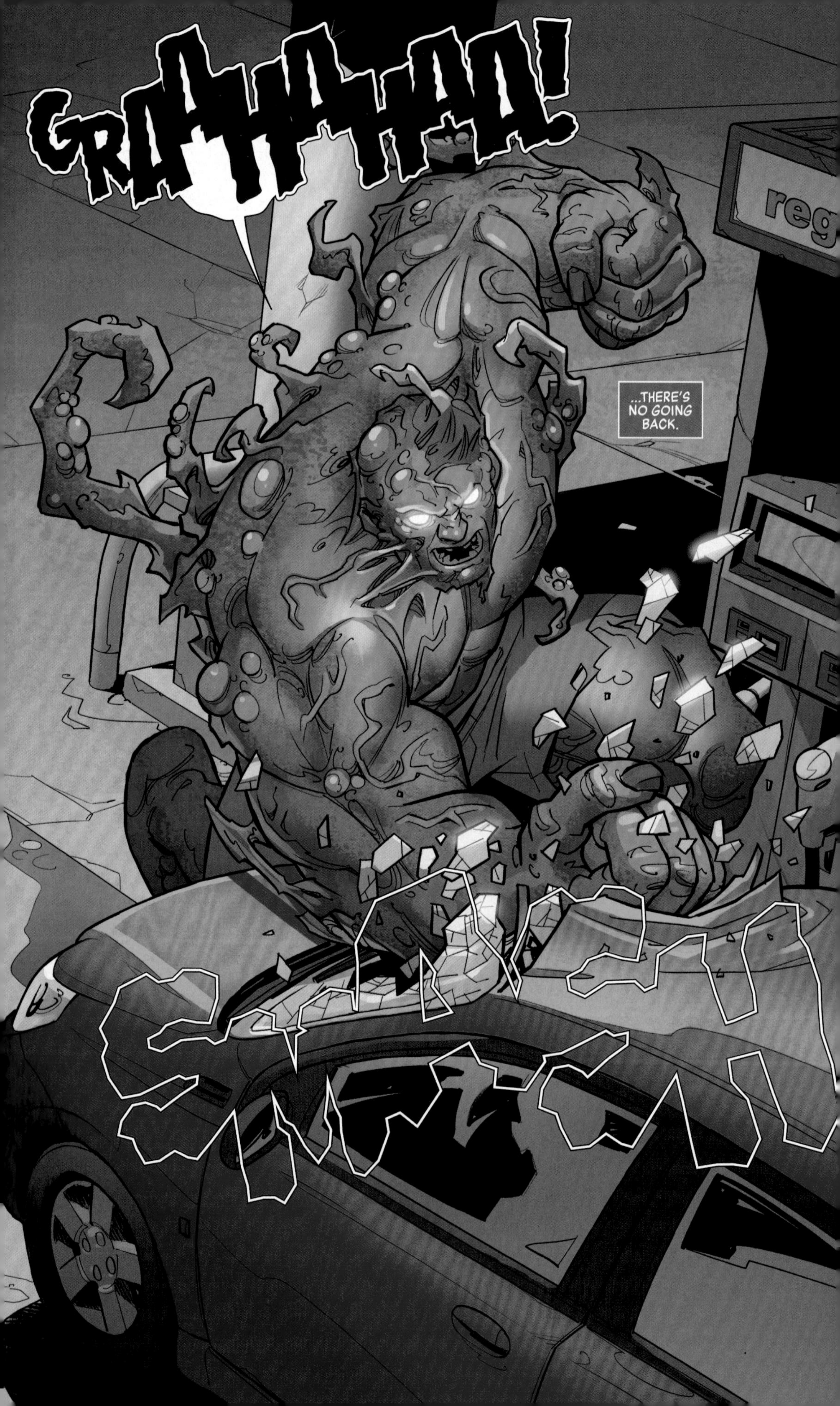
GRAAHAAA!
...THERE'S NO GOING BACK.
reg
SMASH

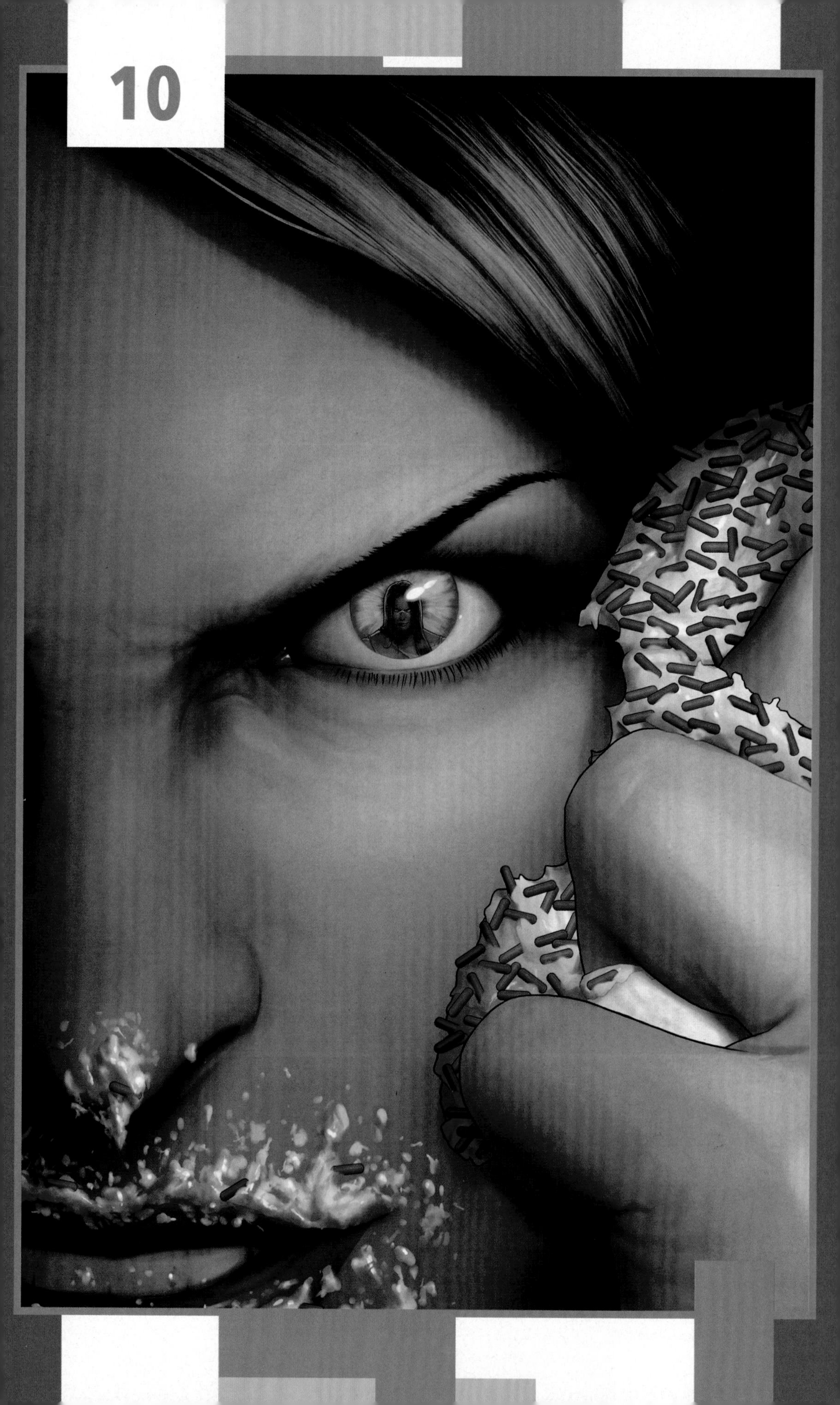
10

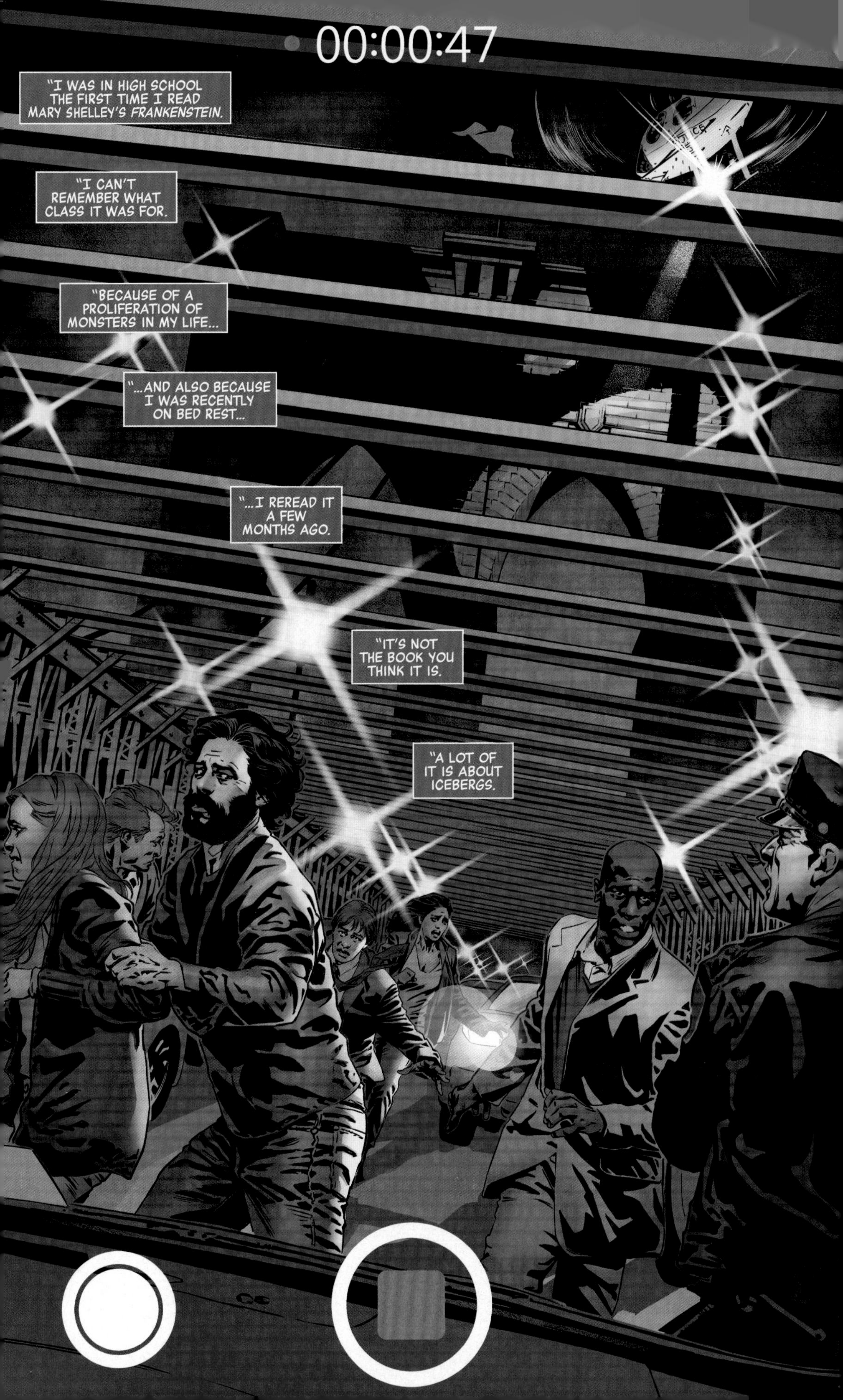
00:00:47
"I WAS IN HIGH SCHOOL THE FIRST TIME I READ MARY SHELLEY'S *FRANKENSTEIN*.
"I CAN'T REMEMBER WHAT CLASS IT WAS FOR.
"BECAUSE OF A PROLIFERATION OF MONSTERS IN MY LIFE...
"...AND ALSO BECAUSE I WAS RECENTLY ON BED REST...
"...I REREAD IT A FEW MONTHS AGO.
"IT'S NOT THE BOOK YOU THINK IT IS.
"A LOT OF IT IS ABOUT ICEBERGS.

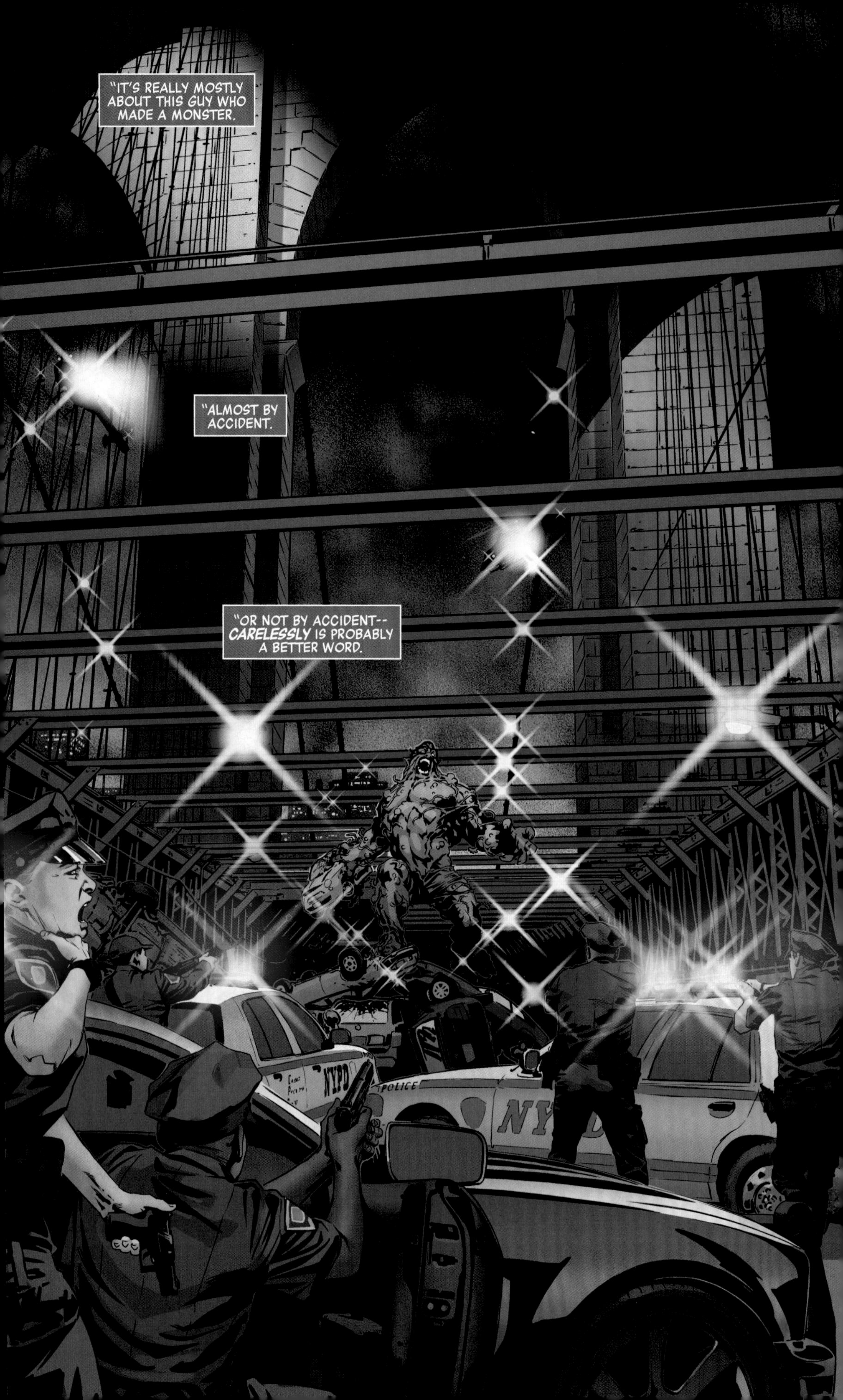
"IT'S REALLY MOSTLY ABOUT THIS GUY WHO MADE A MONSTER.
"ALMOST BY ACCIDENT.
"OR NOT BY ACCIDENT-- *CARELESSLY* IS PROBABLY A BETTER WORD.
NYPD
POLICE
NYPD

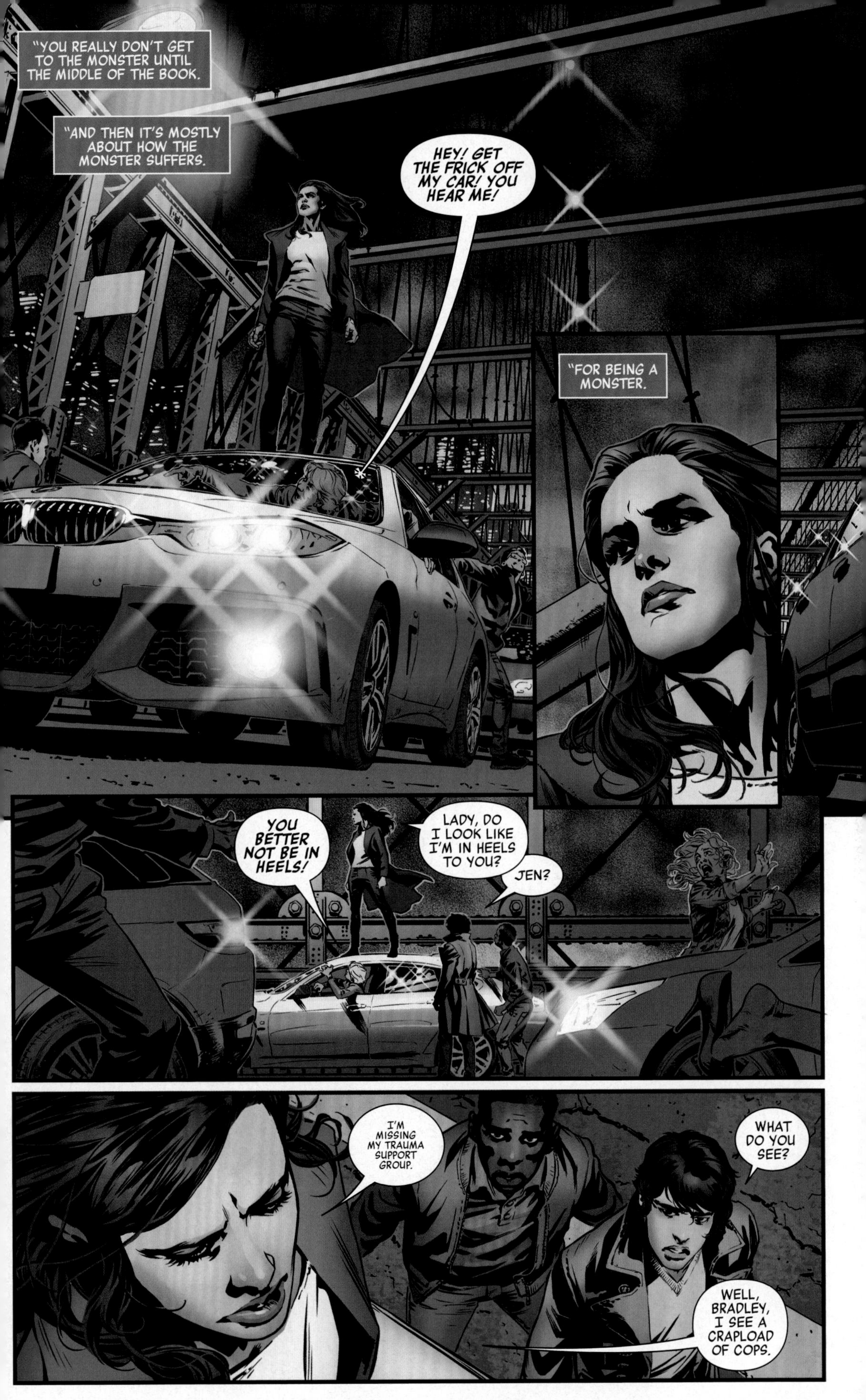
"YOU REALLY DON'T GET TO THE MONSTER UNTIL THE MIDDLE OF THE BOOK.
"AND THEN IT'S MOSTLY ABOUT HOW THE MONSTER SUFFERS.
HEY! GET THE FRICK OFF MY CAR! YOU HEAR ME!
"FOR BEING A MONSTER.
YOU BETTER NOT BE IN HEELS!
LADY, DO I LOOK LIKE I'M IN HEELS TO YOU?
JEN?
I'M MISSING MY TRAUMA SUPPORT GROUP.
WHAT DO YOU SEE?
WELL, BRADLEY, I SEE A CRAPLOAD OF COPS.

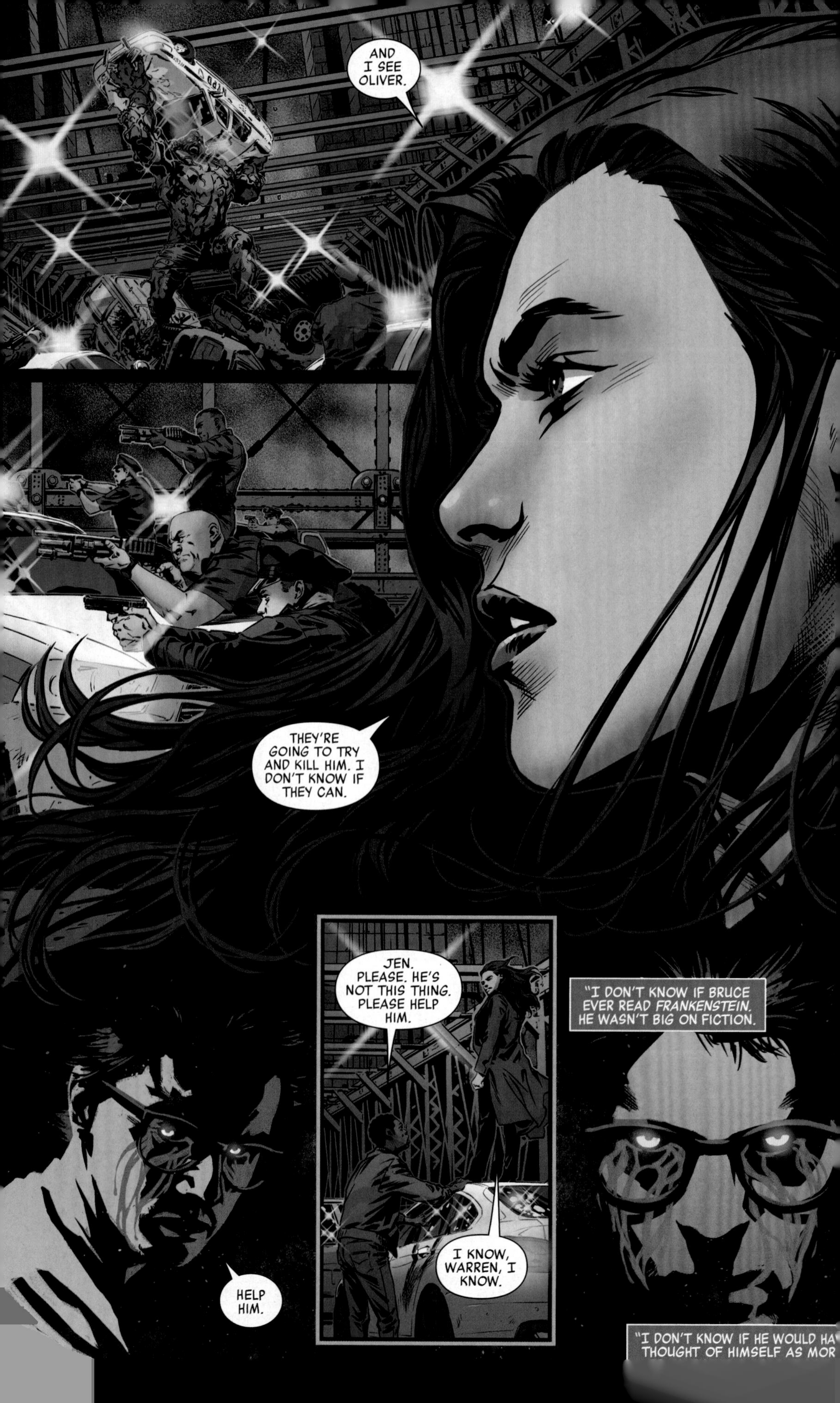
AND I SEE OLIVER.
THEY'RE GOING TO TRY AND KILL HIM. I DON'T KNOW IF THEY CAN.
HELP HIM.
JEN. PLEASE. HE'S NOT THIS THING. PLEASE HELP HIM.
I KNOW, WARREN, I KNOW.
"I DON'T KNOW IF BRUCE EVER READ *FRANKENSTEIN*. HE WASN'T BIG ON FICTION.
"I DON'T KNOW IF HE WOULD HA THOUGHT OF HIMSELF AS MOR

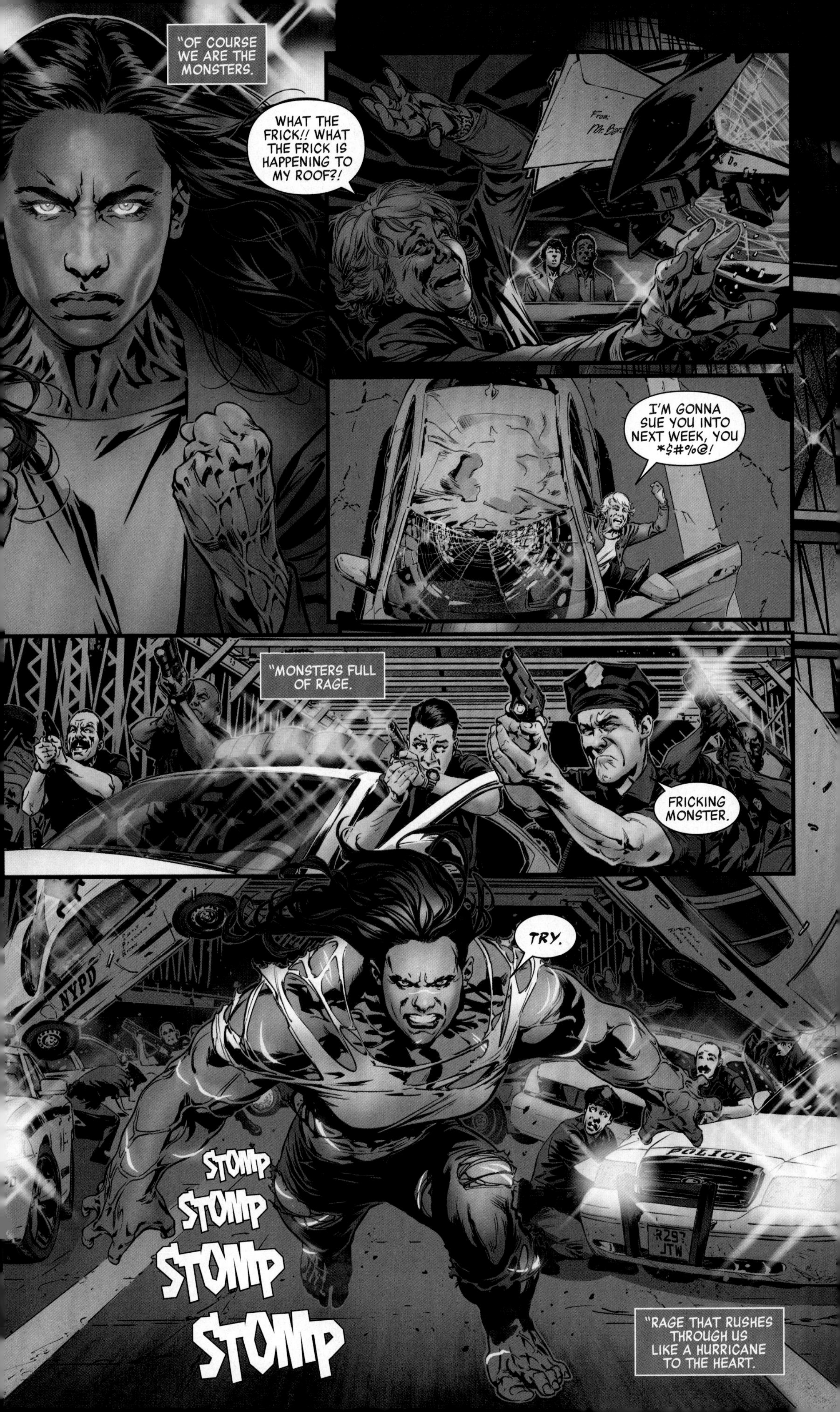
"OF COURSE WE ARE THE MONSTERS.
WHAT THE FRICK!! WHAT THE FRICK IS HAPPENING TO MY ROOF?!
I'M GONNA SUE YOU INTO NEXT WEEK, YOU *$#%@!
"MONSTERS FULL OF RAGE.
FRICKING MONSTER.
TRY.
NYPD
POLICE
STOMP
STOMP
STOMP
STOMP
"RAGE THAT RUSHES THROUGH US LIKE A HURRICANE TO THE HEART.

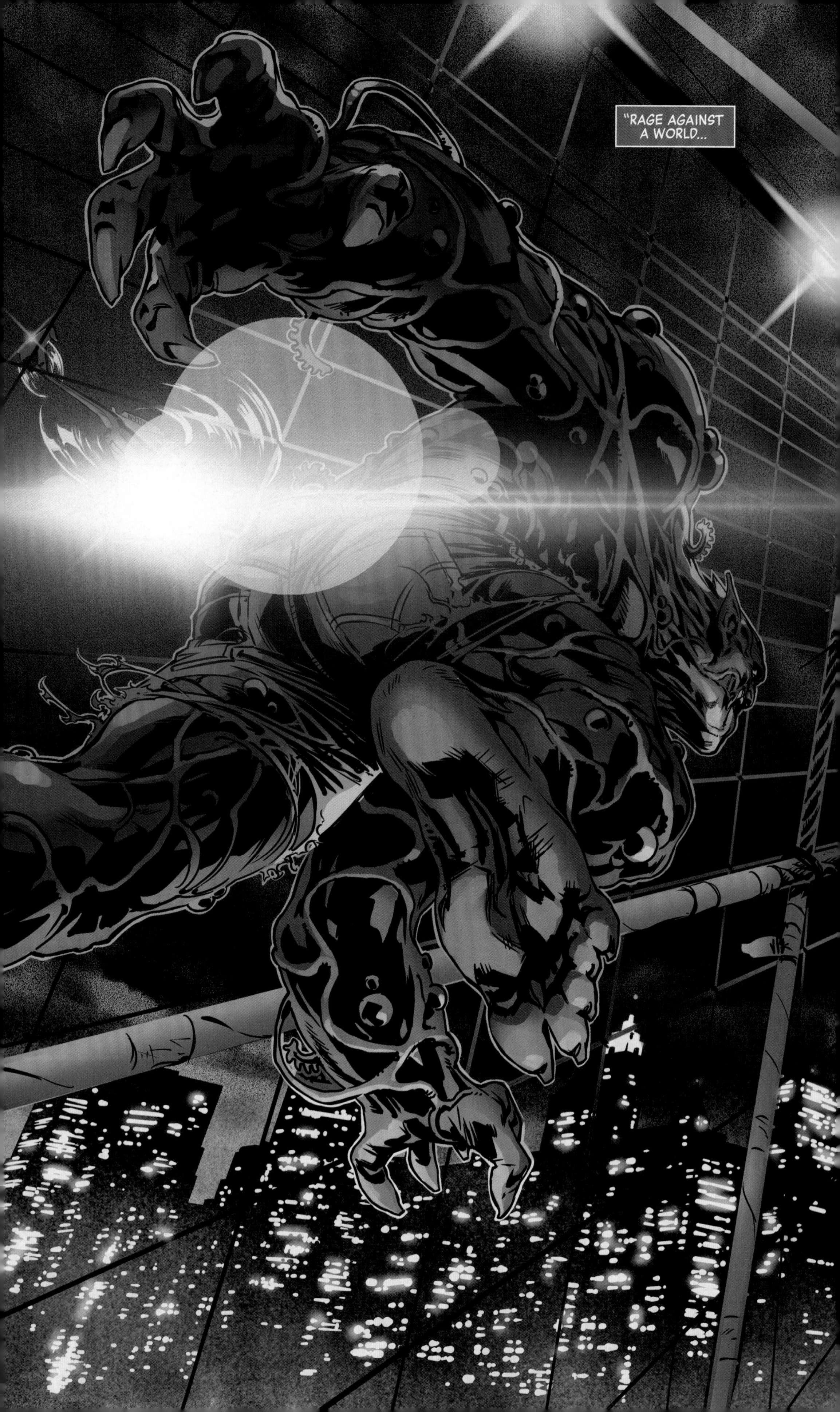
"RAGE AGAINST A WORLD...

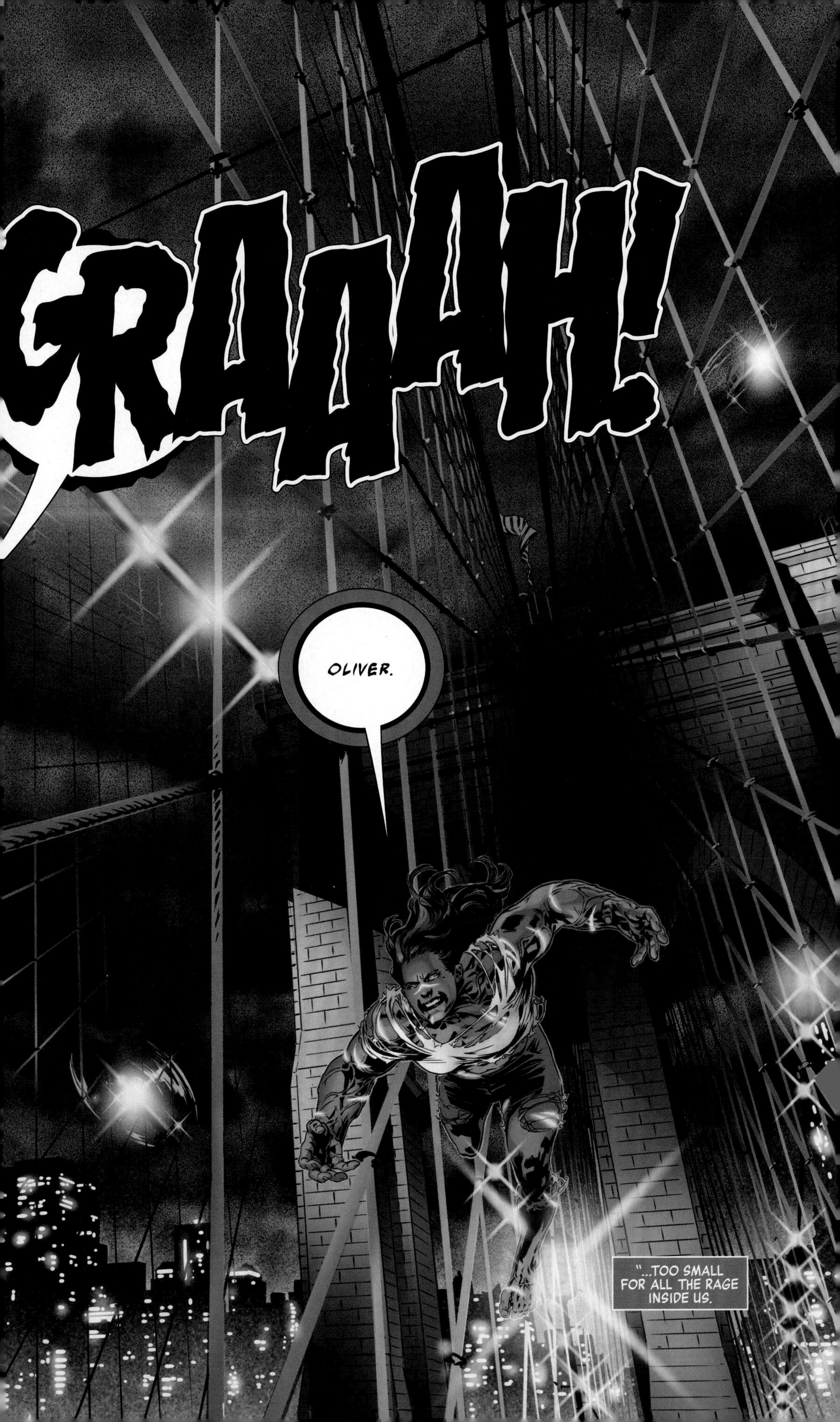
GRAAAH!
OLIVER.
"...TOO SMALL FOR ALL THE RAGE INSIDE US.

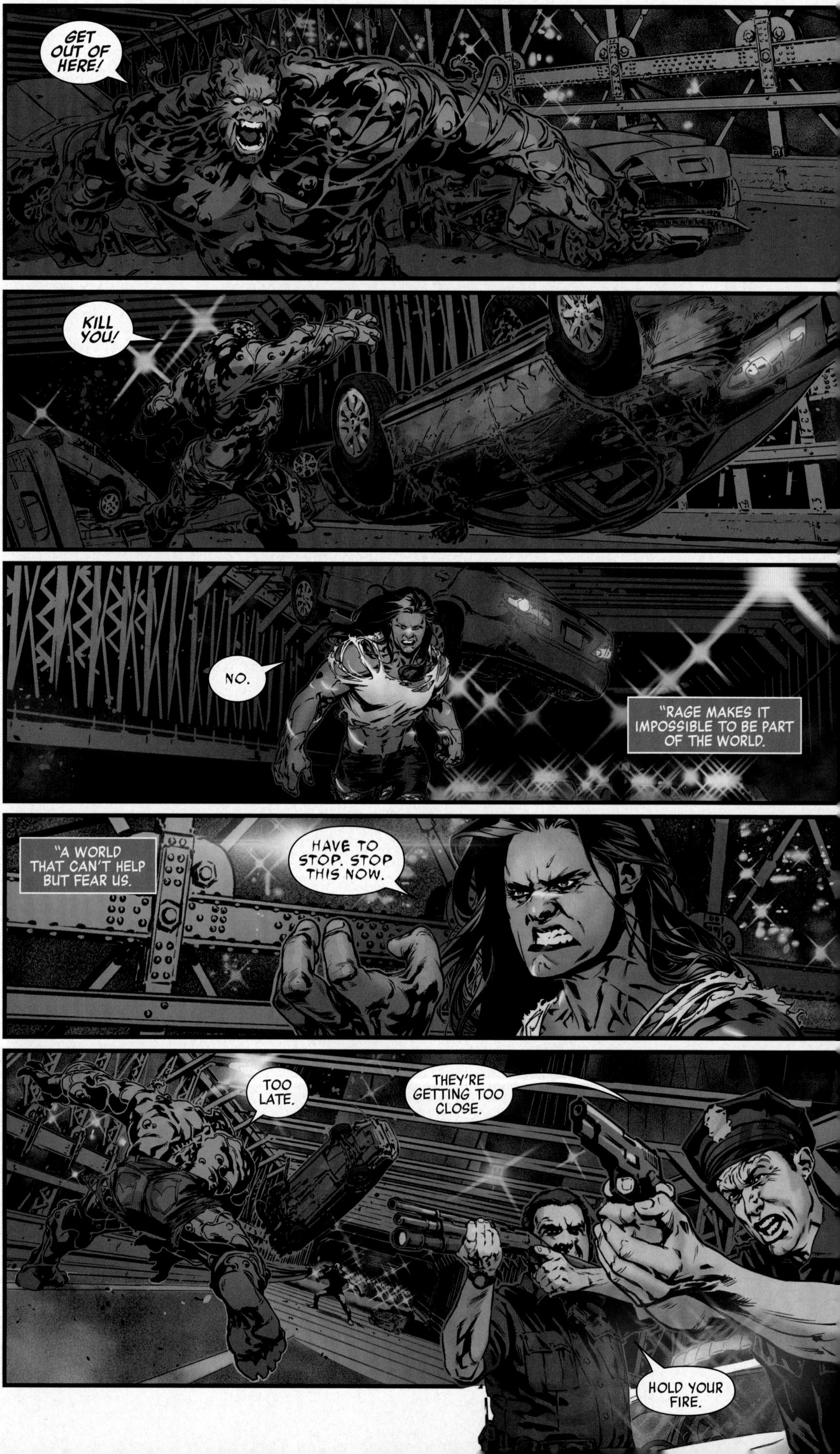
GET OUT OF HERE!
KILL YOU!
NO.
"RAGE MAKES IT IMPOSSIBLE TO BE PART OF THE WORLD.
"A WORLD THAT CAN'T HELP BUT FEAR US.
HAVE TO STOP. STOP THIS NOW.
TOO LATE.
THEY'RE GETTING TOO CLOSE.
HOLD YOUR FIRE.

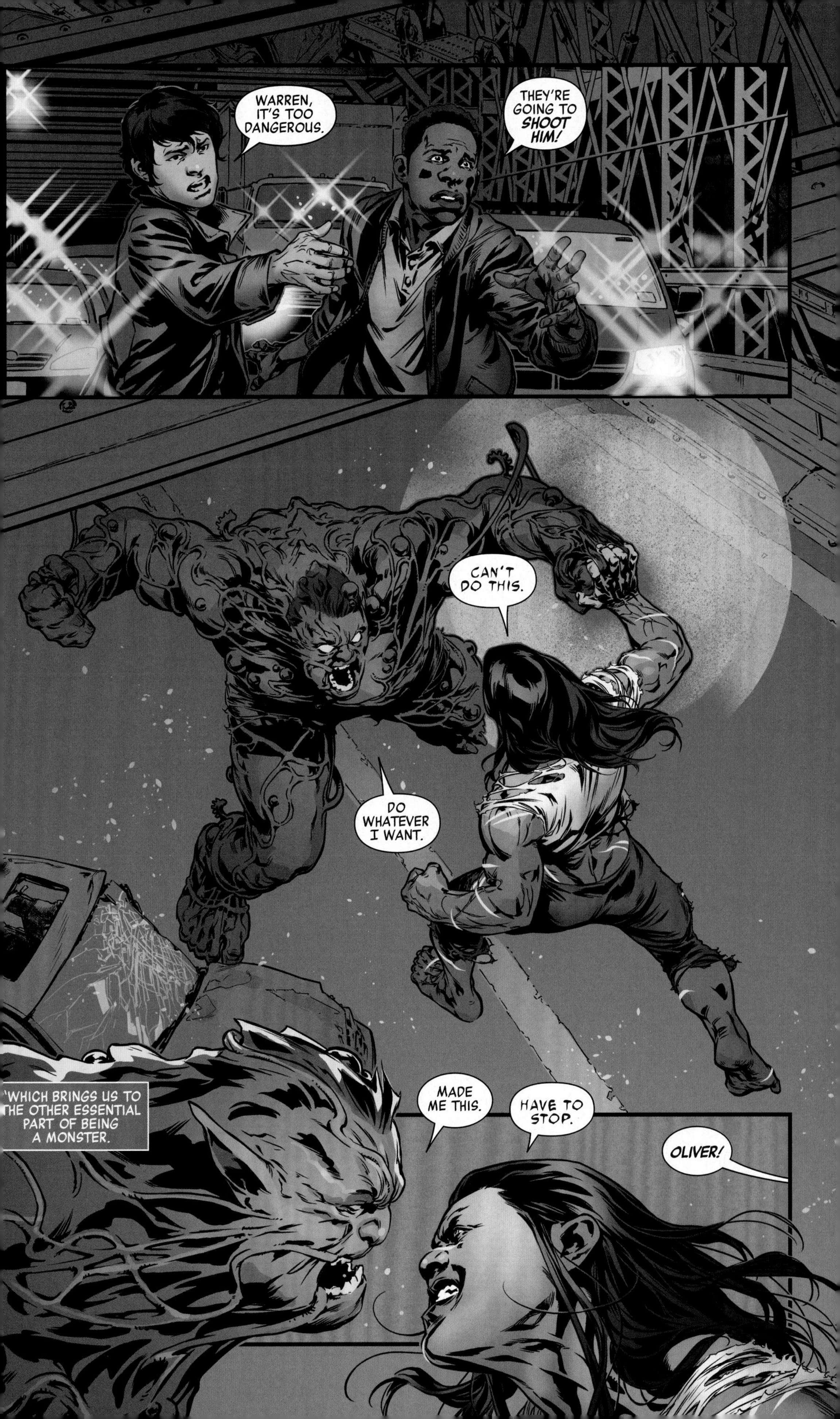
WARREN, IT'S TOO DANGEROUS.
THEY'RE GOING TO SHOOT HIM!
CAN'T DO THIS.
DO WHATEVER I WANT.
WHICH BRINGS US TO THE OTHER ESSENTIAL PART OF BEING A MONSTER.
MADE ME THIS.
HAVE TO STOP.
OLIVER!

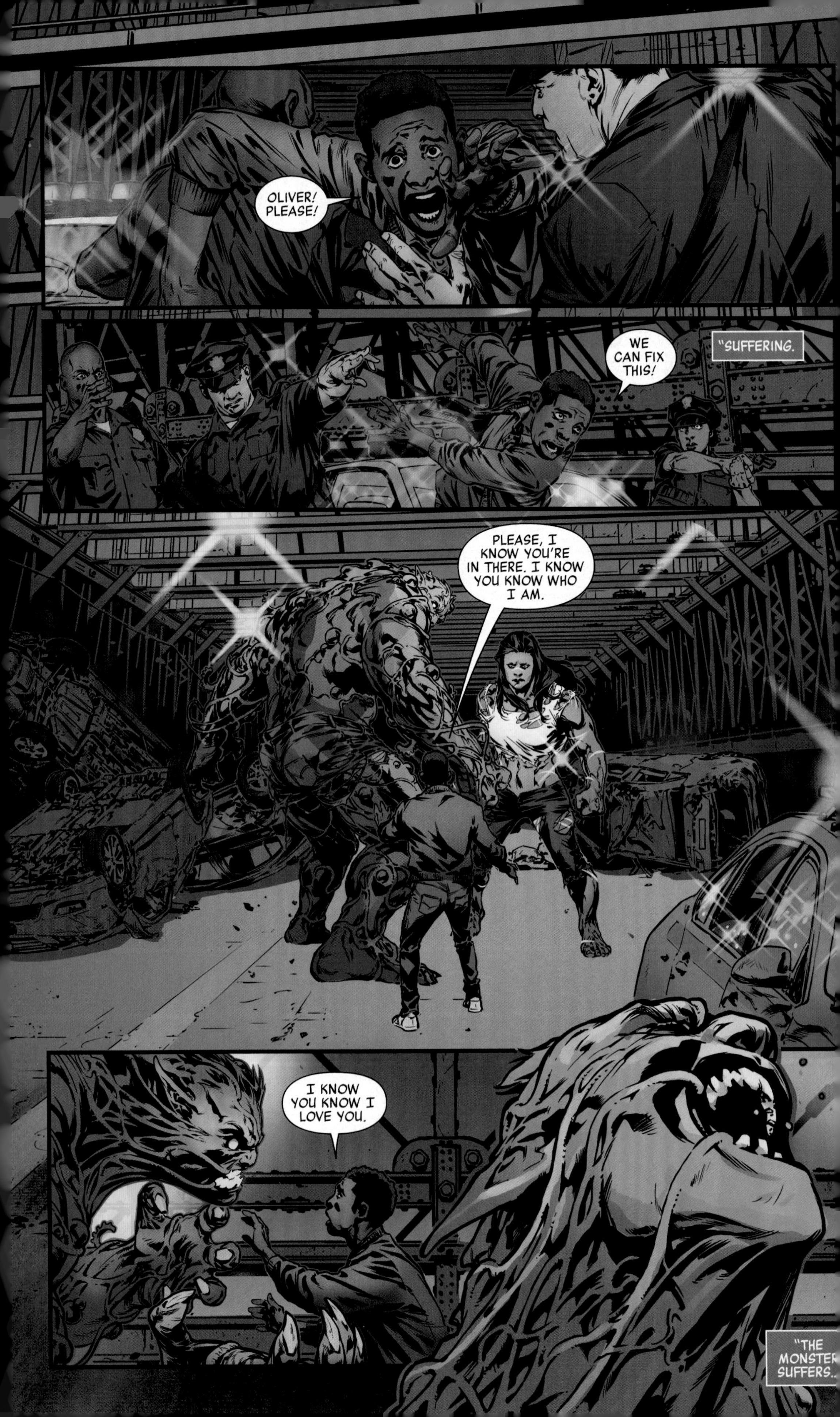
OLIVER! PLEASE!
WE CAN FIX THIS!
"SUFFERING.
PLEASE, I KNOW YOU'RE IN THERE. I KNOW YOU KNOW WHO I AM.
I KNOW YOU KNOW I LOVE YOU.
"THE MONSTER SUFFERS...

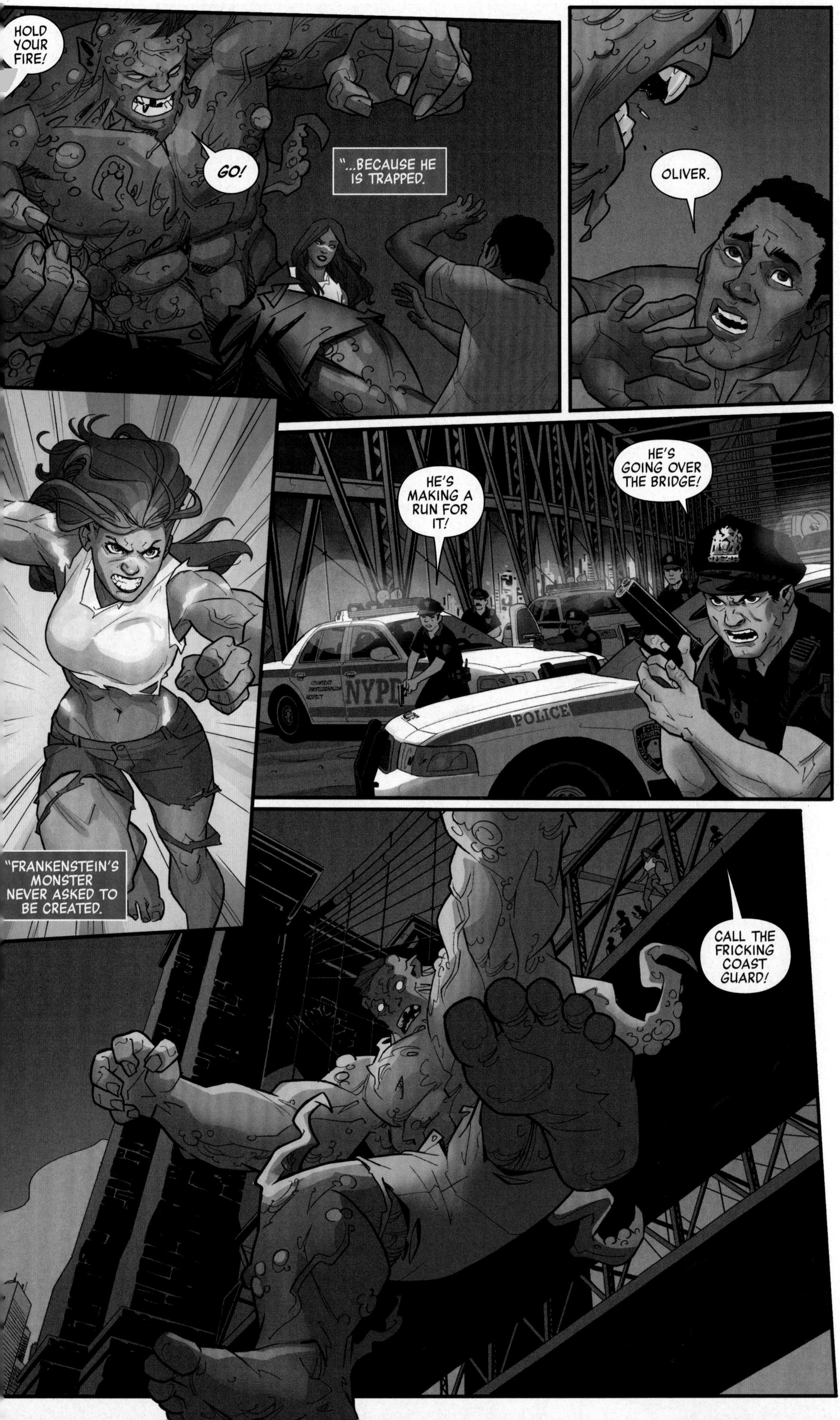
HOLD YOUR FIRE!
GO!
"...BECAUSE HE IS TRAPPED.
OLIVER.
HE'S MAKING A RUN FOR IT!
HE'S GOING OVER THE BRIDGE!
NYPD
POLICE
"FRANKENSTEIN'S MONSTER NEVER ASKED TO BE CREATED.
CALL THE FRICKING COAST GUARD!

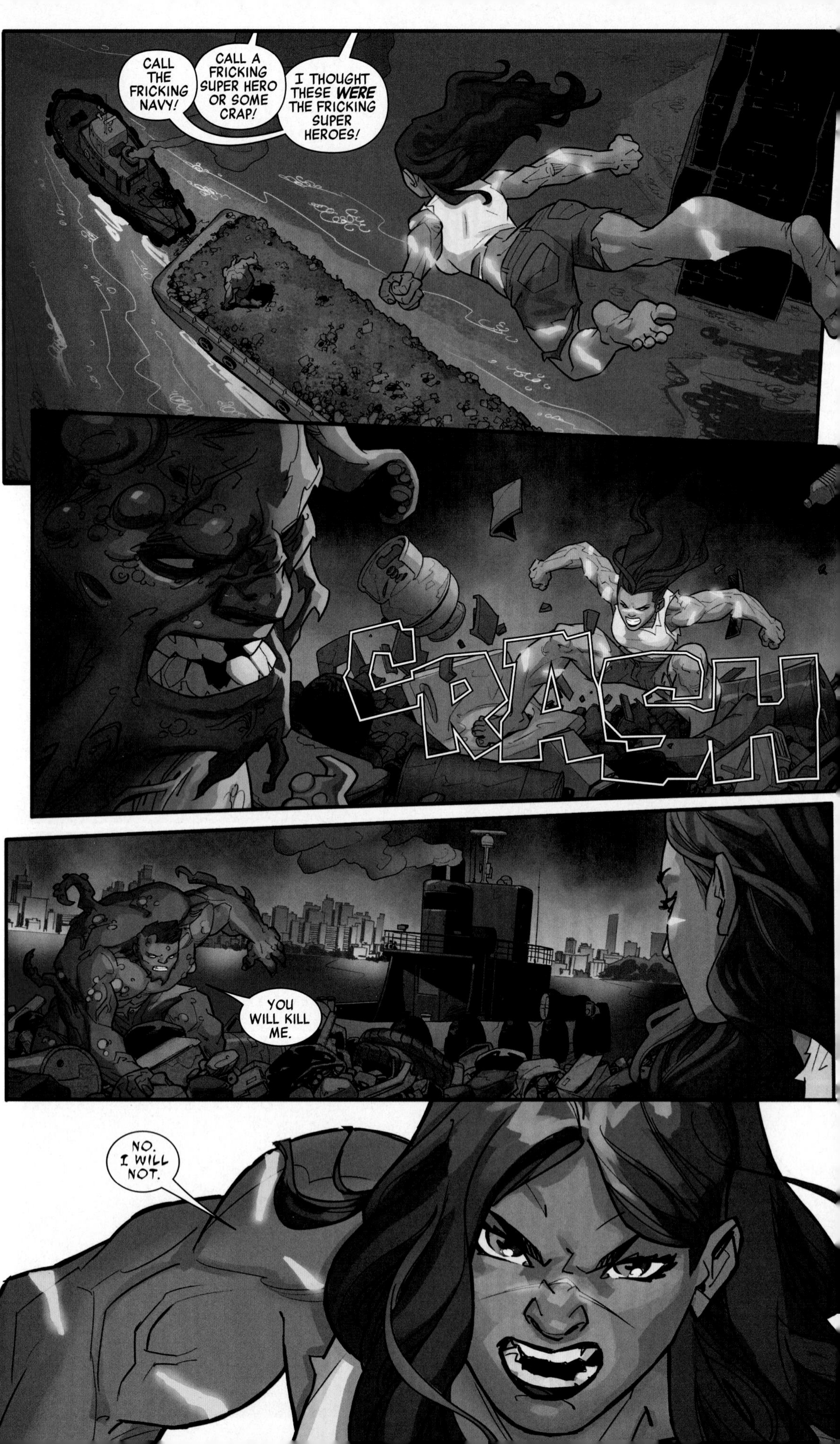

CALL THE FRICKING NAVY!
CALL A FRICKING SUPER HERO OR SOME CRAP!
I THOUGHT THESE WERE THE FRICKING SUPER HEROES!
CRASH
YOU WILL KILL ME.
NO. I WILL NOT.

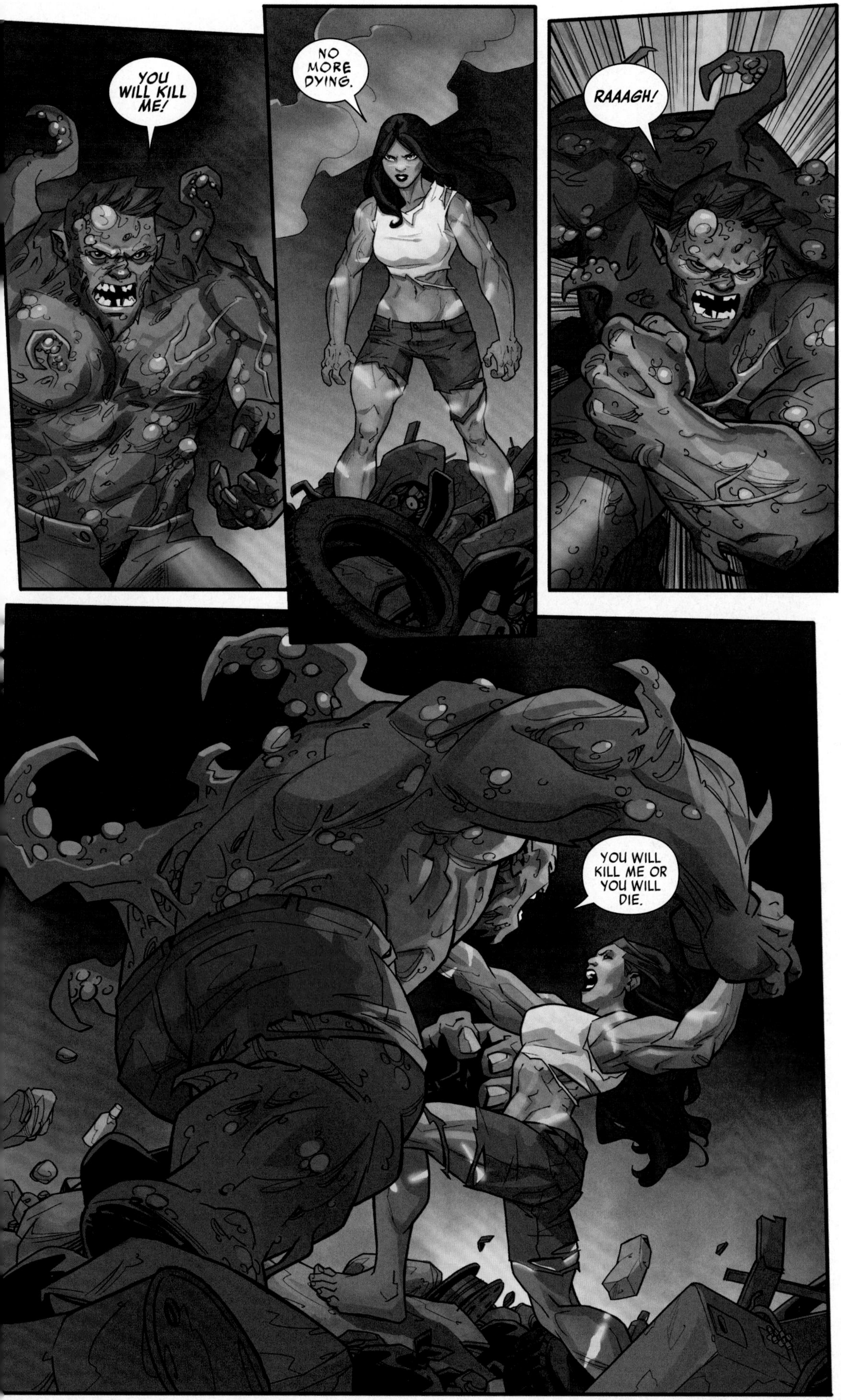
YOU WILL KILL ME!
NO MORE DYING.
RAAAGH!
YOU WILL KILL ME OR YOU WILL DIE.

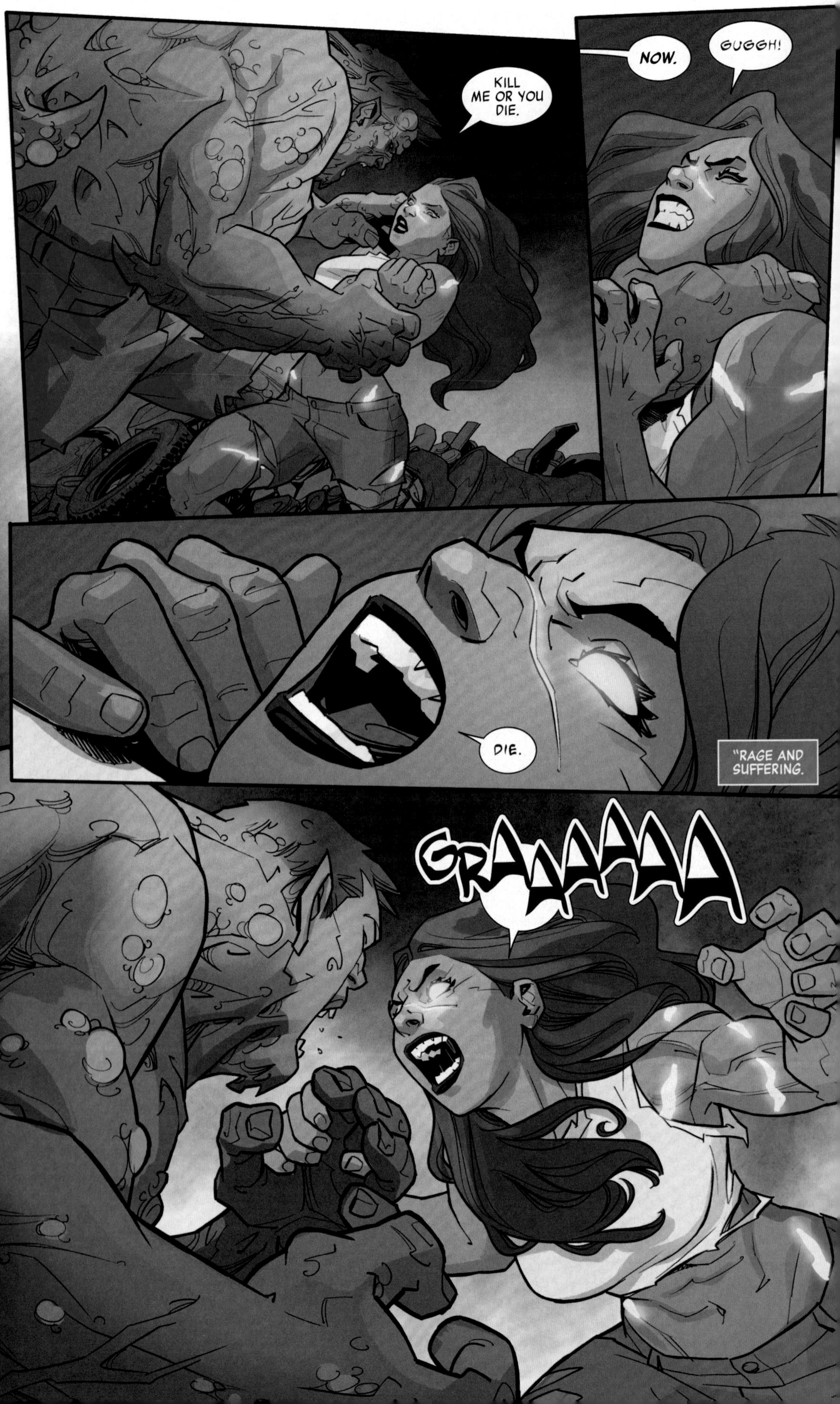
KILL ME OR YOU DIE.
NOW.
GUGGH!
DIE.
"RAGE AND SUFFERING.
GRAAAAAAA

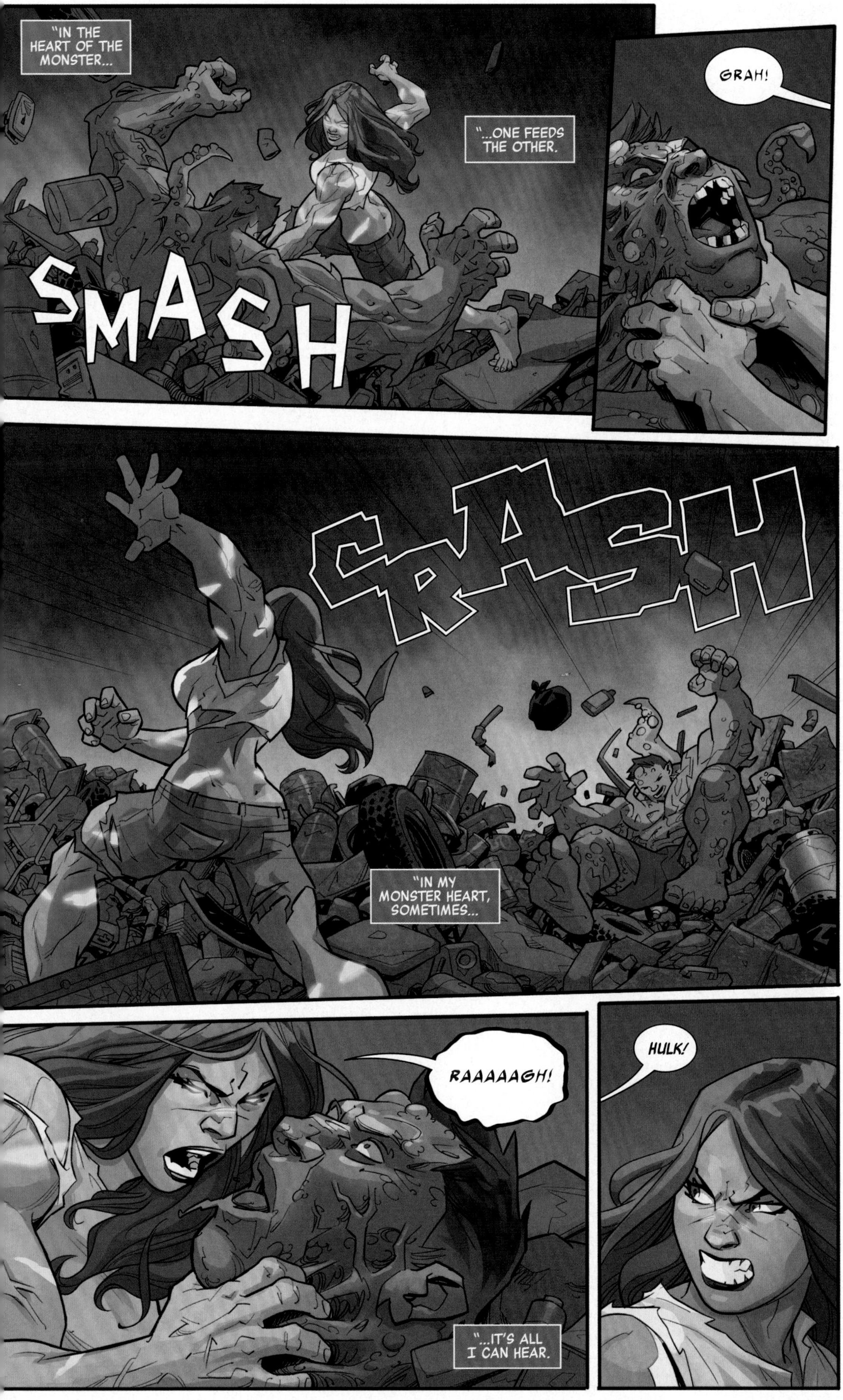
"IN THE HEART OF THE MONSTER...
SMASH
"...ONE FEEDS THE OTHER.
GRAH!
CRASH
"IN MY MONSTER HEART, SOMETIMES...
RAAAAAGH!
"...IT'S ALL I CAN HEAR.
HULK!

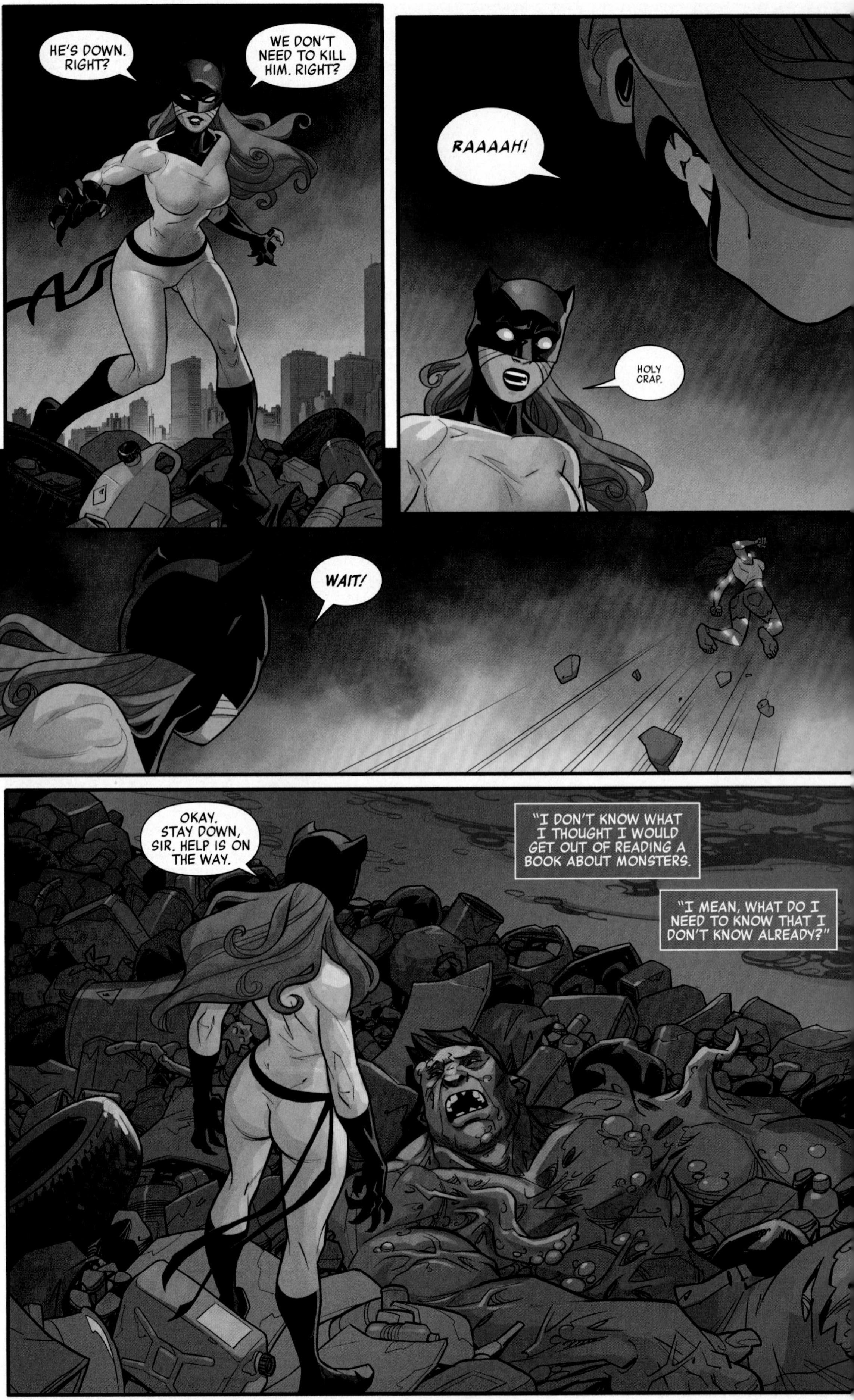
HE'S DOWN. RIGHT?
WE DON'T NEED TO KILL HIM. RIGHT?
RAAAAH!
HOLY CRAP.
WAIT!
OKAY. STAY DOWN, SIR. HELP IS ON THE WAY.
"I DON'T KNOW WHAT I THOUGHT I WOULD GET OUT OF READING A BOOK ABOUT MONSTERS.
"I MEAN, WHAT DO I NEED TO KNOW THAT I DON'T KNOW ALREADY?"

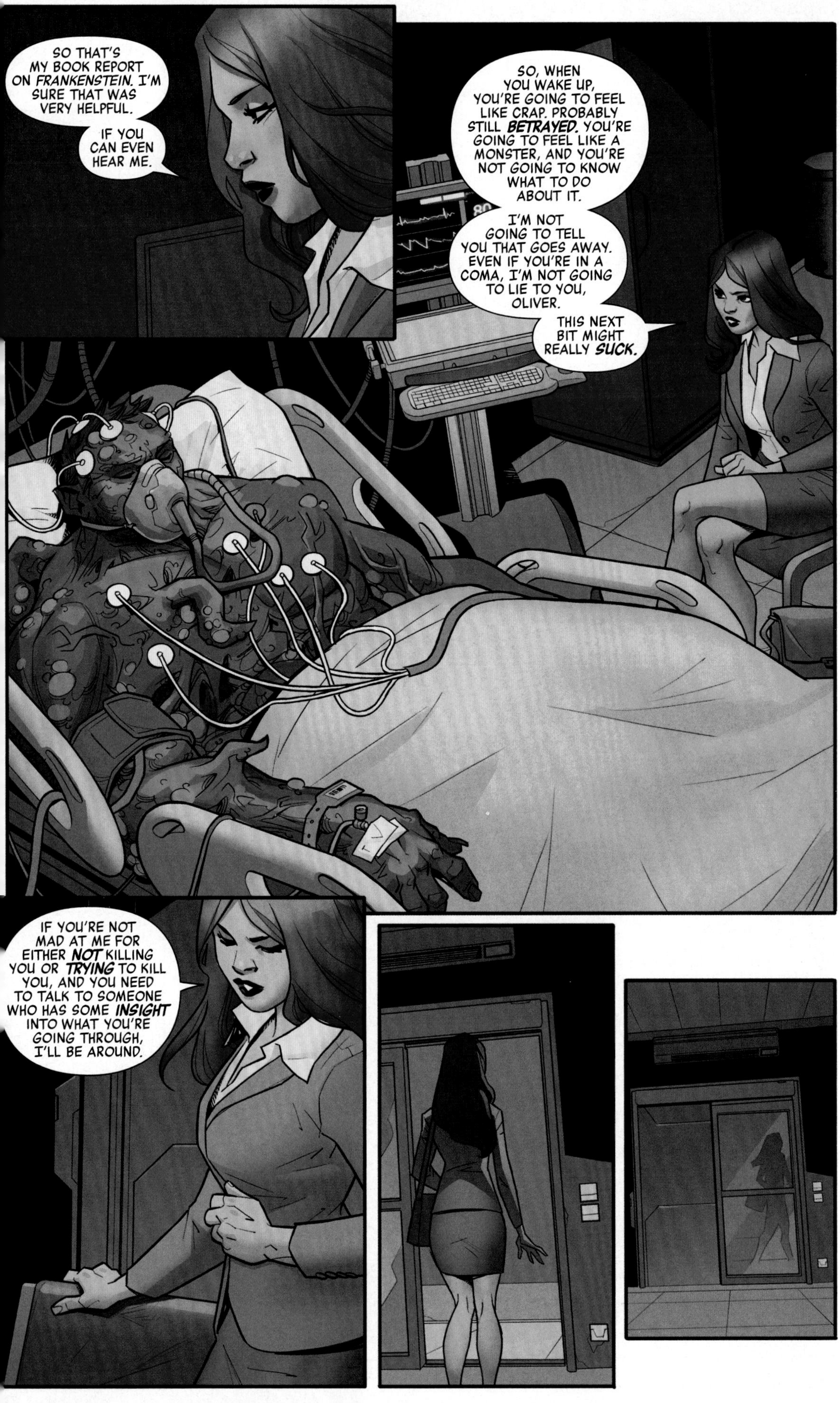

SO THAT'S MY BOOK REPORT ON *FRANKENSTEIN*. I'M SURE THAT WAS VERY HELPFUL.
IF YOU CAN EVEN HEAR ME.
SO, WHEN YOU WAKE UP, YOU'RE GOING TO FEEL LIKE CRAP. PROBABLY STILL ***BETRAYED.*** YOU'RE GOING TO FEEL LIKE A MONSTER, AND YOU'RE NOT GOING TO KNOW WHAT TO DO ABOUT IT.
I'M NOT GOING TO TELL YOU THAT GOES AWAY. EVEN IF YOU'RE IN A COMA, I'M NOT GOING TO LIE TO YOU, OLIVER.
THIS NEXT BIT MIGHT REALLY ***SUCK.***
IF YOU'RE NOT MAD AT ME FOR EITHER ***NOT*** KILLING YOU OR ***TRYING*** TO KILL YOU, AND YOU NEED TO TALK TO SOMEONE WHO HAS SOME ***INSIGHT*** INTO WHAT YOU'RE GOING THROUGH, I'LL BE AROUND.

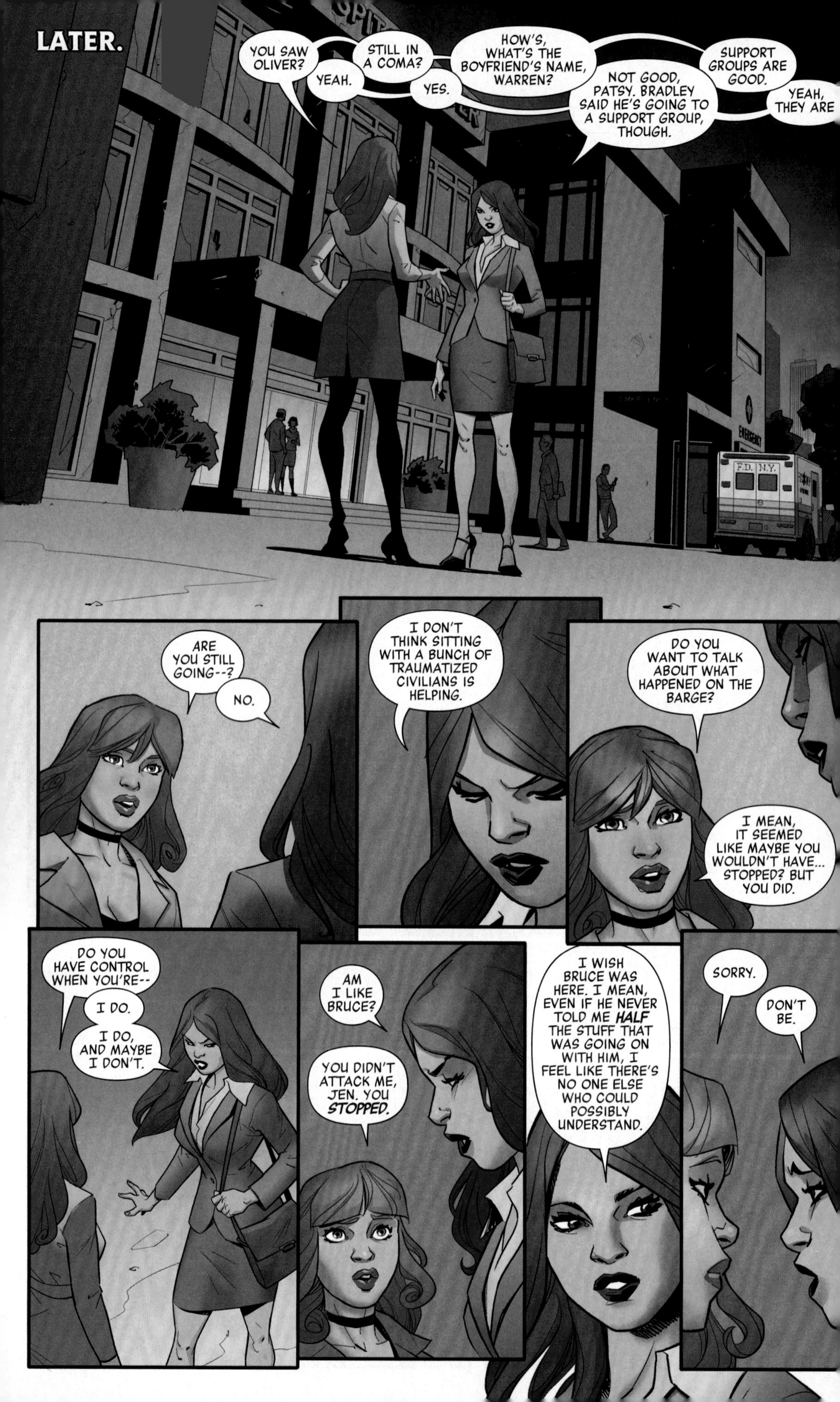
LATER.
YOU SAW OLIVER?
YEAH.
STILL IN A COMA?
YES.
HOW'S, WHAT'S THE BOYFRIEND'S NAME, WARREN?
NOT GOOD, PATSY. BRADLEY SAID HE'S GOING TO A SUPPORT GROUP, THOUGH.
SUPPORT GROUPS ARE GOOD.
YEAH, THEY ARE
EMERGENCY
F.D. N.Y.
ARE YOU STILL GOING--?
NO.
I DON'T THINK SITTING WITH A BUNCH OF TRAUMATIZED CIVILIANS IS HELPING.
DO YOU WANT TO TALK ABOUT WHAT HAPPENED ON THE BARGE?
I MEAN, IT SEEMED LIKE MAYBE YOU WOULDN'T HAVE... STOPPED? BUT YOU DID.
DO YOU HAVE CONTROL WHEN YOU'RE--
I DO.
I DO, AND MAYBE I DON'T.
AM I LIKE BRUCE?
YOU DIDN'T ATTACK ME, JEN. YOU *STOPPED.*
I WISH BRUCE WAS HERE. I MEAN, EVEN IF HE NEVER TOLD ME ***HALF*** THE STUFF THAT WAS GOING ON WITH HIM, I FEEL LIKE THERE'S NO ONE ELSE WHO COULD POSSIBLY UNDERSTAND.
SORRY.
DON'T BE.

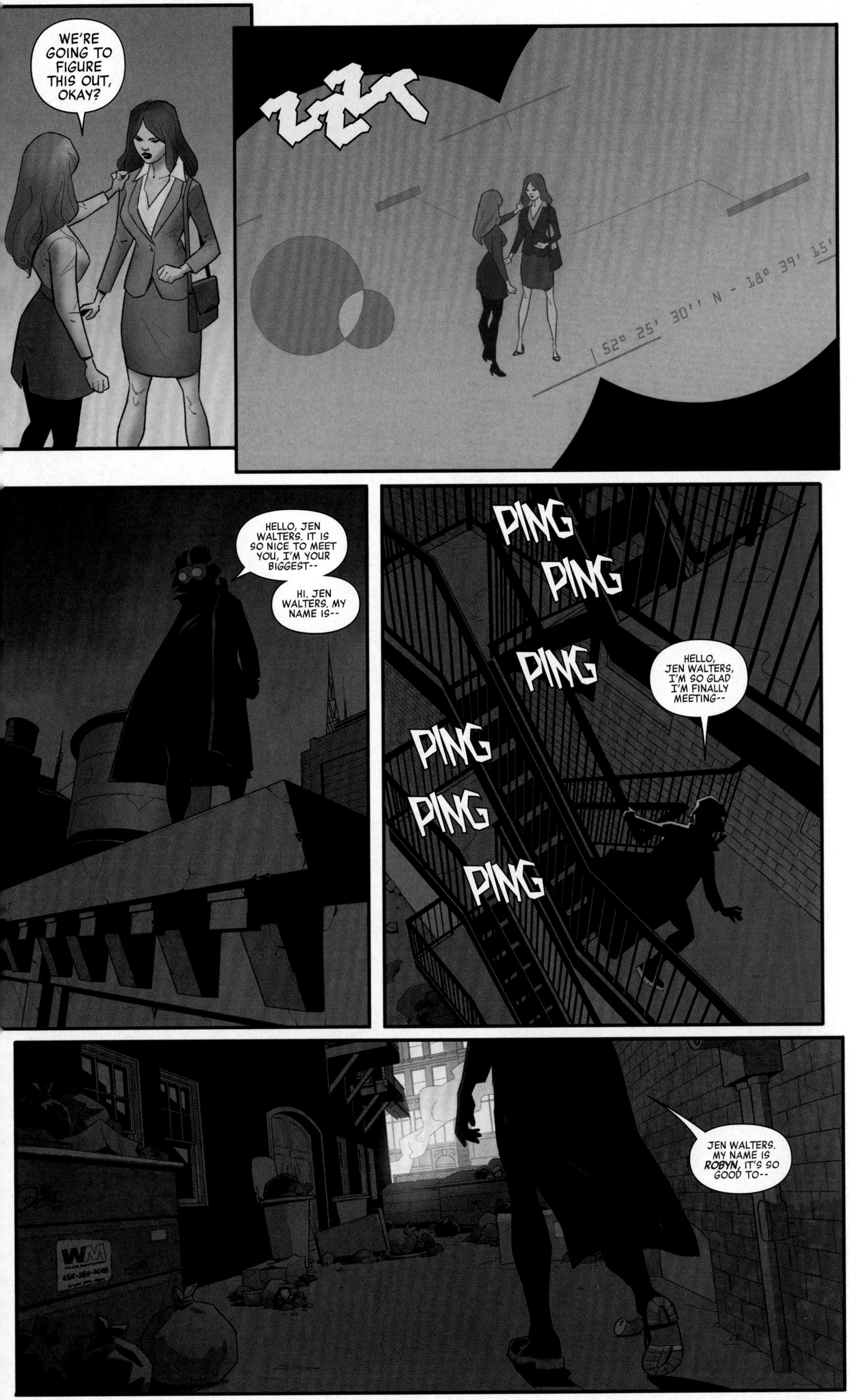
WE'RE GOING TO FIGURE THIS OUT, OKAY?
52° 25' 30'' N - 18° 39' 15'
HELLO, JEN WALTERS. IT IS SO NICE TO MEET YOU, I'M YOUR BIGGEST--
HI. JEN WALTERS. MY NAME IS--
PING
PING
PING
PING
PING
PING
HELLO, JEN WALTERS, I'M SO GLAD I'M FINALLY MEETING--
JEN WALTERS. MY NAME IS ROBYN, IT'S SO GOOD TO--

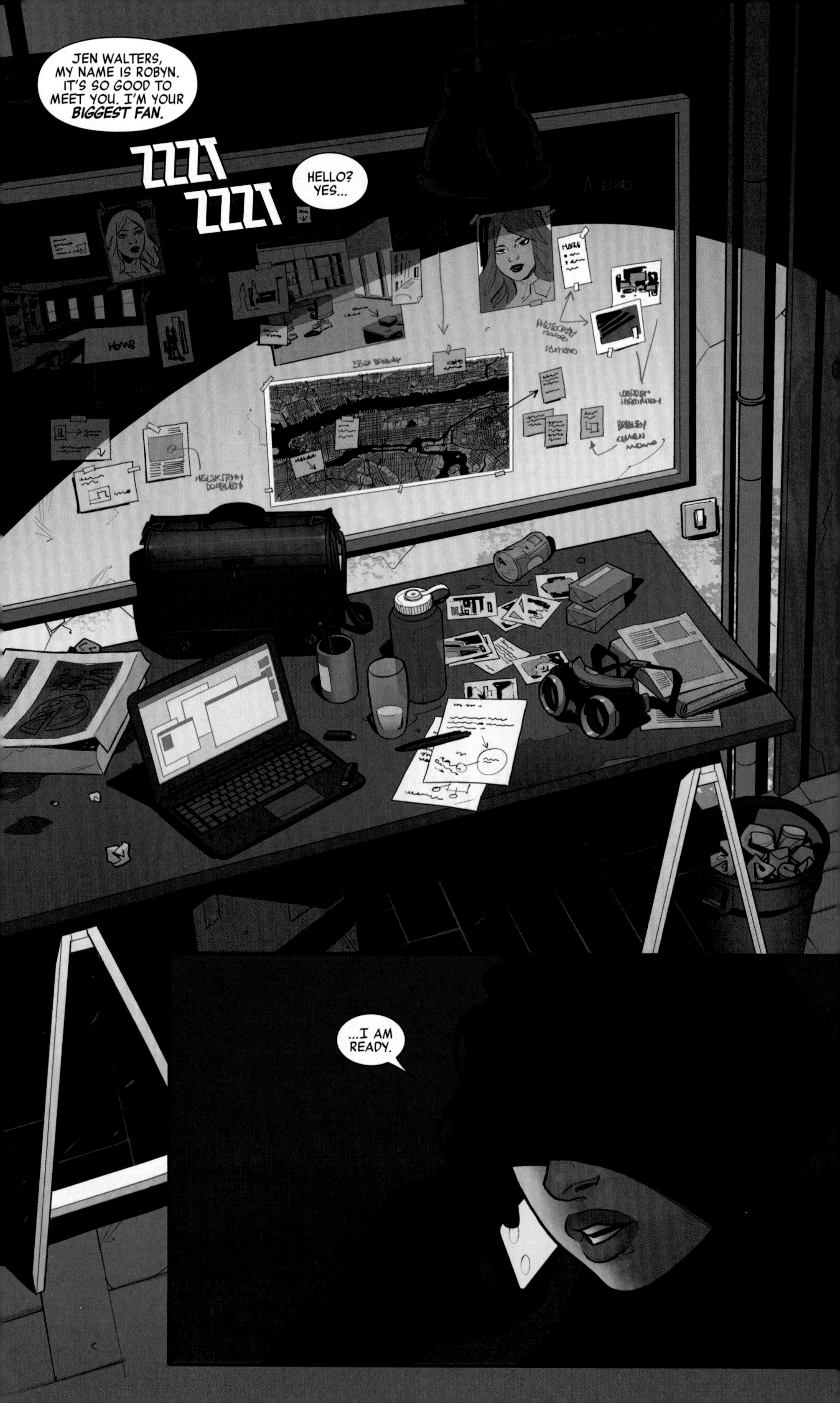

JEN WALTERS, MY NAME IS ROBYN. IT'S SO GOOD TO MEET YOU. I'M YOUR BIGGEST FAN.
ZZZZT
ZZZZT
HELLO? YES...
...I AM READY.

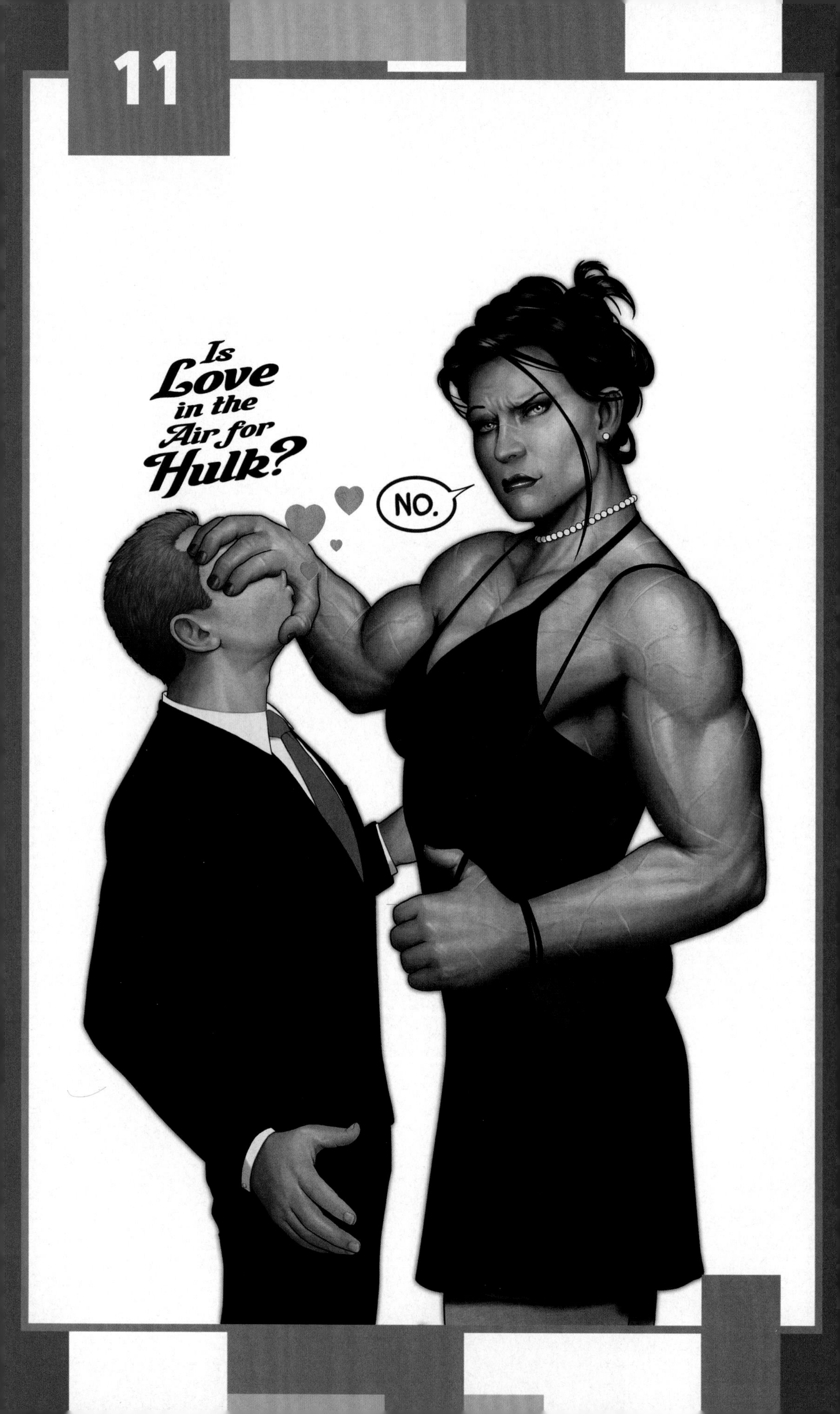
11
Is Love in the Air for Hulk?
NO.

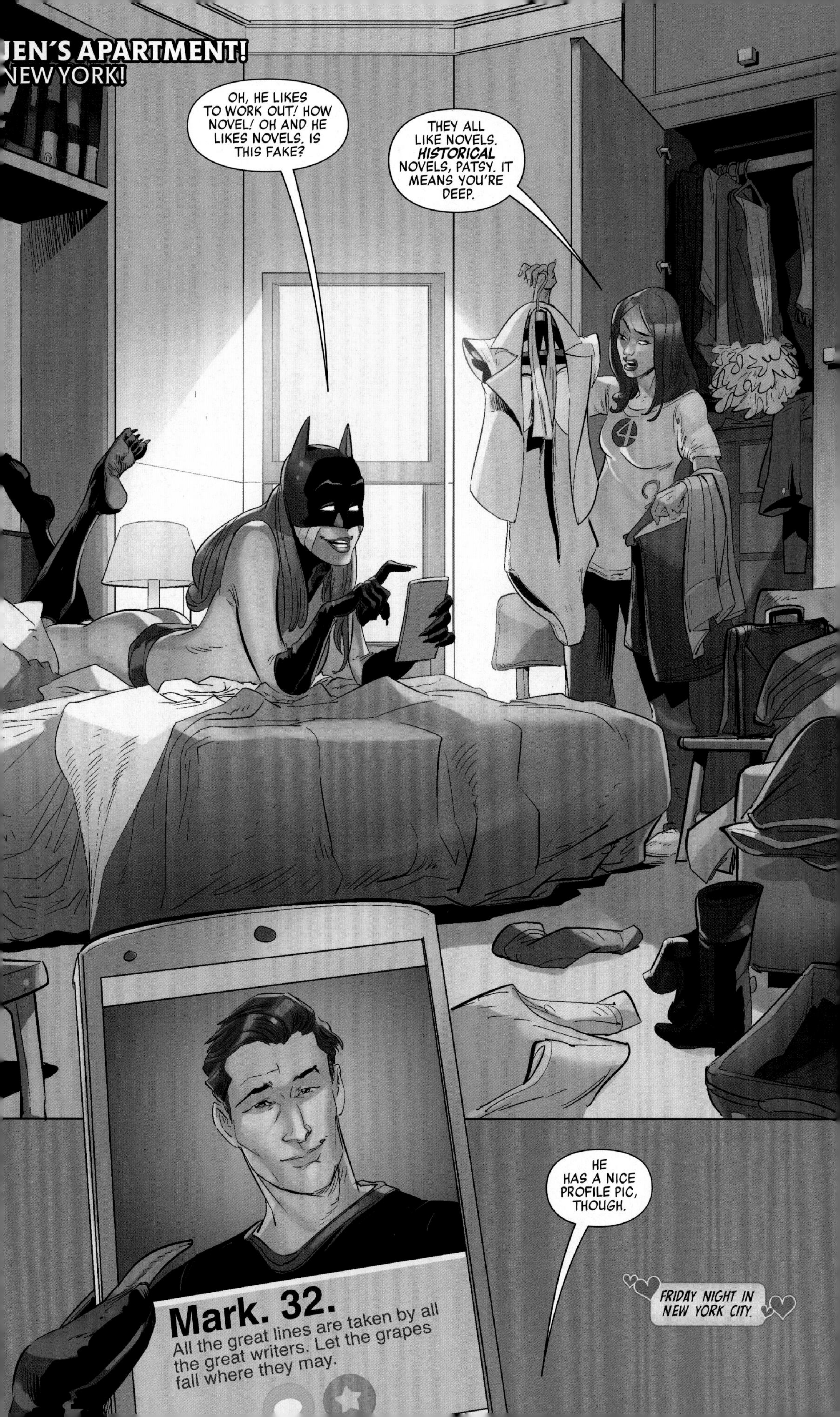

JEN'S APARTMENT!
NEW YORK!
OH, HE LIKES TO WORK OUT! HOW NOVEL! OH AND HE LIKES NOVELS. IS THIS FAKE?
THEY ALL LIKE NOVELS. HISTORICAL NOVELS, PATSY. IT MEANS YOU'RE DEEP.
Mark. 32.
All the great lines are taken by all the great writers. Let the grapes fall where they may.
HE HAS A NICE PROFILE PIC, THOUGH.
FRIDAY NIGHT IN NEW YORK CITY.

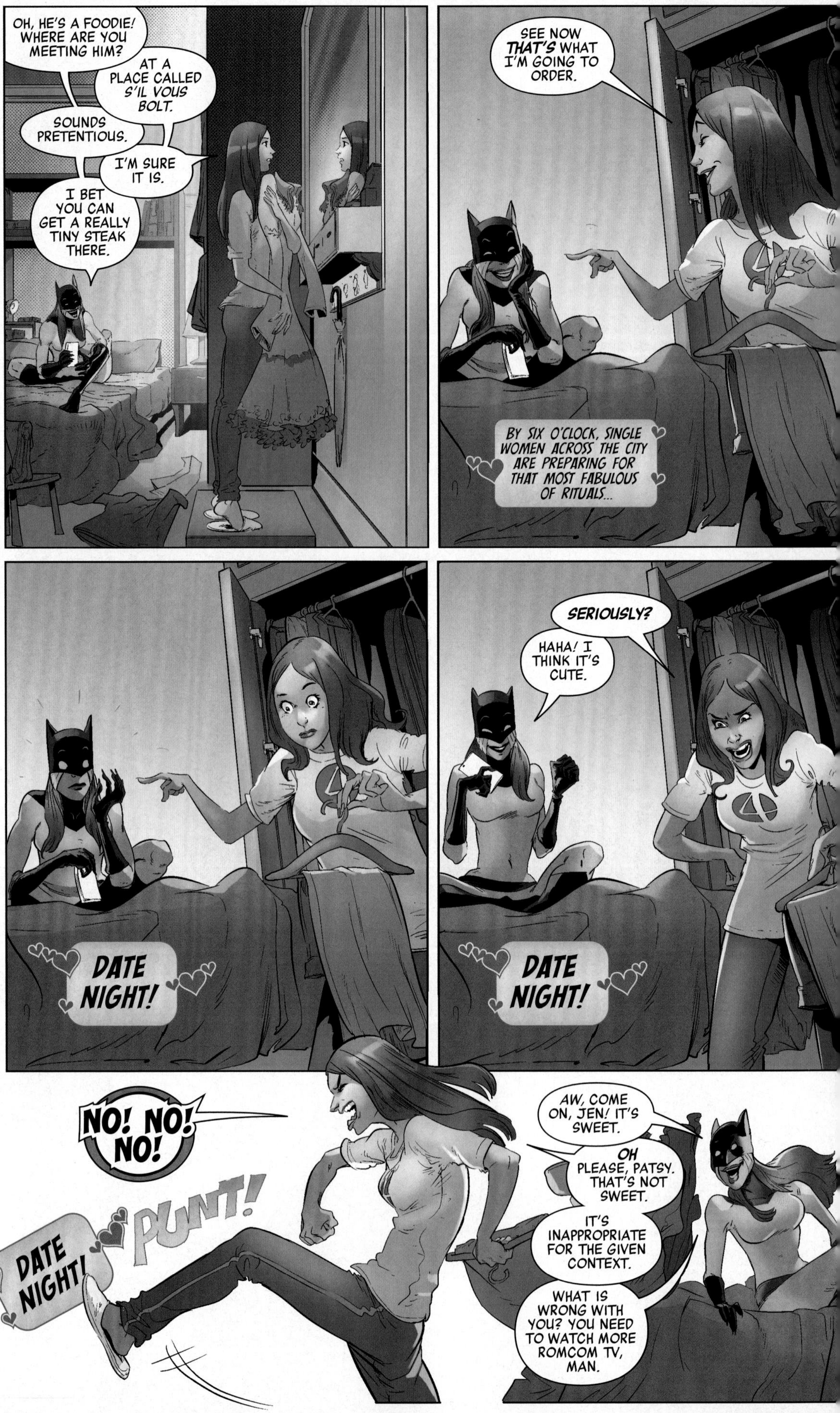

OH, HE'S A FOODIE! WHERE ARE YOU MEETING HIM?
AT A PLACE CALLED S'IL VOUS BOLT.
SOUNDS PRETENTIOUS.
I'M SURE IT IS.
I BET YOU CAN GET A REALLY TINY STEAK THERE.
SEE NOW THAT'S WHAT I'M GOING TO ORDER.
BY SIX O'CLOCK, SINGLE WOMEN ACROSS THE CITY ARE PREPARING FOR THAT MOST FABULOUS OF RITUALS...
DATE NIGHT!
SERIOUSLY?
HAHA! I THINK IT'S CUTE.
DATE NIGHT!
NO! NO! NO!
PUNT!
DATE NIGHT!
AW, COME ON, JEN! IT'S SWEET.
OH PLEASE, PATSY. THAT'S NOT SWEET.
IT'S INAPPROPRIATE FOR THE GIVEN CONTEXT.
WHAT IS WRONG WITH YOU? YOU NEED TO WATCH MORE ROMCOM TV, MAN.

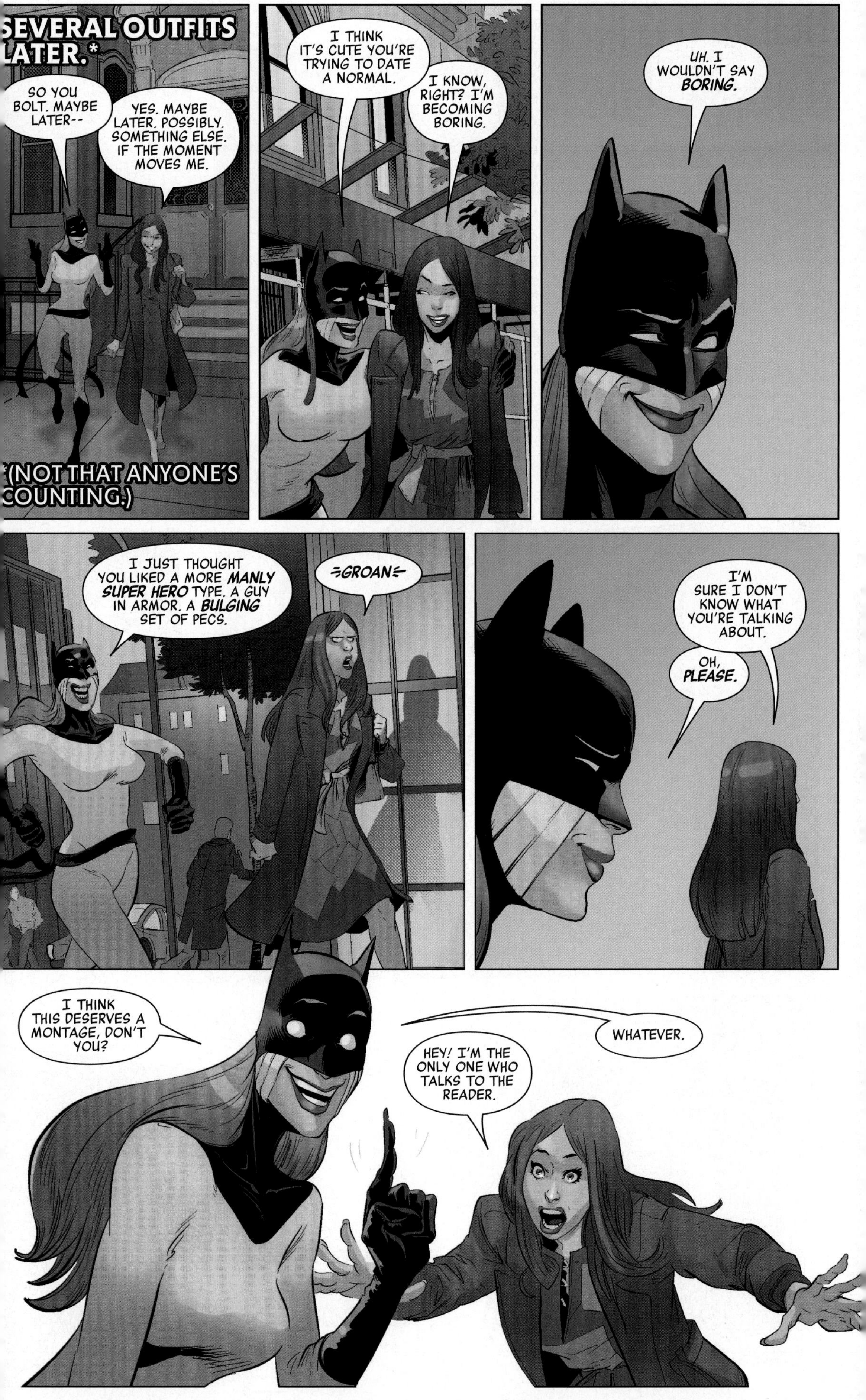

SEVERAL OUTFITS LATER.*
SO YOU BOLT. MAYBE LATER--
YES. MAYBE LATER. POSSIBLY. SOMETHING ELSE. IF THE MOMENT MOVES ME.
*(NOT THAT ANYONE'S COUNTING.)
I THINK IT'S CUTE YOU'RE TRYING TO DATE A NORMAL.
I KNOW, RIGHT? I'M BECOMING BORING.
UH. I WOULDN'T SAY *BORING.*
I JUST THOUGHT YOU LIKED A MORE *MANLY SUPER HERO* TYPE. A GUY IN ARMOR. A *BULGING* SET OF PECS.
=GROAN=
I'M SURE I DON'T KNOW WHAT YOU'RE TALKING ABOUT.
OH, *PLEASE.*
I THINK THIS DESERVES A MONTAGE, DON'T YOU?
WHATEVER.
HEY! I'M THE ONLY ONE WHO TALKS TO THE READER.

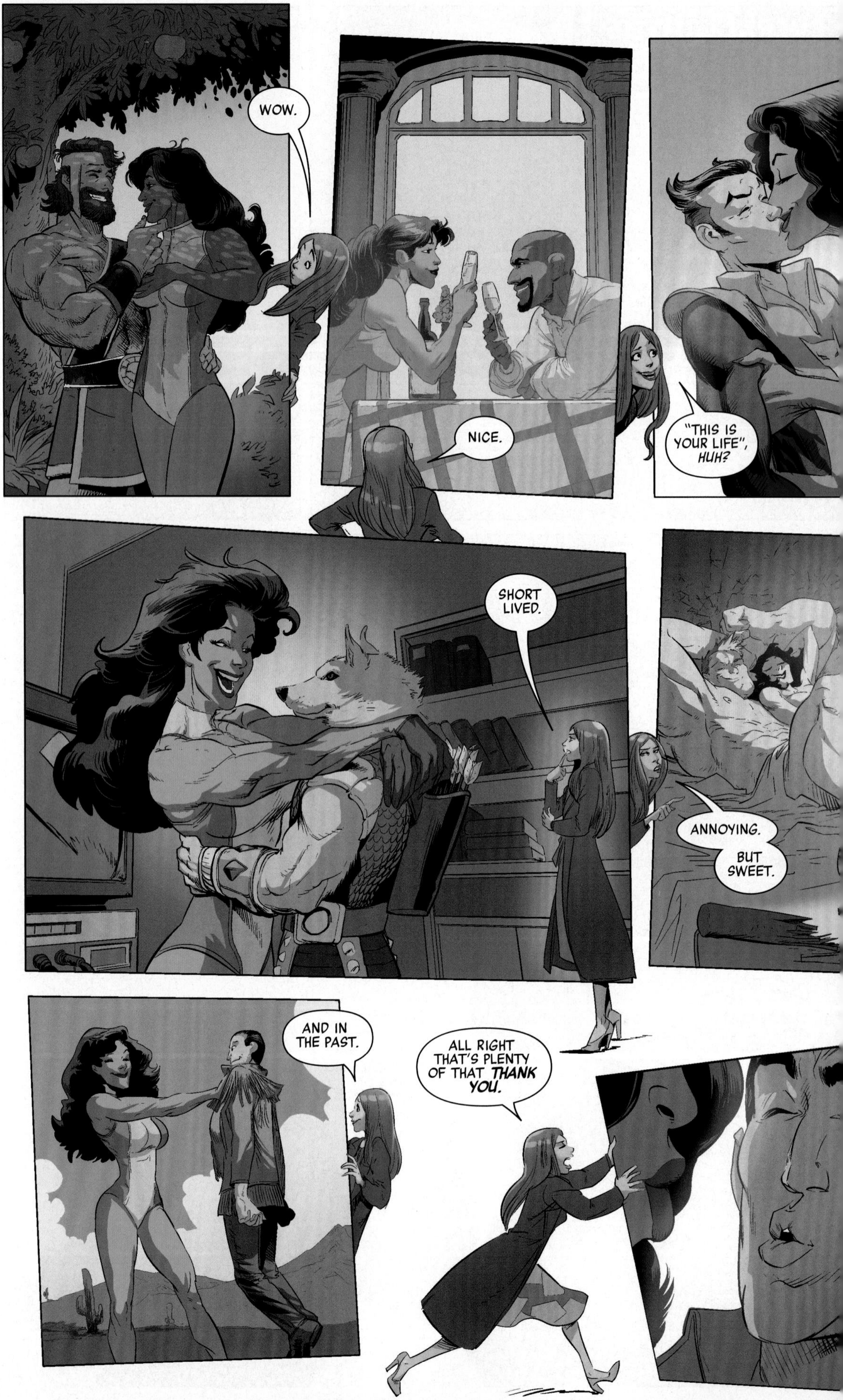
WOW.
NICE.
"THIS IS YOUR LIFE", HUH?
SHORT LIVED.
ANNOYING.
BUT SWEET.
AND IN THE PAST.
ALL RIGHT THAT'S PLENTY OF THAT THANK YOU.

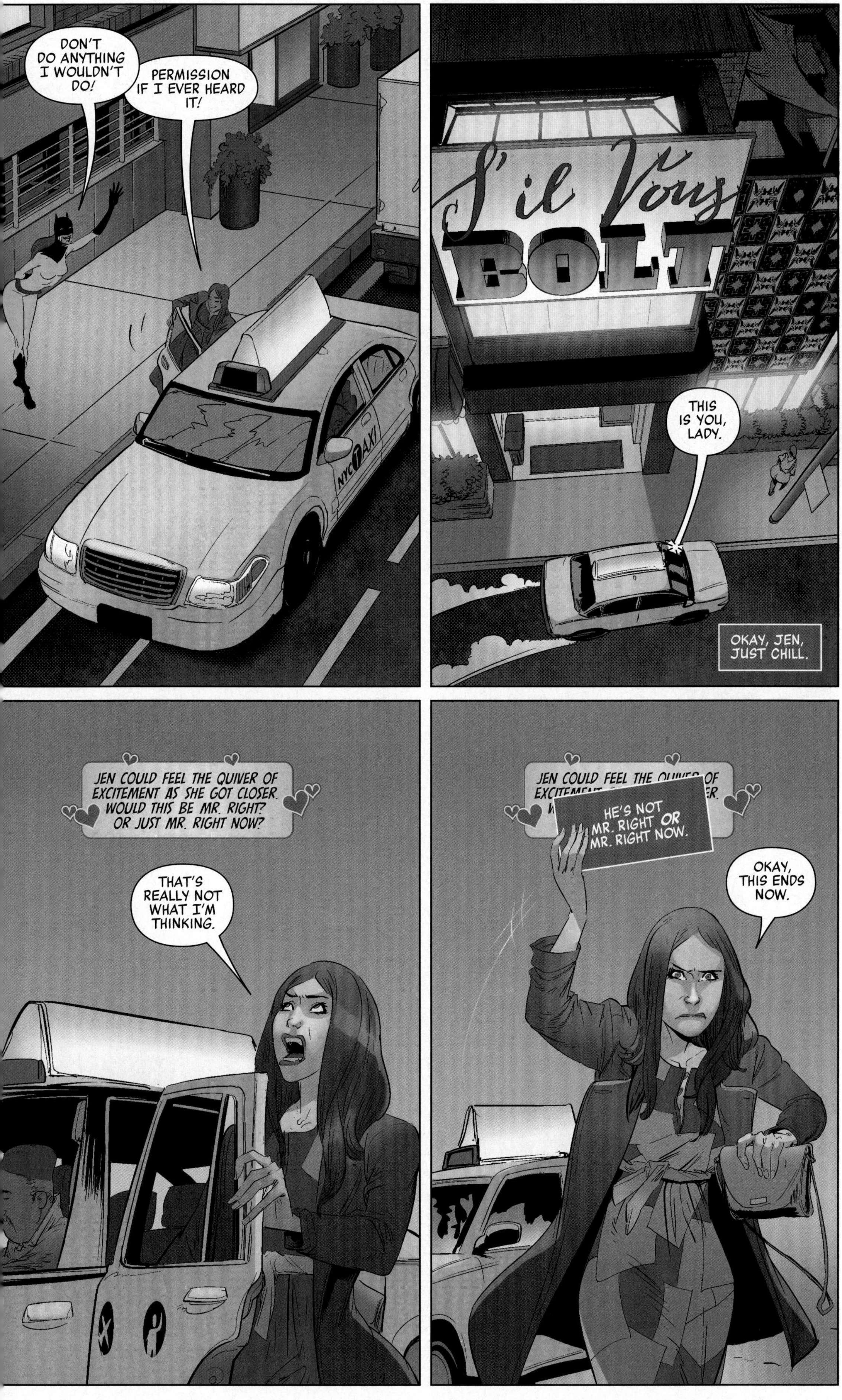
DON'T DO ANYTHING I WOULDN'T DO!
PERMISSION IF I EVER HEARD IT!
S'il Vous BOLT
THIS IS YOU, LADY.
OKAY, JEN, JUST CHILL.
JEN COULD FEEL THE QUIVER OF EXCITEMENT AS SHE GOT CLOSER. WOULD THIS BE MR. RIGHT? OR JUST MR. RIGHT NOW?
THAT'S REALLY NOT WHAT I'M THINKING.
HE'S NOT MR. RIGHT OR MR. RIGHT NOW.
OKAY, THIS ENDS NOW.

HELLO! IT'S JEN, SORRY I'M LATE.

HI! MARK! I ORDERED WINE, I HOPE THAT'S OKAY. I'M KIND OF A WINE SNOB.

JEN COULD FEEL THE QUIVER OF EXCITEMENT AS SHE GOT CLOSER. WOULD THIS BE MR. RIGHT? OR JUST MR. RIGHT NOW?

HE'S JUST A GUY AND I NEED TO GET OUT MORE.

I DIDN'T PUSH YOUR CHAIR IN.

YOU DIDN'T HAVE TO.

IT'S A GENTLEMAN THING AND I'M TRYING TO BE A GENTLEMAN.

JEN COULD FEEL THE QUIVER OF EXCITEMENT AS SHE GOT CLOSER. WOULD THIS BE MR. RIGHT? OR JUST MR. RIGHT NOW?

OBVIOUSLY I DID A FULL CRIMINAL RECORD SEARCH ON HIM. WHAT AM I, A ROOKIE?

WOW. THAT IS A *TINY* STEAK.

IS IT... OKAY?

YEAH, IT'S JUST, INSIDE JOKE. SORRY.

JEN COULD FEEL THE QUIVER OF HE WAS A GREAT DATE. COURTEOUS. FUNNY. OR JUST MR. RIGHT NOW?

SO YOU'RE STILL PRACTICING CRIMINAL LAW?

COULD SHE HOPE? COULD THIS BE... THE ONE?

YEAH IT'S... FULFILLING. I FEEL LIKE THIS CITY NEEDS BETTER CRIMINAL LAWYERS.

COUL HOPE? THIS THE O

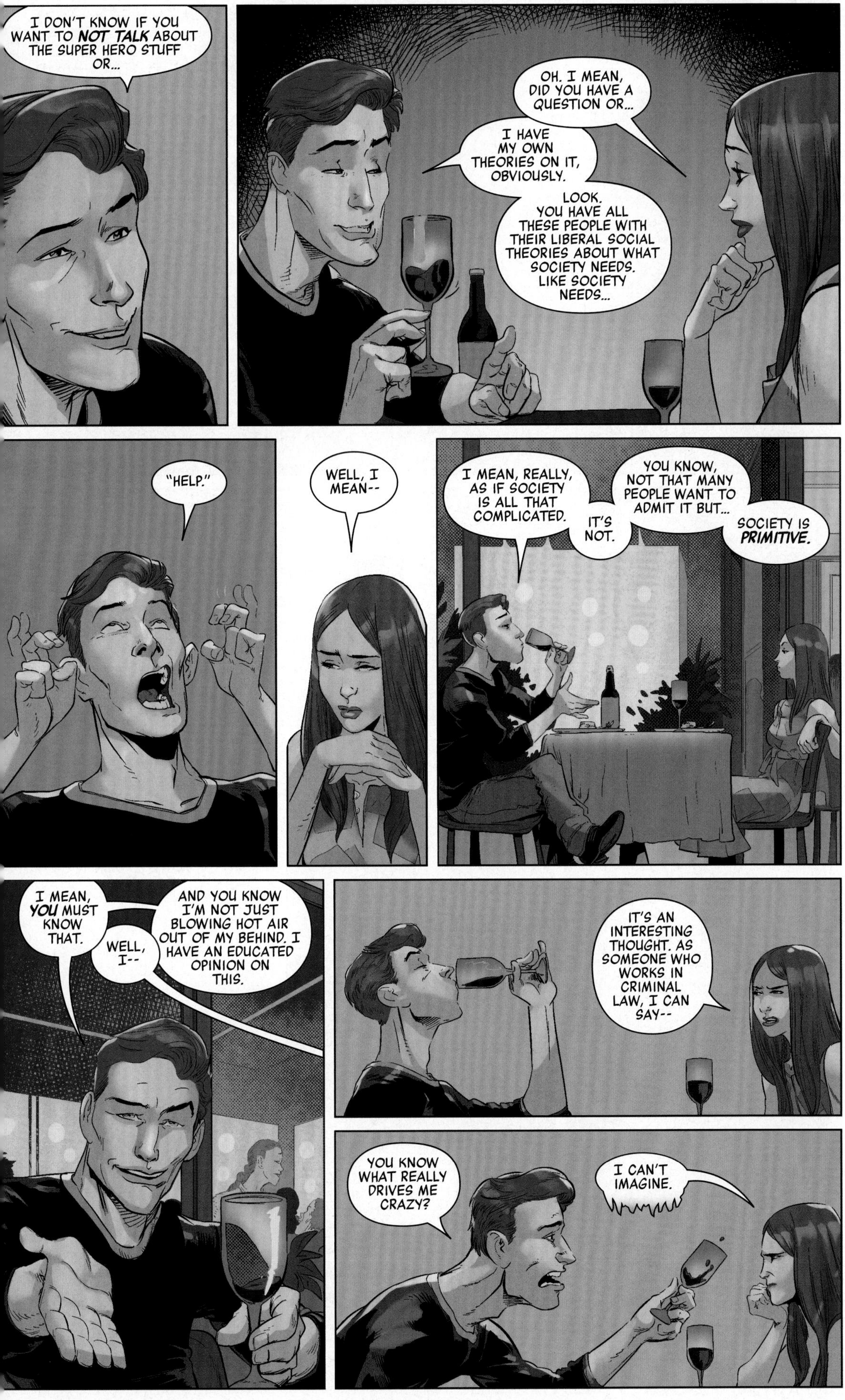

I DON'T KNOW IF YOU WANT TO **NOT TALK** ABOUT THE SUPER HERO STUFF OR...
OH. I MEAN, DID YOU HAVE A QUESTION OR...
I HAVE MY OWN THEORIES ON IT, OBVIOUSLY.
LOOK. YOU HAVE ALL THESE PEOPLE WITH THEIR LIBERAL SOCIAL THEORIES ABOUT WHAT SOCIETY NEEDS. LIKE SOCIETY NEEDS...
"HELP."
WELL, I MEAN--
I MEAN, REALLY, AS IF SOCIETY IS ALL THAT COMPLICATED.
IT'S NOT.
YOU KNOW, NOT THAT MANY PEOPLE WANT TO ADMIT IT BUT...
SOCIETY IS ***PRIMITIVE.***
I MEAN, ***YOU*** MUST KNOW THAT.
WELL, I--
AND YOU KNOW I'M NOT JUST BLOWING HOT AIR OUT OF MY BEHIND. I HAVE AN EDUCATED OPINION ON THIS.
IT'S AN INTERESTING THOUGHT. AS SOMEONE WHO WORKS IN CRIMINAL LAW, I CAN SAY--
YOU KNOW WHAT REALLY DRIVES ME CRAZY?
I CAN'T IMAGINE.

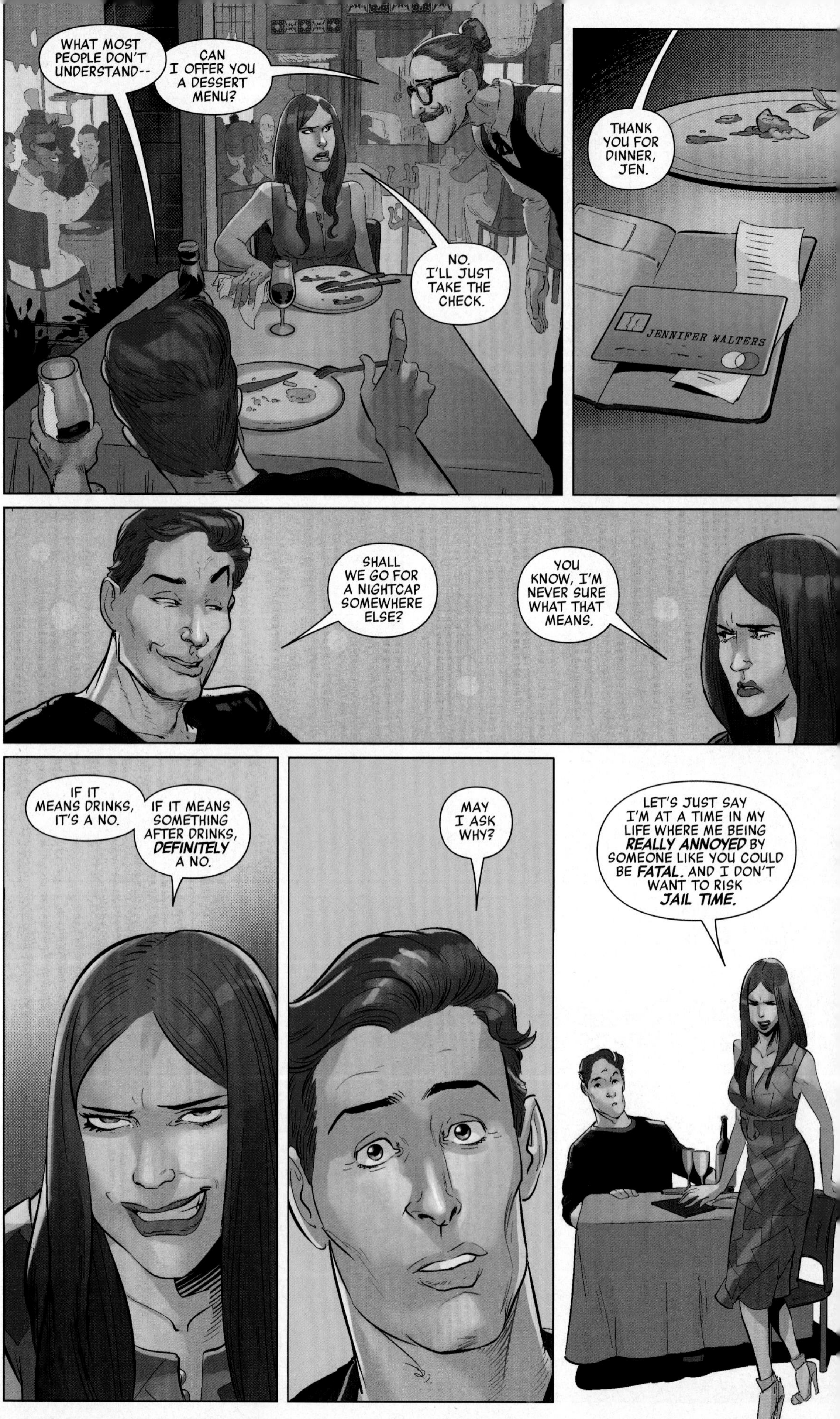
WHAT MOST PEOPLE DON'T UNDERSTAND--
CAN I OFFER YOU A DESSERT MENU?
NO. I'LL JUST TAKE THE CHECK.
THANK YOU FOR DINNER, JEN.
JENNIFER WALTERS
SHALL WE GO FOR A NIGHTCAP SOMEWHERE ELSE?
YOU KNOW, I'M NEVER SURE WHAT THAT MEANS.
IF IT MEANS DRINKS, IT'S A NO.
IF IT MEANS SOMETHING AFTER DRINKS, DEFINITELY A NO.
MAY I ASK WHY?
LET'S JUST SAY I'M AT A TIME IN MY LIFE WHERE ME BEING REALLY ANNOYED BY SOMEONE LIKE YOU COULD BE FATAL. AND I DON'T WANT TO RISK JAIL TIME.

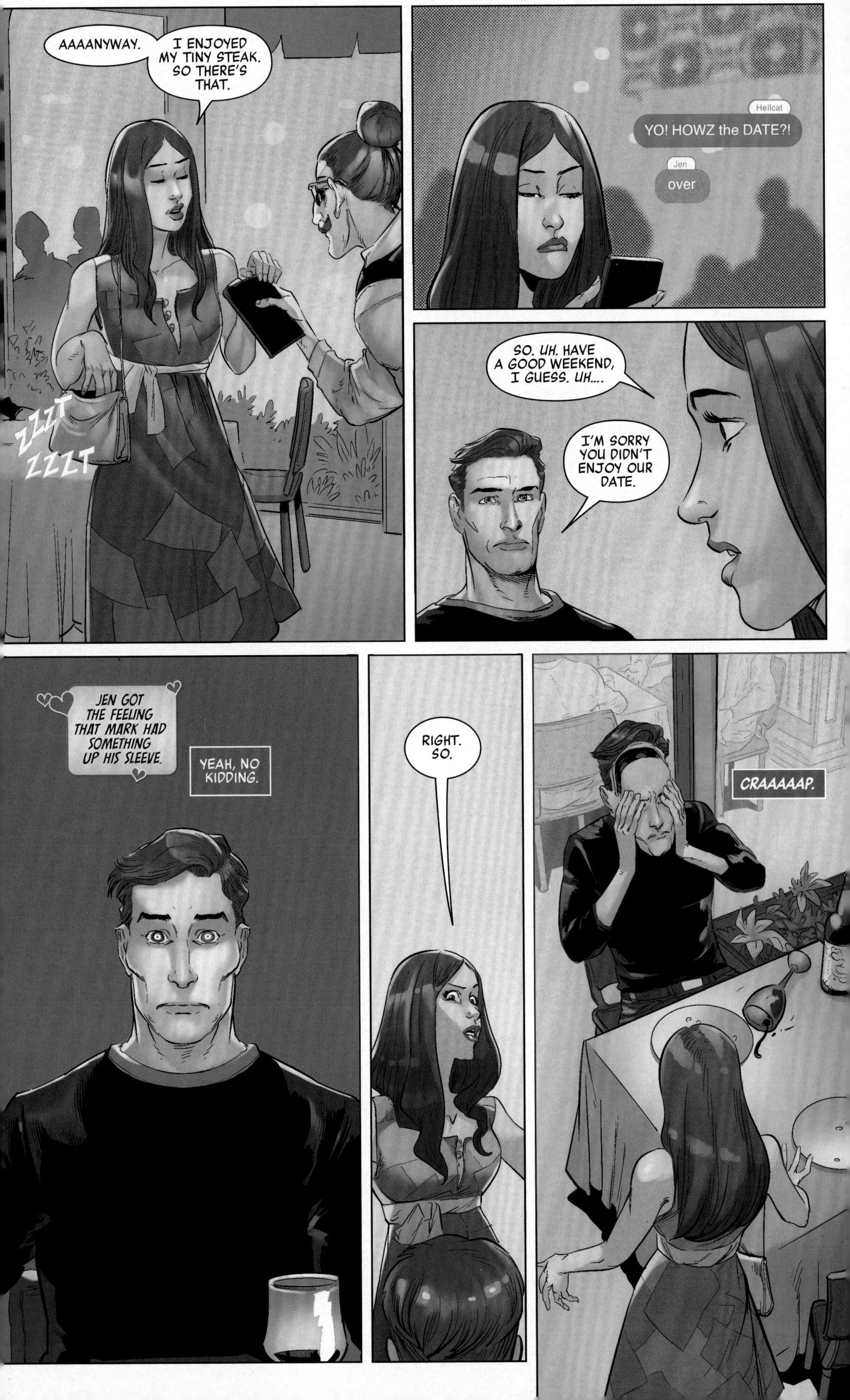

AAAANYWAY.
I ENJOYED MY TINY STEAK. SO THERE'S THAT.
ZZZT
ZZZT
Hellcat
YO! HOWZ the DATE?!
Jen
over
SO. UH. HAVE A GOOD WEEKEND, I GUESS. UH....
I'M SORRY YOU DIDN'T ENJOY OUR DATE.
JEN GOT THE FEELING THAT MARK HAD SOMETHING UP HIS SLEEVE.
YEAH, NO KIDDING.
RIGHT. SO.
CRAAAAAP.

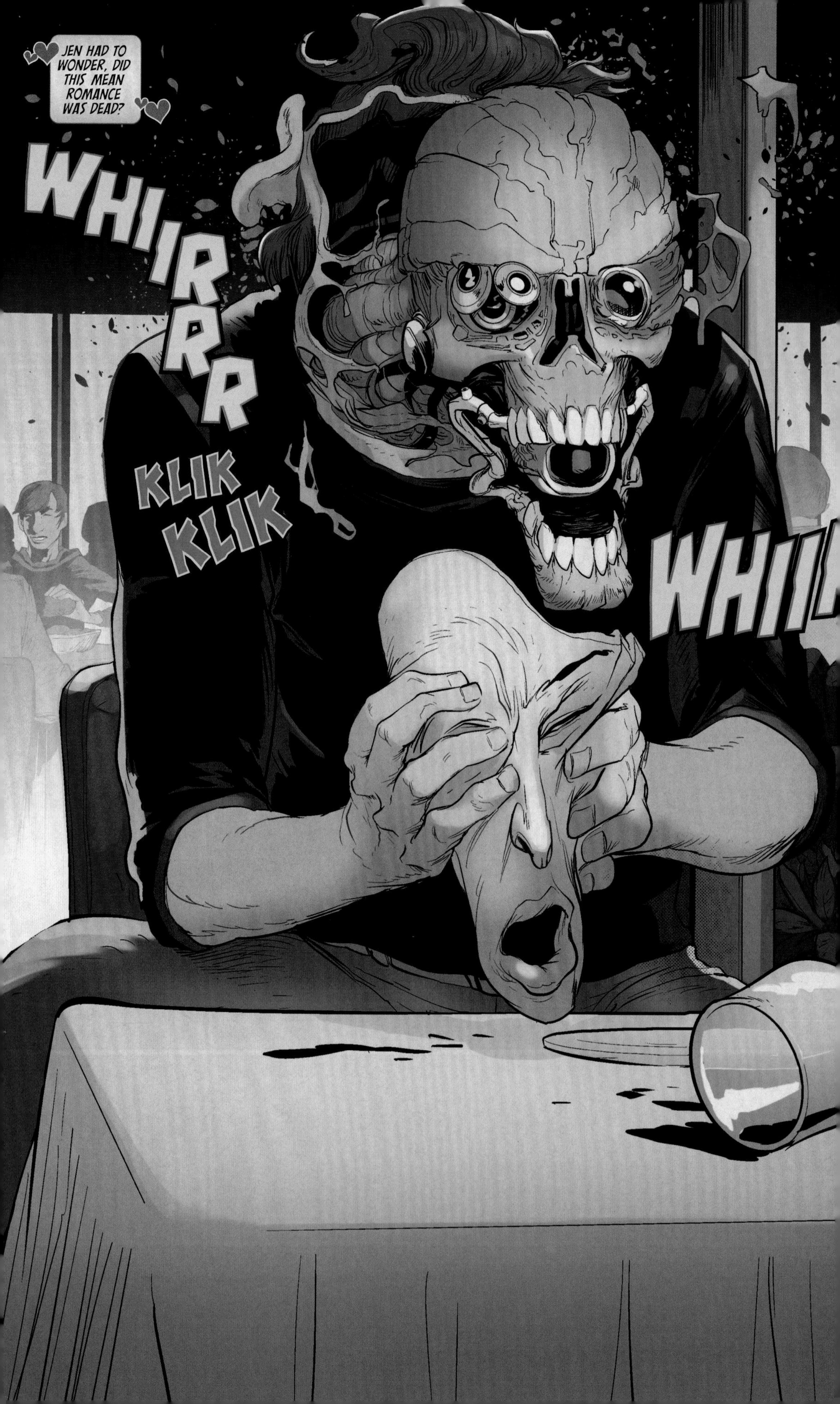
JEN HAD TO WONDER, DID THIS MEAN ROMANCE WAS DEAD?
WHIIRRR
KLIK KLIK
WHII

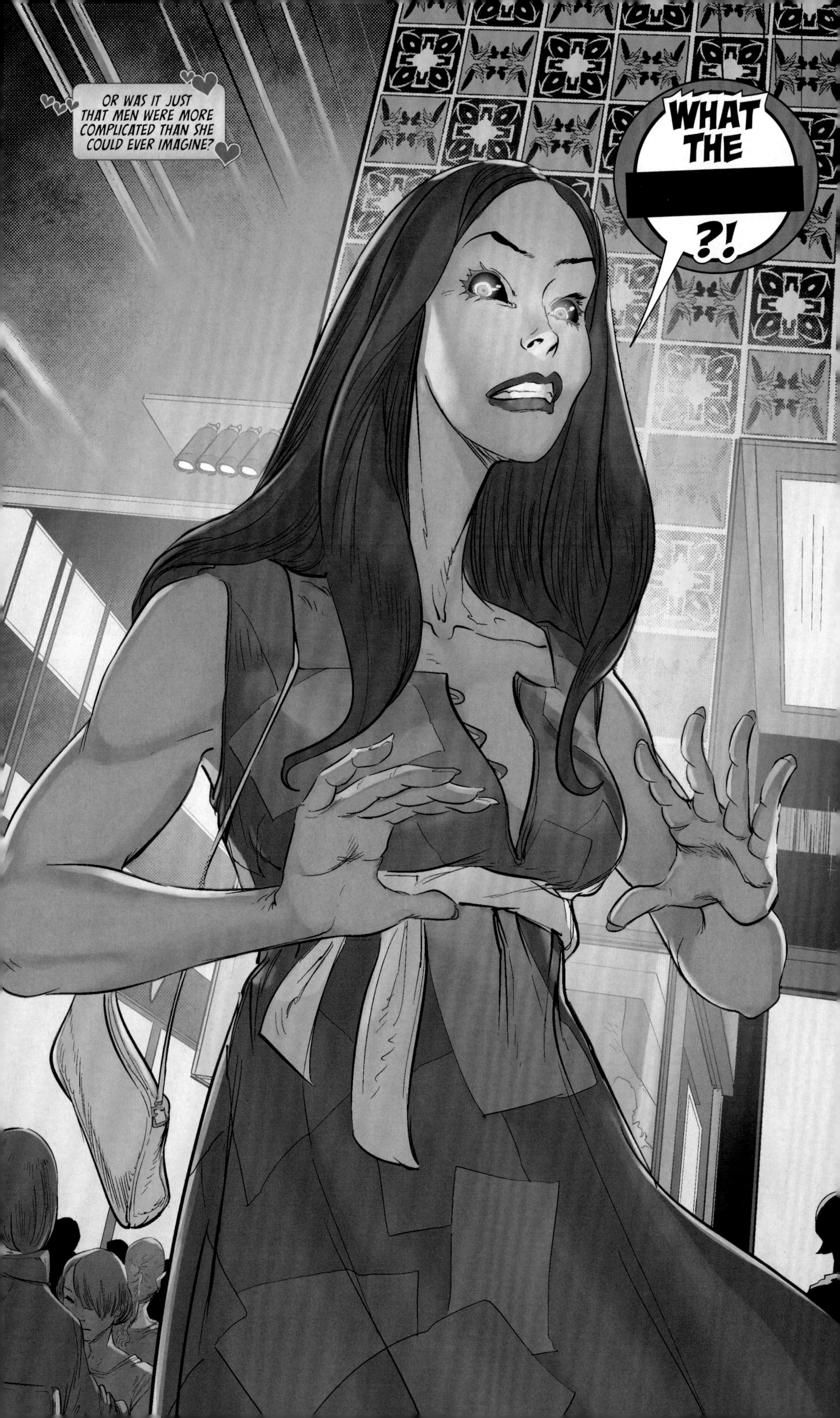
OR WAS IT JUST THAT MEN WERE MORE COMPLICATED THAN SHE COULD EVER IMAGINE?
WHAT THE [redacted] ?!

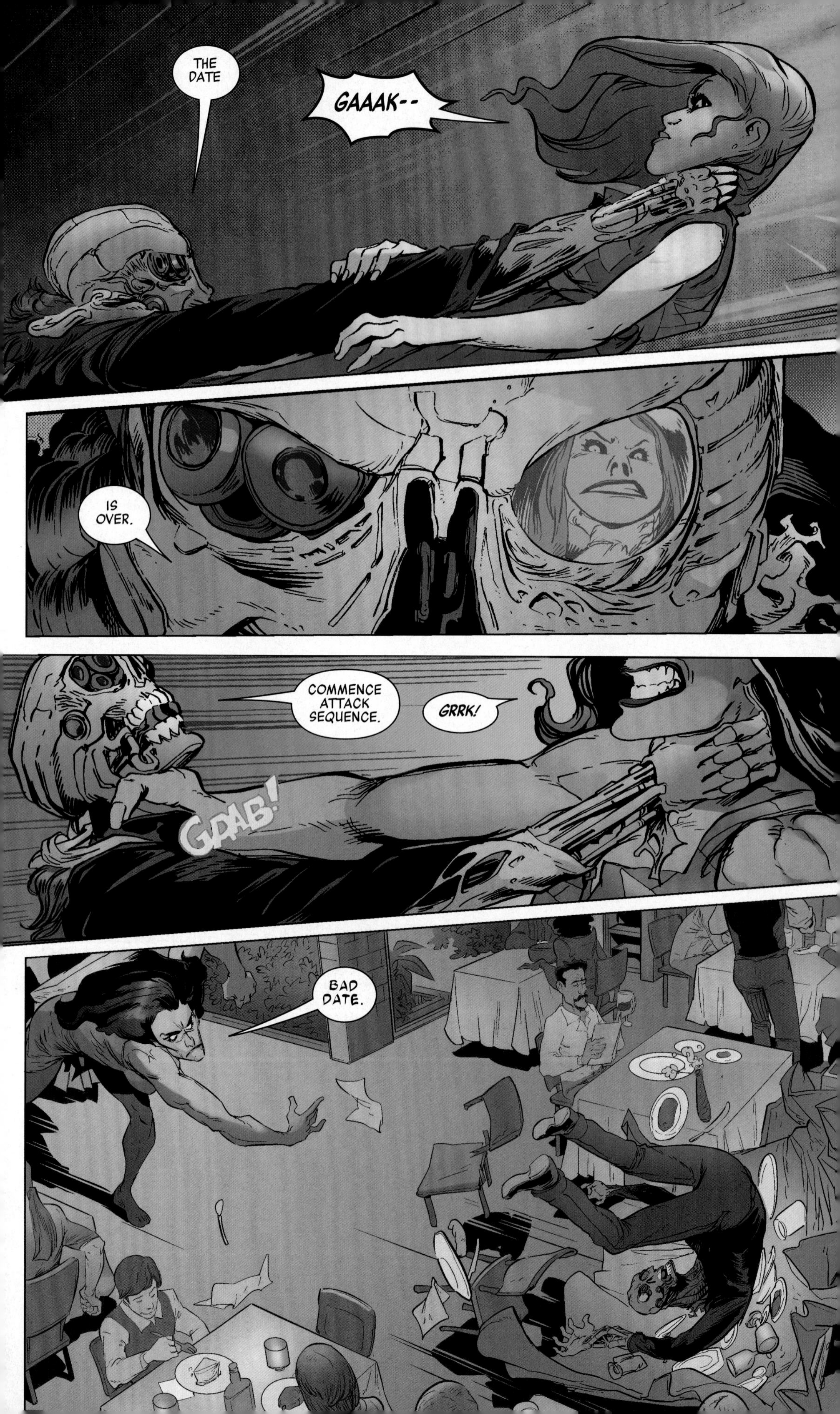
THE DATE
GAAAK--
IS OVER.
COMMENCE ATTACK SEQUENCE.
GRRK!
GRAB!
BAD DATE.

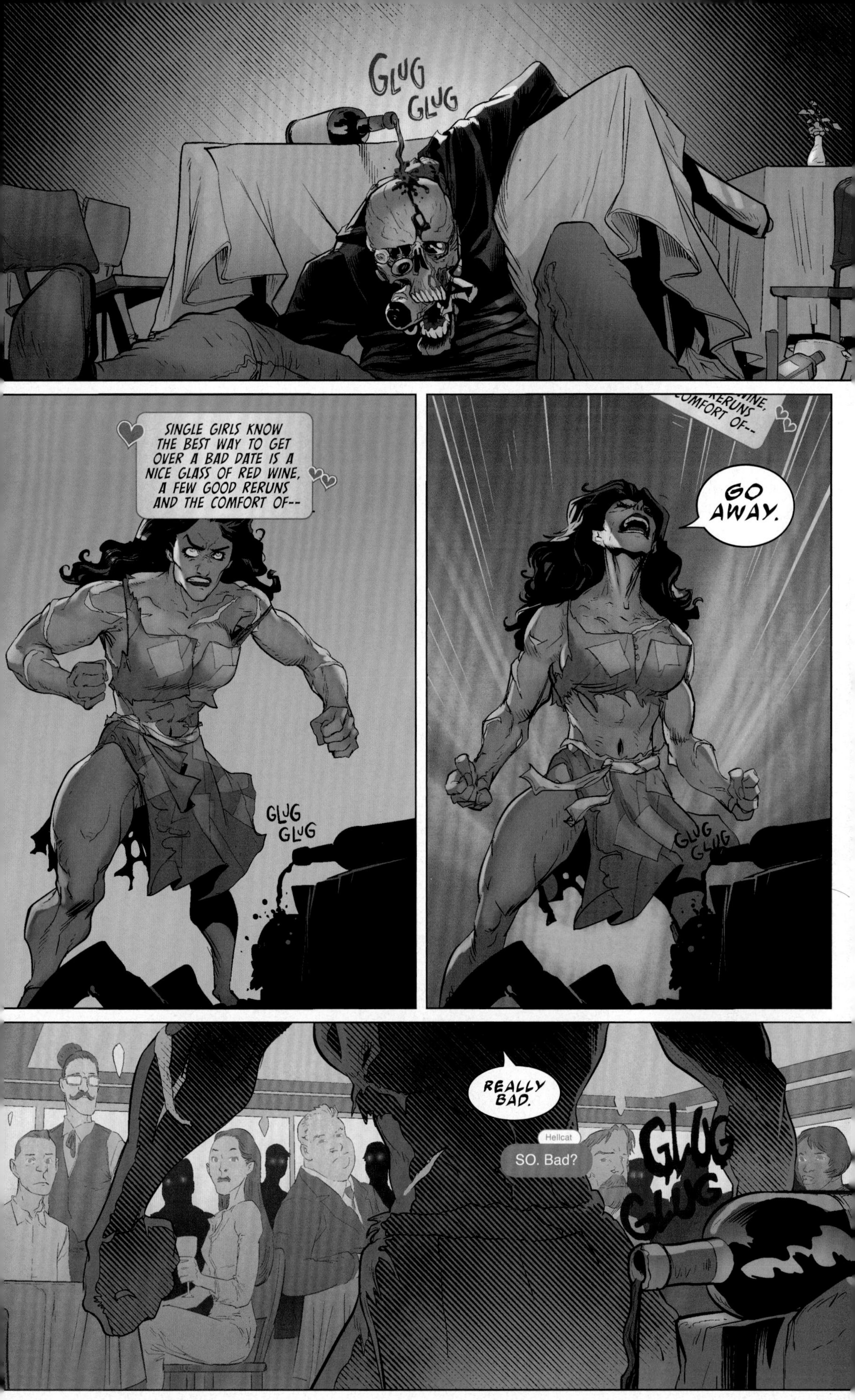
GLUG GLUG
SINGLE GIRLS KNOW THE BEST WAY TO GET OVER A BAD DATE IS A NICE GLASS OF RED WINE, A FEW GOOD RERUNS AND THE COMFORT OF--
GLUG GLUG
GO AWAY.
GLUG GLUG
REALLY BAD.
Hellcat
SO. Bad?
GLUG GLUG

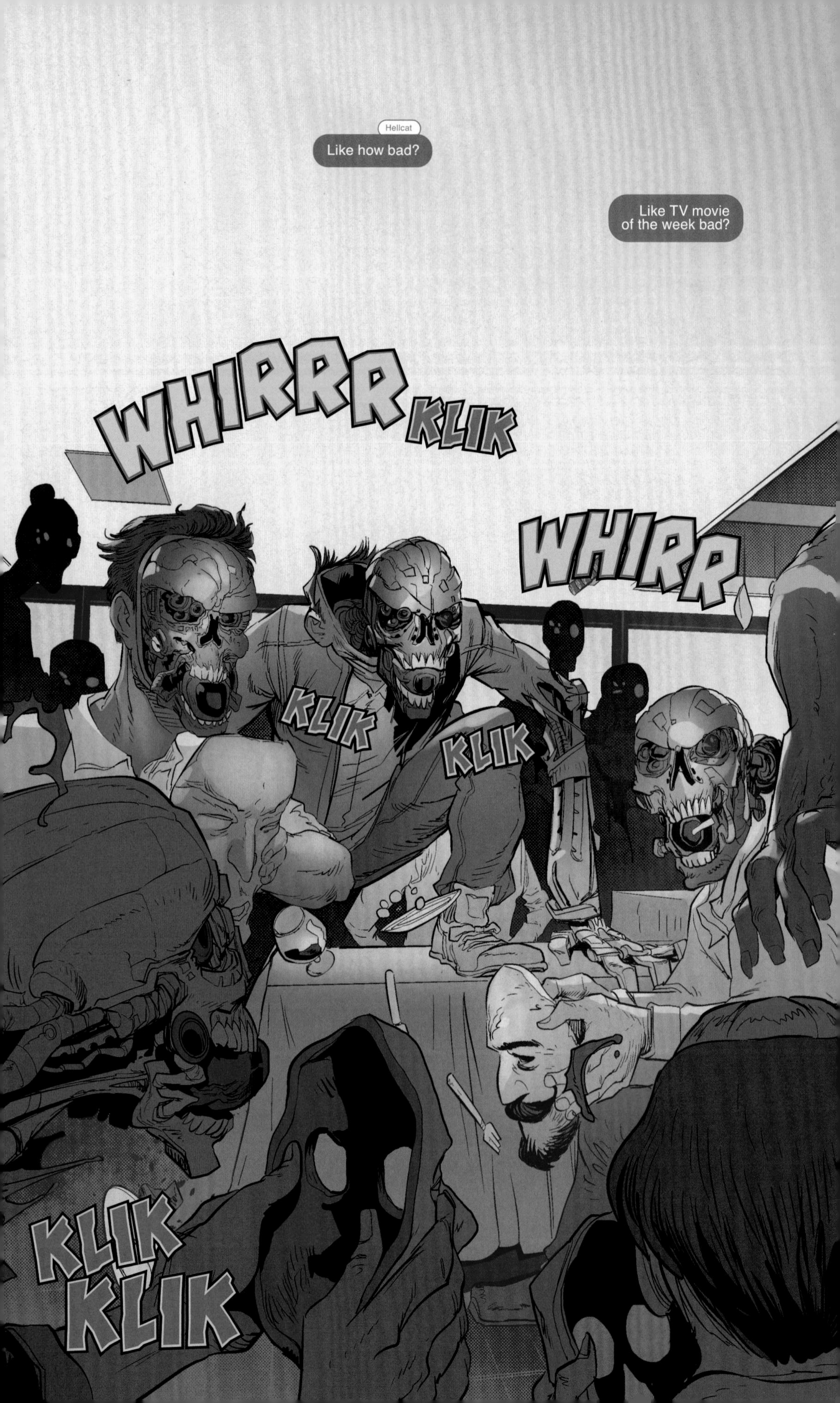

Hellcat
Like how bad?
Like TV movie of the week bad?
WHIRRR
KLIK
WHIRR
KLIK
KLIK
KLIK
KLIK

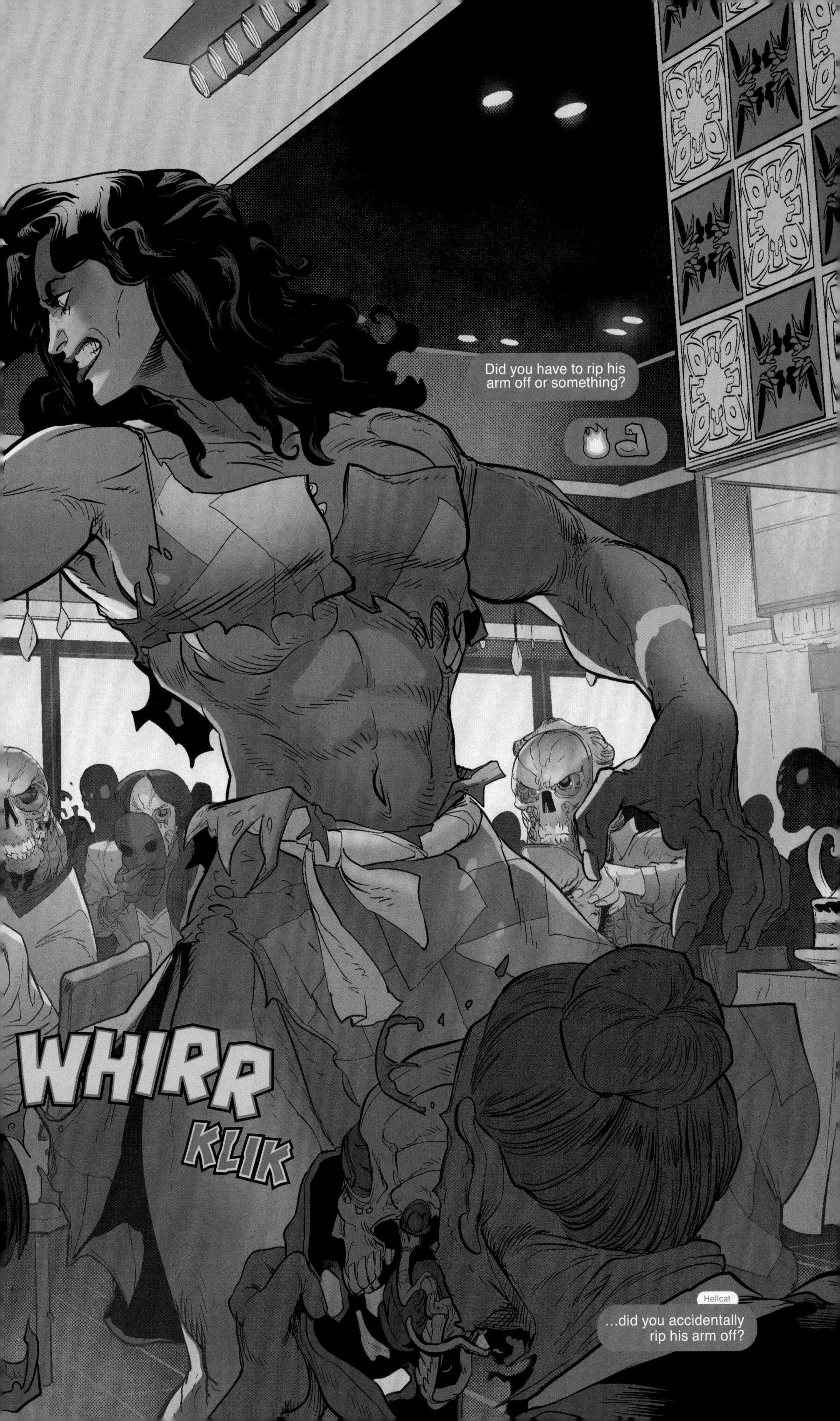
Did you have to rip his arm off or something?
WHIRR
KLIK
Hellcat
...did you accidentally rip his arm off?

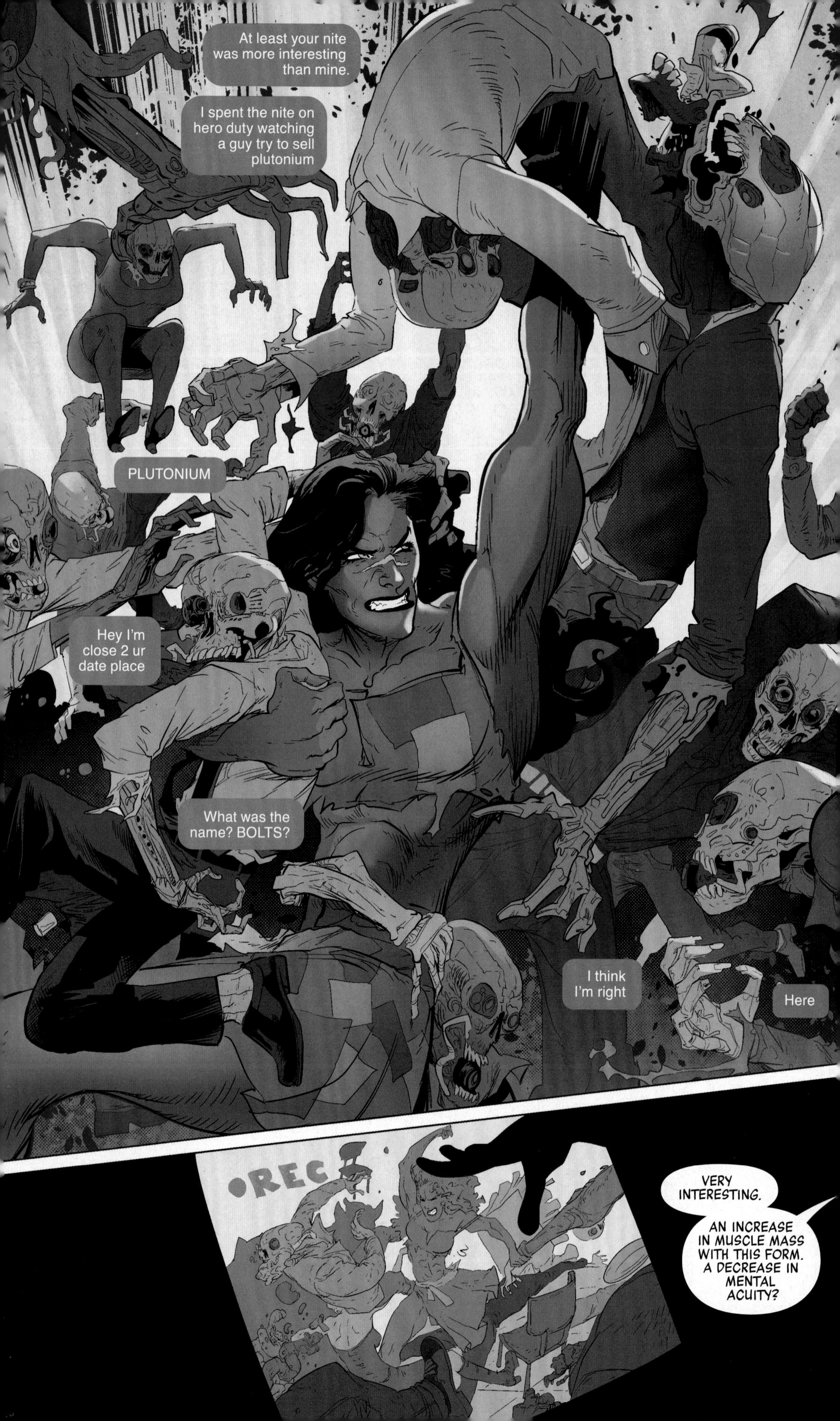
At least your nite was more interesting than mine.
I spent the nite on hero duty watching a guy try to sell plutonium
PLUTONIUM
Hey I'm close 2 ur date place
What was the name? BOLTS?
I think I'm right
Here
REC
VERY INTERESTING.
AN INCREASE IN MUSCLE MASS WITH THIS FORM. A DECREASE IN MENTAL ACUITY?

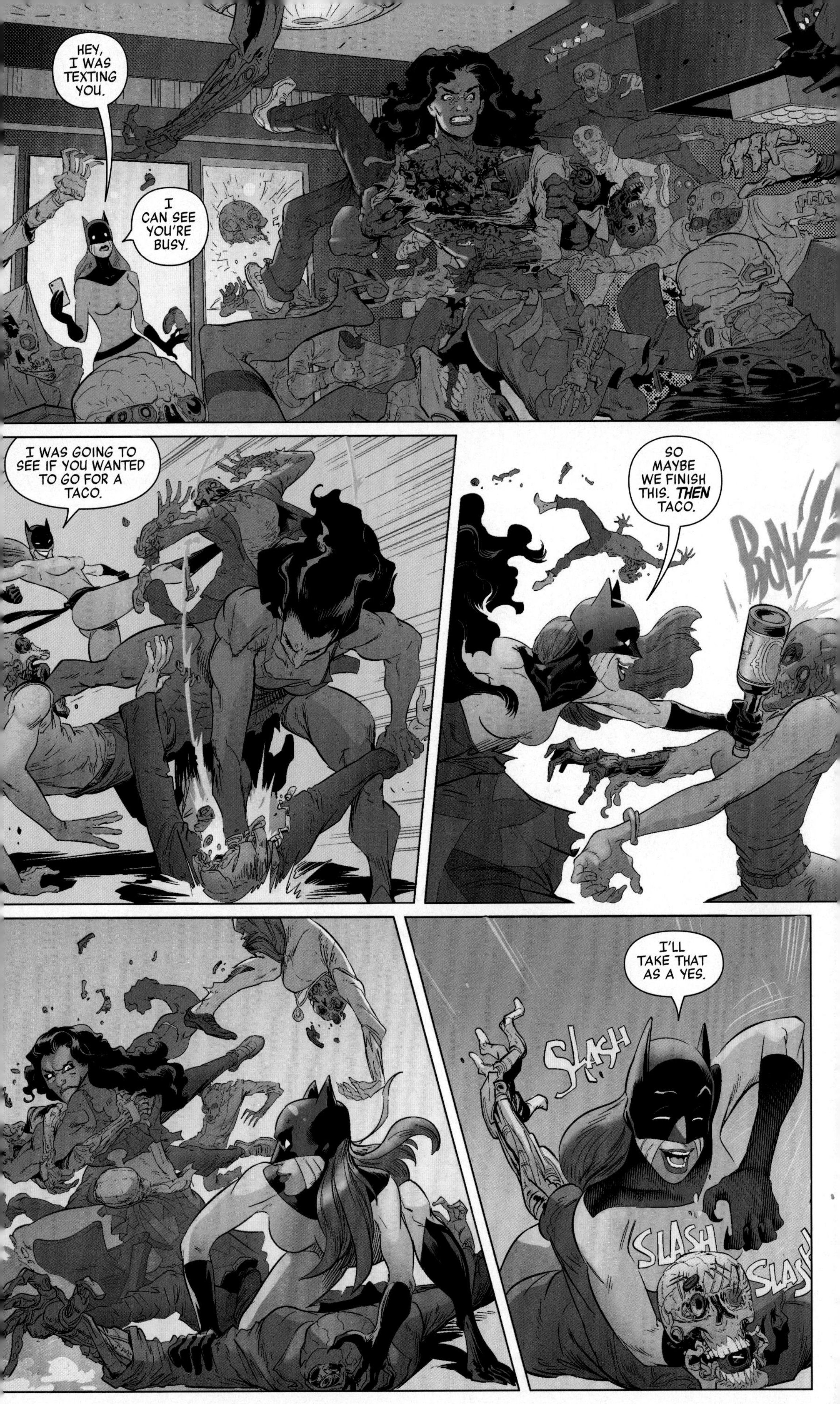
HEY, I WAS TEXTING YOU.
I CAN SEE YOU'RE BUSY.
I WAS GOING TO SEE IF YOU WANTED TO GO FOR A TACO.
SO MAYBE WE FINISH THIS. THEN TACO.
I'LL TAKE THAT AS A YES.
SLASH
SLASH

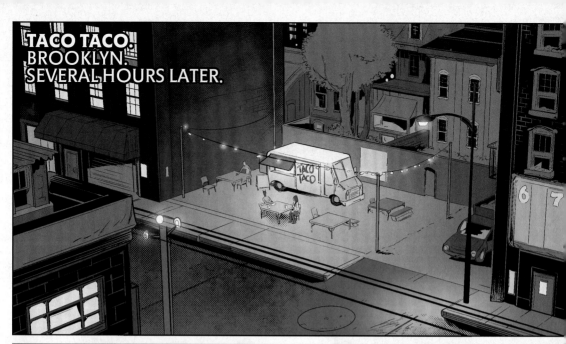

TACO TACO: BROOKLYN. SEVERAL HOURS LATER.

WAS IT AN EXPENSIVE DRESS?

EHH. YOU KNOW, PART OF THE DEAL.

I CAN'T HAVE NICE THINGS.

SO. BAD DATE?

NOT GREAT, NO.

GOOD STEAK, THOUGH.

SO, NOT A COMPLETE LOSS.

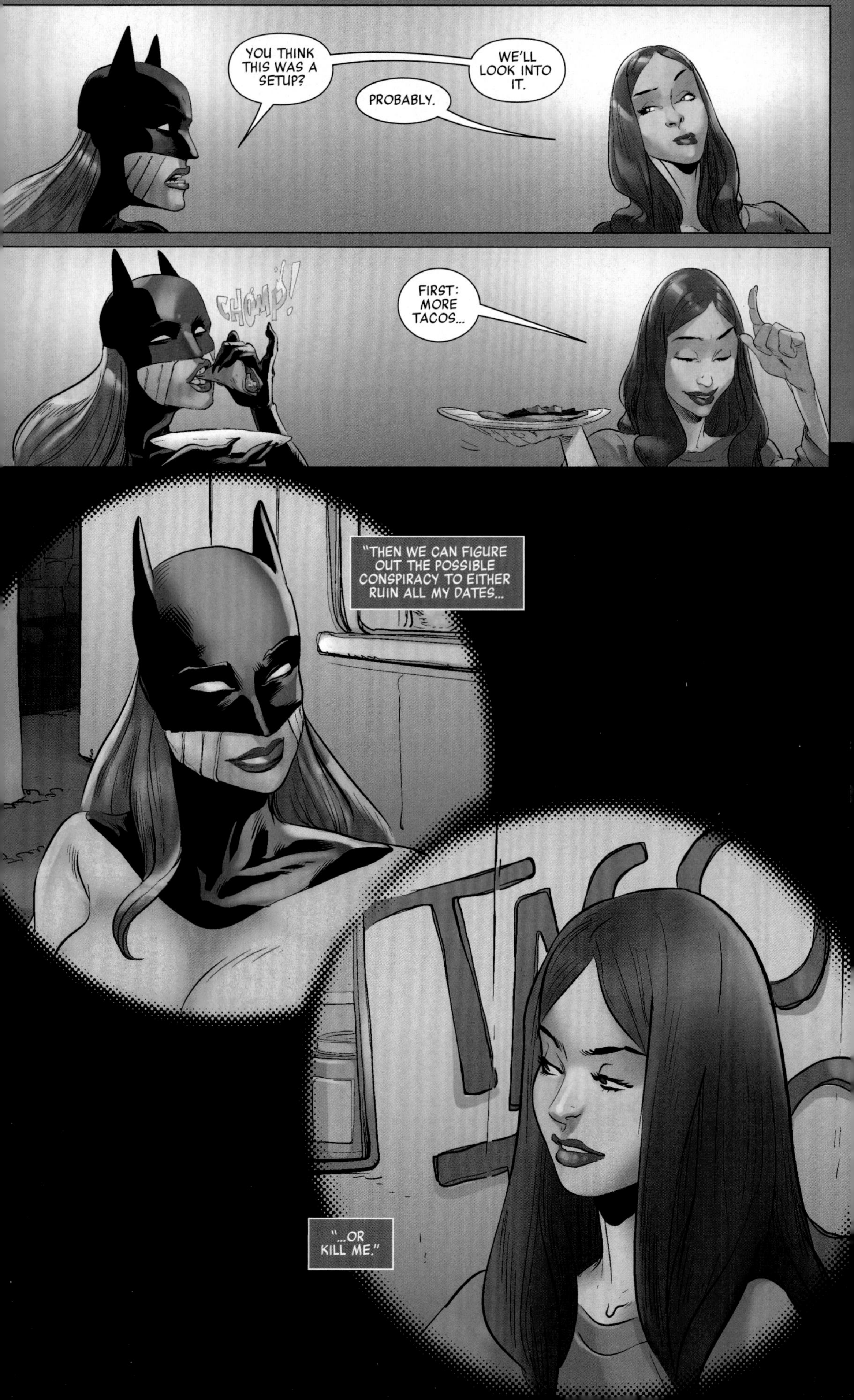
YOU THINK THIS WAS A SETUP?
PROBABLY.
WE'LL LOOK INTO IT.
CHOMP!
FIRST: MORE TACOS...
"THEN WE CAN FIGURE OUT THE POSSIBLE CONSPIRACY TO EITHER RUIN ALL MY DATES...
"...OR KILL ME."

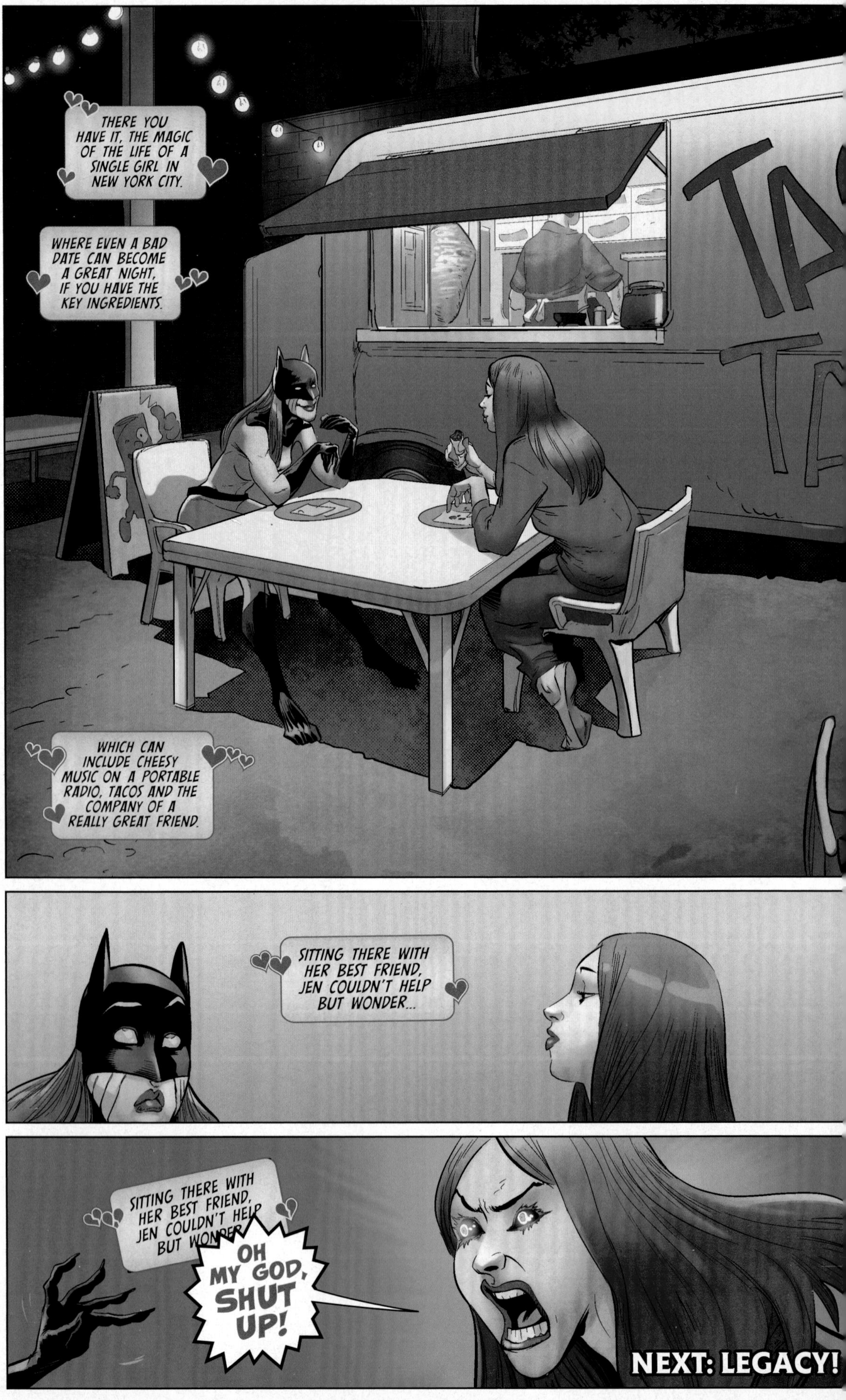
THERE YOU HAVE IT, THE MAGIC OF THE LIFE OF A SINGLE GIRL IN NEW YORK CITY.
WHERE EVEN A BAD DATE CAN BECOME A GREAT NIGHT, IF YOU HAVE THE KEY INGREDIENTS.
WHICH CAN INCLUDE CHEESY MUSIC ON A PORTABLE RADIO, TACOS AND THE COMPANY OF A REALLY GREAT FRIEND.
SITTING THERE WITH HER BEST FRIEND, JEN COULDN'T HELP BUT WONDER...
SITTING THERE WITH HER BEST FRIEND, JEN COULDN'T HELP BUT WON
OH MY GOD, SHUT UP!
NEXT: LEGACY!